Men's Sexual Health

Men's Sexual Health

FITNESS FOR SATISFYING SEX

BARRY W. MCCARTHY AND MICHAEL E. METZ

Routledge
Taylor & Francis Group
New York   London

Routledge
Taylor & Francis Group
270 Madison Avenue
New York, NY 10016

Routledge
Taylor & Francis Group
2 Park Square
Milton Park, Abingdon
Oxon OX14 4RN

Printed in the United States of America on acid-free paper
10 9 8 7 6 5 4 3 2

International Standard Book Number-13: 978-0-415-95638-3 (Softcover)

Visit the Taylor & Francis Web site at
http://www.taylorandfrancis.com

and the Routledge Web site at
http://www.routledge.com

To my grandsons Torren Michael McCarthy and Liam Karl McCarthy with the hope that they grow up in a world that celebrates healthy male, female, and couple sexuality

Barry McCarthy

To all the men and women; parents; and healthcare, clergy, media, and teaching professionals who are promoting positive, healthy sexuality

Michael E. Metz

Contents

Acknowledgments   ix

1   The Truth About Sex   1

2   Healthy Thinking About Male Sexuality: What You
Need to Know and Learn   17

3   Boys to Men: What Is Normal and Healthy?   37

4   Vive le Difference: His Sexuality and Her Sexuality   59

5   The Mantra of Healthy Sexuality: Intimacy, Pleasuring,
Eroticism, and Satisfaction   87

6   Good-Enough Male and Couple Sexuality   99

7   Fitness, Physical Well-Being, and Sexual Function   121

8   Lifelong Healthy Sexuality—You Are a Sexual
Man Until You Die   135

9   Dealing With Sexual and Health Problems   147

10 Valuing an Intimate, Erotic Sexual Life   181

Epilogue: The Nuts and Bolts for Your Sexual Health   189

Appendix A: Choosing an Individual, Couple, or Sex Therapist   193

Appendix B: Resources   197

References   201

Index   205

Acknowledgments

This book represents what we have learned in our combined seventy years as clinical psychologists, sex and marital therapists, and teachers and researchers. We are especially indebted to our clients and students who have taught us so much and added to the quality of the material in this book.

We want to acknowledge the outstanding contributions of the publishing team at Routledge/Taylor & Francis, especially our very wise editor, George Zimmar; his editorial assistant, Fred Coopersmith; Stephanie Pekarsky, who has taught us a great deal about the marketing world; and Michael Davidson, for his editorial production work and for putting up with all our requests. Thank you all.

Request for Feedback and How to Reach Us

We are very interested in your reactions to this book, especially

- What has been the most helpful?
- What was least helpful?
- What could we have addressed more fully?

Please feel free to contact us with your questions, comments, or requests:

Barry McCarthy, Ph.D.
Washington Psychological Center
5225 Wisconsin Avenue, NW Suite 513
Washington, DC 20015
mccarthy160@comcast.net

Michael E. Metz, Ph.D.
Meta Associates
821 Raymond Ave., Suite 440
St.Paul, MN. 55114
MMetzMpls@aol.com
www.MichaelMetzPhD.com

CHAPTER 1

The Truth About Sex

Men Deserve to Feel Proud of Their Sexuality

Remember a time when a buddy made a bragging sexual comment and you felt intimidated; you wondered if you were sexually "normal"; a TV program described male sexuality in a negative way; the time you felt confused about what to do sexually with a woman; whether your sexual fantasies were healthy; whether your expectations of lovemaking were realistic; when you thought, "Yes, I really like sex, but I feel differently than what other men feel." If you've ever had moments or thoughts like these (and the great majority of men have), this book will help you develop a healthier, more confident, and satisfying sex life. What's different about this book? We'll tell you the honest truth—no hype, no magic, no "BS." We will share with you the best available scientific, psychological, medical, and relationship information. The truth about sex is that every man deserves to feel proud, confident, and healthy about his masculinity and sexuality. The truth is that sex is an essential part of who we are as men.

To begin, we ask you to take our 21-item true–false quiz to assess your understanding of male sexuality. Don't worry about performance anxiety; you can score this yourself to see how knowledgeable you are, and you don't have to tell anyone your score.

Exercise 1.1: Sexual Knowledge Questionnaire

1. _____ Penis size is the most important factor in pleasing your partner.
2. _____ Real men are always interested and ready to perform sexually. *(Continued)*

1

(*Continued*)

3. _____ The best sex happens when you are single; committed sex squelches good sex.
4. _____ All men are potential rapists.
5. _____ Perfect sexual performance is the most important factor in satisfying your partner.
6. _____ Women control men with sex. It's just the way it is.
7. _____ Women expect to be fucked hard, but don't honestly say it.
8. _____ The Internet is the best source for accurate sexual information.
9. _____ Sex is such a basic physical need, men should be able to perform perfectly regardless of their level of physical conditioning, lifestyle, or age.
10. _____ What men most want and need in a relationship is sex.
11. _____ Men will do or say anything to get sex.
12. _____ Men inevitably think with their penis.
13. _____ Sex is natural and requires no learning, management, or regulation.
14. _____ Sex requires an erection because sex equals intercourse.
15. _____ Men need a lot of sex; lack of sex causes major physical problems.
16. _____ It is the man's responsibility to give his partner an orgasm each time.
17. _____ The man leads sex: "Men are supposed to run the sex show."
18. _____ Sex equals performance and performance is what counts.
19. _____ Real men have penises that are "two feet long, hard as steel, and able to go all night."
20. _____ Men can't control their sex drives.
21. _____ Men should never view women as sex objects.

How many "True" responses did you record? Compare your responses to the fact that this is a male sex myth test; all of these items are false. In the following chapters, we will coach you how to think about your sexuality in an accurate, honest, reasonable, confident manner. You can learn to increase sexual pleasure and satisfaction for the rest of your life.

The Truth and Nothing but the Truth

We've written this book to coach you (and your partner) in the truth about healthy, pleasurable, satisfying sex—not hype or promises that only lead to disappointment and "is that all there is?" We coach you in the scientific and medical facts, the reality of real men who have real jobs and real stresses, living real life with real women, with real failures as well as successes. We wrote this book to coach you with integrity, openness, candor, frankness, and details that you can apply to your life. We wrote this book because we believe there is too much BS out there about men and sex. We wrote this so that you can avoid the myriad of mistakes we have seen in our clinical practices, mistakes made out of ignorance, misinformation, unrealistic expectations, anxiety, shame, and following hyped-up promises—"Use this cream and your 'dick' will grow two inches." We've seen too many lies told to men. We want to give you the facts! So, we have written this book with the promise—to ourselves and to you—that this is a book with *integrity*.

We've counseled and coached thousands of men (and their partners) how to develop positive male sexual health, address sexual problems, and overcome worries, misunderstandings, and other barriers to sexual satisfaction. We have heard legions of men individually, in educational workshops, in couples therapy, and in men's group therapy express hidden thoughts and conflicts about sex. These men are scientists, construction workers, college students, professional football players, Fortune 500 CEOs, politicians, government employees, computer geeks, police officers, investment bankers, bakers, hockey stars, medical doctors, waste management truck drivers, pilots, prisoners, clergymen, chefs, military personnel, lawyers, factory workers, diplomats, teachers. You name the occupation, and we've heard from them over the years of our clinical work. They are young, middle-aged, older, single, married, divorced, sexually active, celibate, in good health, in poor health. Like their jobs and status in life, men are different emotionally and sexually. We are not stereotypes but have incredible diversity and ranges of thoughts, feelings, experiences, and sexual preferences. Some of us are saintly, some are villainous, while most of us are in the broad expanse in between. While we are different from each other in many ways, we all seek sexual health. Here are principles and facts that are common to all of us when it comes to sexual health. Men's sexual health is grounded on psychological and physical facts and truths.

Fact #1: Healthy Men Are Proud of Their Sexuality

Feeling good about your body and sexuality is essential to being sexually healthy. The truth about great sex is that every man deserves to feel proud and confident of his masculinity. Okay, there are jokes that sexual health for men is impossible or an oxymoron—that men are sexual idiots or "only think with their penis." These are simplistic stereotypes. Trash talk!

Each man can feel proud of his masculinity. Sex is a good part of a man's (and a woman's) life, not something to feel ashamed or embarrassed about.

Feeling proud of your body, unashamed of your powerful sex drive and sexual desires, buoyed by your sexual function, and clear with yourself of the importance of feeling pleased and satisfied with sex are important principles of men's sexual health. This confidence is based in physical, psychological, and relationship principles that accept masculinity with pride and self-respect.

Fact #2: Sexually Healthy Men Are Confident and Strong

What *is* men's sexual health? How do I get a solid grip on it? How do I determine if I am a sexually healthy man? These are not simple questions with simple answers. Sexual health is a lifelong process, with subtly different dimensions at each stage. For example, sexual health of a boy is part of the lifelong process but is different from that for a teen or young adult and different from a middle years and older adult. However, at each stage of life, common elements characterize sexual health. Here is the description of sexual health from the United Nations' World Health Organization (WHO, 1975):

> Sexual Health may be defined as a dynamic and harmonious state involving erotic and reproductive experiences and fulfillment, within a broader physical, emotional, interpersonal, social, and spiritual sense of well-being, in a culturally informed, freely and responsibly chosen, and ethical framework; not merely the absence of sexual disorders.

A translation may be helpful. Sexual health is the integration of your psychological, biological, and interpersonal sexual energies in a comfortable, meaningful, and satisfying way. In short, you feel confident and strong about yourself as a sexual man and know that others feel comfortable with you as well. Sex is a physiological, natural function, and sex is part of sexuality. Sexuality is a learned, psychosocial function. Sexuality is an integral part of every man's personality and is expressed in all that we do. In the broadest sense, sexuality is the psychic *energy* that finds physical and emotional expression in the desire for contact, warmth, tenderness, eroticism, and love. This energy is part of a man's balanced self-confidence and strength.

Fact #3: Men Have a Wide Range of Sexual Concerns

Every man (and woman) has concerns about what is sexually normal. There is a wide range of concerns about what is normal physically (like penis size); how your sexual body functions (erections, ejaculation); what thoughts or fantasies are normal (e.g., being sexually aggressive, group sex, attracted to a coworker, sex with animals); how to make love (how to "turn a woman on"); and what are appropriate sexual feelings (e.g., "horny"), sexual interest (e.g., "Am I addicted to strip bars?"), or behaviors ("Is my use of porn okay?"). We hear real men say things like:

- "Am I normal?"
- "Is my partner normal?"
- "I love sex; it's great. But I am not like men in the movies or TV. Is there something wrong with me?"
- "My testicles hang differently. Is there something wrong with me?"
- "I don't want to get older, 55 or 75, because sex surely must decline and end."
- "I'm embarrassed that I don't know how to be a super lover."
- "I had really great sex with her, but is that all there is?"
- "I feel so dumb! Nobody talked to me about what healthy sex is. I don't trust all the braggadocio I hear from male friends in the locker room or sports bar."
- "Sex with a long-term partner gets boring."
- "I use pornography regularly because it is my guarantee for variety. It ensures that I can get aroused and erect. Is that healthy?"
- "I feel inadequate; I doubt my ability to perform and satisfy my partner."
- "Penis size seems so important to women. I worry, am I big enough?"
- "Sex is supposed to be natural, but I have difficulty letting go."
- "My sexuality as a man seems more complex than what other men say, TV or movies show, or what the Internet says. Am I peculiar or inadequate?"
- "There are times that I feel very ashamed of my honest sexual desires, that they are 'bad.'"
- "I often doubt my ability to perform, to sexually satisfy my partner."
- "Are my fantasies, my body, my lovemaking style normal?"
- "I'm afraid she's judging me, my sexual skills and performance; this makes me anxious."
- "I have some weird thoughts and desires. How do I know if I'm deviant?"

These and other thoughts and feelings represent common concerns men have about their masculinity and sexual performance. If you are a man who wants to be honest with yourself and not live in the world of beer commercials, simplistic promises of Viagra ads, and sexual hype, you'll find yourself in this book. You can learn to feel proud of your masculinity and sexuality. This is a book for honest, strong, thoughtful men. We will explore common anxieties that many of us experience. Most men have little opportunity to learn from other men about healthy sexuality. We will confront common barriers to growing and developing an adult, healthy, and satisfying male sexuality.

This book takes men's sexuality seriously. Rather than trivializing men and sex, we consider complexity. This is a book for real men, not politically correct men. We will give you essential facts and discuss how sexual health can confirm your masculinity and promote life satisfaction.

Fact #4: What Is Good for Your Body Is Good for Your Sex Life. What Is Good for Your Sex Life Is Good for Your Body

The interrelationship between your physical body and sexual function is crucial to sexual health. Good lifestyle habits and choices—such as proper sleep, regular exercise for physical conditioning, healthy diet, moderation in your use of alcohol—provide the foundation for easy sexual function. Taking good care of your physical body is a prerequisite for satisfying sex. Positive, realistic expectations and cooperation with your partner are good for your sexual function. This interrelationship makes sense in the context of physiological sexual response and the importance of relaxation and comfort with your partner.

Fact #5: Satisfying Sex Is Important to Your General Health

When men feel sexually healthy and satisfied, men walk tall. Our sexual feelings, emotional well-being, confidence in the world, and even our physical health are essentially intertwined. On the other hand, a man who is troubled with his sexuality is at risk for low self-esteem, irritability, anxiety, and even physical illness. This interrelationship is an important reason that sexual dysfunction is considered both a psychological and a medical concern. The mind–body connection is valid.

Fact #6: Satisfying Sex Involves Lovemaking Skills

Good sex is more than performing as a "stud." Healthy physical conditioning, realistic psychological thinking, emotional health, and interpersonal cooperation for mutual pleasure are all part of good psychosexual (lovemaking) skills. While procreation may be biologically natural, satisfying lovemaking skills are not automatic but are developed through healthy attitudes, behaviors, and emotional intimacy. You can develop comfort and confidence with psychosexual skills and strengthen your desire, arousal, and orgasm response.

Fact #7: Knowledge Is Power

Accurate and realistic knowledge about men's bodies and male sexuality is crucial. Sexual health for men involves understanding physical, psychological, and relationship factors. Being realistic and thinking accurately about your body and your sexual function is a crucial component of sexual health.

This is essential because the public presentation of sex has nearly no relationship to the truth. The media, marketing, and public discourse is about getting your attention more than teaching you the truth about sex in real people's lives. This is a major problem and one of the most important motivations for our writing this book.

You also need a good understanding of your emotional life. It is important to understand the differences between your sex drive ("feeling horny") and positive and negative emotions like anxiety, loneliness, enjoyment, or pride in a job success. All energy in the body is not sexual energy, although there is a tendency for men to interpret a variety of emotions as sexual and try to manage their emotions by sexualizing them. For example, most men have masturbated to relieve anxiety or stress.

You also need to understand what healthy sexual behaviors are. Men care about sexual performance. Sexual function (performance) for men is fundamental, and to dismiss this important component of male sexuality is self-defeating. We'll coach you how to put sexual function into perspective; otherwise, it becomes a huge barrier to sexual pleasure, sexual acceptance, and relationship intimacy.

Fact #8: Sexual Health Is a Lifelong Developmental Process

Your health as a sexual man is a lifelong process. Sex can be a positive, integral part of your life at every stage. You are sexual from the day you are born to the day you die. Realize that your sexuality is a lifelong, progressive, and developmental process. It changes as you go through your life—from boyhood, adolescence, young adulthood, middle age, and older. Your sexuality as a 15-, 25-, 45-, 65-, or 85-year-old has both underlying similarities and also differences. We can be sexually healthy at each stage of our lives.

> "To be what we are, and to become what we are capable of becoming, is the only end of life."—Robert Louis Stevenson

The best research indicates that the quality of sex—like fine wine—improves with age. If you take good care of your psychological, physical, and relationship health, lifelong sexual satisfaction is a realistic expectation.

Fact #9: There Are Many Barriers to Healthy Sex

Detrimental messages, stereotypes, and erroneous beliefs about men and sex can set you up for sexual self-doubts, dysfunction, and dissatisfaction. The quiz you took earlier presented common myths. Some incorrect stereotypes include "Good women really don't like sex" or it's antithesis, "Hot women expect perfect sex performance"; others, "Great sex is what you see in porn videos" or "Marital sex is inevitably boring and mediocre."

Do not be duped by such damaging messages—recognize where they come from. Don't get faked out! Pay attention to positive sexuality. The following sources can undermine your sexual health.

Negative Messages About Men and Sex in the Media. Product marketing: It is important to realize that we live in a commercial culture and that media is a primary source for selling products. Sex sells. Because of its natural power, sex is used to get our attention and even to create a need by associating sexualized women to attract us to a product—whether a car, shaving lotion, beer, or athletic club. Be aware that marketing typically trivializes men and sexuality.

News and entertainment: Male sexuality attracts attention—often associated with shame. For example, news reports often and sadly focus on rape, lust killings, child sexual abuse, arrests of men making or distributing child porn, sexual abuse by clergymen, and voyeurism. Men are frequently portrayed as sexually troubled and even dangerous, addicted to Internet pornography, sex harassers, or sex offenders. Some TV shows engage in male-bashing. Men who try to be sexually healthy may unfortunately take on by osmosis subtle collective shame, feeling that as a man he is somehow implicated, suspect, bad.

Avoidance ("Silence") About Honest Male Sexual Feelings. Men's cautiousness about expressing honest sexual feelings is a significant barrier to sexual health. This silence in expressing honest sexual feelings subverts feeling proud of masculinity and sexuality. Men (and women) get faked out, believing that male sexuality is simplistic, one-dimensional (e.g., intercourse), impersonal, and about perfect performance and proving masculinity. This may fit an adolescent emerging from childhood to manhood, but men seeking lifelong sexual health do not live in such a one-dimensional world of sex.

Male "Bravado": Bragging and Trivializing. Seldom do men honestly talk with other men about sex in a personal way. Locker-room teasing, joking about another man, and exaggerating sexual escapades are accepted as normal male interaction. Sex is simple, no questions, automatic; it is about how often one "scores" (gets "laid"). This competitive bantering is the usual public discourse for men. When that is the only level on which men communicate with each other about sex, it reinforces a lack of understanding and acceptance and sets up self-defeating sexual expectations.

Typical male language can also be a barrier—language that is object focused (third person) rather than an expression of personal thoughts or feelings. Objectifying language depersonalizes and trivializes sexuality. For example, when a man says to his partner "Your body is hot" he may actually mean "I'm lonely and want to feel special and close to you"; "You've got great tits" may mean "When you invite me to enjoy you and get close to you I feel special"; or "You don't want sex? What's wrong with you?" may mean "I'm confused. When you flat out just say 'no,' I think you don't love me. I feel rejected and controlled."

Unrealistic Sex Expectations.   Sex as presented in our society has virtually nothing to do with what we know of realistic sex according to the best scientific research. The public impression and discussion of sex in America is almost silly. When accurate information is undermined by myths, political distortions, and hype, people do not learn and accept facts about men's bodies, women's bodies, and how people function sexually. Without accurate information, we are susceptible to myths, "Hollywood" or pornographic notions of what is supposed to be "real" sex. You will not find men's sexual health portrayed in a porn movie because pornography is purely about sexual fantasy.

Fantasy is "what you don't have and can't reasonably have in real life with a real woman." That doesn't make it "bad"—just fantasy. Pornographic fantasy has the message that sexual drive does not need to be regulated, that anything goes. Major unrealistic expectations are encouraged. There is an absence of positive societal messages that teach boys (and men) to regulate their sex drive. Instead, the cultural message about sex drive is negative and shaming (such as in radical feminist philosophy, anti-porn zealots, or negative religious messages of sin). Paradoxically, this shame serves to powerfully contribute to sexual impulsivity and impede men's sexual health.

Fact #10: You Need a Model for Your Sexuality as a Man

So, what is your model for male sexuality? Who is your role model for a sexually healthy man? How can you think positively about the multiple dimensions of your masculinity? How can you create your standard for healthy sexuality? Your model defines what—for you—is sexual health. It includes your assumptions about what is good sex and what causes sexual problems. This framework determines your understanding of the nature and purposes of sex, your attitude toward your body and your partner's body, your feelings, the value of fantasies, sexual growth and maturity, your expectations about sex, your relationship expectations, what a sexual dysfunction is, your attitudes toward friendships with men and women, your philosophy of life, the relationship between spirituality and sex, and your definition of sexual satisfaction.

Your sexual model will have a valence; sex is either fundamentally positive or negative—sex is good or sex is bad. Your model needs to focus on you as an individual and on your sexual relationship. Focus your model on accurate knowledge, feelings (satisfaction), and behavior (sexual function). You want to avoid being simplistic or one-dimensional. Ensure that your model of sexuality is inclusive, multidimensional, and well integrated with your body and mind. As much as we all wish important things in life could be simple, the fact is that life is complex, and so is sexuality.

Exercise 1.2: Creating Your Model of Male Sexual Health

Consider the following questions about your thoughts, beliefs, and values about male sexuality:

Do you think that you can be in poor physical condition and still have a good quality sex life?

How do you understand your body to be "programmed"? What is it sexually designed to do?

For you, what are the most important purposes for sex?

If you feel that you are ugly or have a small penis, can you find sexual satisfaction?

What do you think is the relationship between your physical and sexual health?

Could you be happy as a celibate man?

What are your specific sexual needs?

What is the interaction between your sexual thoughts, feelings, and actions?

Do you think sex is the one area of your life where you should be free and not need to regulate feelings or behavior?

Is your sexuality your own, or is sex meant to be shared with a loving partner?

Do you believe that sex is serious or playful?

Where does your sex drive come from? Body? Emotions? Relationship?

Do you think playfulness during sex is valuable for your relationship?

Can you sexually disappoint your partner and still have satisfying sex and feel good about yourself?

How important is a good sex life to an intimate, long-term relationship?

Do you think sex should rely more on physical desire than emotional closeness?

How much do you value intimacy? How much eroticism? Can these be integrated into your relationship?

(Continued)

(*Continued*)

Reflection: There are no simple responses, no correct or incorrect responses to these considerations. Ask yourself:

What thoughts stand out as you reflect on these questions? What do you learn about yourself? Your values? Your model of male sexual health?

Fact #11: Men's Sexuality Is Complex

An honest model for men's sexual health grapples with its complexity. We are not the simple, testosterone-driven, google-eyed, lap dogs for women portrayed in beer commercials. Men who model their sex on a Bud Light commercial (think wet T-shirt contest and female mud wrestling) may have fun in college, but this will restrict your adult sexual growth and health.

We propose a new psycho-biosocial, integrative model, that can be valuable for the man (and his partner) from his 20s to his 80s. We label our model the "Good-Enough Sex" model. What is different about our integrative psycho-biosocial model is that it includes multidimensional aspects of each component (mind, body, relationship) plus positive, realistic expectations based on accurate, scientific information and personally relevant guidelines. For example, the psychological dimension appreciates that we have important sexual thoughts (cognitions), feelings (emotions), and actions (behaviors) that need to be integrated. We want you to see the complexity of male sexuality, not trivialize it; to feel confident; to respect your manliness; to understand how to build your sexual satisfaction individually and in a relationship. These features vary and develop throughout your life. Sexuality is not set in stone, immutable, but rather evolving and contributing to the distinctive man that you are at each age.

Fact #12: Male Sexuality Has Multiple Dimensions

Men's sexual health involves multiple dimensions that help understand and integrate the physical, psychological, relational, cultural, and psychosexual lovemaking skills. These five factors are illustrated in Figure 1.1. The 5 Components of Integrative Sexual Health. Each dimension is indispensable and warrants attention to ensure sexual health throughout life.

The biological factors are the physiologic dimensions of sexual function—sexual drive, getting and keeping erections, ejaculation and orgasm, and physiological sexual satisfaction. The physical systems are the vascular, neurologic, hormonal, and behavioral health habits. Good physical condition and healthy habits are the foundation for your biological sexual health.

The psychological dimensions (CBE) are your cognitions, behaviors, and emotions. You can understand and ensure healthy sexual cognitions or thoughts (C); actions or behaviors (B); and your feelings or emotions (E).

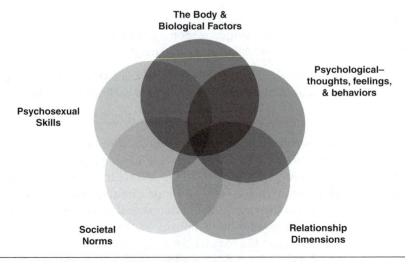

Figure 1.1 The 5 Components of Integrative Sexual Health.

The relationship dimension, includes the identity you and your partner share as a couple (e.g., couple expectations such as balancing autonomy and cohesion); your style of cooperation and interactions such as mutual conflict resolution; and emotional intimacy—especially empathy with your partner.

Societal norms refers to the social and cultural environment within which sexuality is understood, moderated, and regulated. This dimension includes prevailing societal attitudes, scientific understanding of sexuality, the laws regulating sexual behavior, as well as religious, moral, and ethical principles. Integrating your sexuality within the social norms and freedoms as well as restrictions of your culture are important aspects of healthy male sexuality.

The psychosexual skills for lovemaking include the cognitive, behavioral, emotional, and interpersonal factors in sexual response. These are important aspects for facilitating your sexual comfort and confidence.

This approach is worth your investment because when you understand how things work and what's involved, it makes sense, and you can integrate it into your cognitions, behaviors, and emotions. This allows you to feel more comfortable and natural. What you understand, you can do. What you can do well, you feel good about!

Fact #13: Pornography May Be Fine Fantasy
but Healthy Sex Is Reality Based

Fantasy for both men and women is a natural part of sexuality. Its role in sexual health depends on its function. Like any other area of life, it needs to fit your realistic lifestyle. A soldier's use of a group sex fantasy may bring relief through masturbatory arousal. For a married man who avoids his spouse sexually, pornography may serve an anti-intimate role. For the couple who mutually integrate erotic materials into their sexual relationship it may serve to freshen their lovemaking. The debates about the appropriate use of pornography in men's sexual lives should be about situation-appropriate sexual arousal. In a sexual relationship, pornography use should be about the comfort of both partners as an intimate team.

Fact #14: Ultimately Sex Is About Relationship Intimacy and Satisfaction

From the psycho-biosocial and developmental perspective, the ultimate function for a long-term sexual bond is relationship satisfaction. Consider that over the course of your life, there is a developmental flow from the biological and physiological development and growth of youth, the psychological and sexual development of young adulthood, and the integration of biological, psychological, and relationship dimensions of sexuality in adulthood and older age. It would be unusual for a teenager to achieve the level of relationship intimacy that is developmentally possible for middle years and older adults. At the same time, among older adults, it would not be reasonable to expect the biological intensity of adolescence. This perspective can enrich the quality of lifelong sexuality.

Fact #15: Long-Term, Satisfying Sexuality Varies in Quality

One of the most important facts is that the quality of lovemaking is naturally variable. It is a perfectionistic myth to believe that lovemaking will always be exceptional. The best research clearly indicates that while lovemaking may vary in quality, satisfaction can still be high. In short, the major criterion for sexual satisfaction is not performance but acceptance and pleasure.

The Truth About Great Sex

The truth is that if you think healthy and act healthy, you'll feel healthy sexually. Thinking well about male sexuality involves taking good care of your body, your partner's body, realistic expectations of sex, and adopting the Good-Enough Sex model. This approach is focused on being an "intimate team;" on pleasure-oriented sexual function rather than falling into the perfect performance trap; understanding the multiple purposes for sex, the three basic arousal styles and how to use them in partner sex, and maintaining positive, realistic sexual expectations.

Who We Are and Why We Wrote This Book

Barry McCarthy and Michael Metz are Ph.D. clinical psychologists, certified sex and marital therapists, and between us have more than 60 years of clinical experience dealing with men and sexual issues. We have coauthored two well-respected books on male sexual dysfunction—*Coping With Premature Ejaculation* (2003) and *Coping With Erectile Dysfunction* (2004). In addition, we have authored over 120 professional articles on sexual issues separately and together. Over the past several years, we have presented workshops or invited addresses to over 40 professional groups including the World Congress of Sexology, Society for Sex Therapy and Research, American Psychological Association, Smart Marriages, American Association of Marriage and Family Therapy, Psychotherapy Networker, Association for Behavioral and Cognitive Therapies, and American Association of Sex Educators, Counselors, and Therapists.

Barry McCarthy, Ph.D., practices at the Washington Psychological Center, is a professor of psychology at American University, has written over 70 professional articles and 20 book chapters, coauthored 11 books for the lay public, and presented over 250 workshops nationally and internationally.

Michael Metz, Ph.D., is in private practice with Meta Associates in St. Paul, Minnesota, is an adjunct assistant professor of family social science at the University of Minneapolis, and was on faculty for 12 years in the University of Minnesota Medical School, Department of Family Practice, where he directed the marital and sex therapy program. He has written over 60 professional publications and presented over 100 workshops nationally and internationally.

We bring a new voice in the field of male sexuality by explaining the Good-Enough Sex model of satisfying, realistic, and healthy male and couple sexuality.

Our reason for writing this book is to promote healthy male sexuality. This is a primary prevention book. We also discuss how to deal with common sexual problems in the acute phase. In our psychotherapy practices, we see men whose sexuality has been subverted by inaccurate information, unrealistic performance demands, who view women as critics they have to perform for and who worry that they are not good enough. Our goal in this book is to present a new integrative Good-Enough Sex model of healthy male and couple sexuality that will enhance your life from your 20s to your 80s so that you can truly enjoy your body and sexuality. Sexuality can play a positive, strong 15–20% role in your life and relationship satisfaction.

Overview of the Book

We want to share with you helpful strategies and techniques to integrate into your sexual health, now and in the years ahead, features that we have learned from our many years of teaching and clinical experience with men and couples.

Chapter 2, "Healthy Thinking About Male Sexuality," summarizes important knowledge for healthy sex. We explain how to organize your thinking (cognitions), understand your feelings (emotions), as well as wisely manage your actions (behaviors). Among 10 features to integrate into your personal sexual style are appreciating the multiple purposes for sex, how to use the three styles of sexual arousal, the importance of regulating your sex drive, viewing sex through the lens of being an intimate team, and understanding why and how Good-Enough Sex is the best sex model.

Chapter 3, "Boys to Men: What Is Normal and Healthy?" describes how we learn about sex as boys and summarizes behaviors of children, adolescents, and young adults. These data help you understand normal and healthy developmental sexuality and the influences and experiences that have formed who you are as a man.

Chapter 4, "Vive le Difference: His Sexuality and Her Sexuality," summarizes points of reference about male and female sexuality. Learnings from history, male and female sexual physiology, the three physiological forms of love, differences and similarities in men and women's sexual desire, and guidelines for cooperating as an intimate team are explained.

In Chapter 5, "The Mantra of Healthy Sexuality," the importance of intimacy, non-demand pleasuring, eroticism, and positive, realistic expectations as a man and couple are explored.

Chapter 6, "Good-Enough Male and Couple Sexuality," discusses realistic, satisfying and fulfilling sex in a long-term relationship. It is crucial to understand that satisfying sex varies in quality, intensity, and function. We discuss creating flexible lovemaking scenarios, understanding "get by" or "survival" sex, as well as the importance of playfulness during lovemaking, which allows you to integrate sex into your daily life.

Chapter 7, "Fitness, Physical Well-Being, and Sexual Function," examines the importance of attentiveness to your physical conditioning to ensure lifelong, adequate, and satisfying sexual function. Becoming and staying physically, psychologically, and interpersonally fit are smart practices. The importance of adequate sleep, exercise, appropriate diet, and other health habits are vital aspects of good sex. The particular risks of smoking and alcohol misuse are explained.

Chapter 8, "Lifelong Healthy Sexuality," describes sexual behavior of men in their 60s, 70s, and 80s. The facts—based in science—about what aging men do sexually can serve as reference points for understanding normal male sexual behavior as well as help you determine what is healthy for you. Adapting to the various sexual health challenges and vulnerabilities of older age is a part of flexible, variable male sexuality. You are a sexual man from the day you are born until the day you die.

Chapter 9, "Dealing With Sexual and Health Problems," addresses the sexual problems and concerns men may face. These include sexual dysfunctions such as inhibited sexual desire, premature ejaculation, erectile dysfunction, and ejaculation inhibition. Other difficulties may include compulsive sexual behavior, variant arousal patterns, affairs, or sexual misuse of the Internet. In addition, we examine illnesses and medication side effects, infertility, fears of aging, and sexual problem relapse prevention. Appreciating the range of sexual difficulties men may encounter encourages us to appreciate the diversity and complexity of male sexuality and address these issues so they do not subvert male sexual health.

Chapter 10, "Valuing an Intimate, Erotic Sexual Life," consolidates the truth about men's sexual health, healthy thinking, and the Good-Enough Sex model.

The epilogue, "The Nuts and Bolts for Your Sexual Health," summarizes the indispensable features of sexual health for men such as honesty with yourself, reasonable thinking, working with your partner as an intimate team, genuinely accepting with pride your masculinity, regulating your sexual drive, promoting Good-Enough Sex, and increasing sexual satisfaction with your partner.

We hope you will accept our invitation to enhance your sexual health. We're confident you won't be disappointed.

CHAPTER 2

Healthy Thinking About Male Sexuality
What You Need to Know and Learn

We want to share with you core concepts about healthy male sexuality. These are scientifically accurate and personally relevant to you. They position you to have a solid and satisfying sexual relationship. We will explain how to organize your thinking (cognitions), understand your feelings (emotions), as well as wisely manage your actions (behaviors). We discuss the 10 things men need to learn for individual sexual health (Table 2.1). These are the attitudes and understandings that serve as the principles for you to be a sexually healthy man and will facilitate a sexually healthy relationship. These features include appreciating the multiple purposes for sex, the three styles of sexual arousal and how to use them, the importance of comfortably regulating your sex drive, and viewing sex as sharing as an intimate team.

These sound easy but actually are very difficult for most men to accept and integrate into their lives. We will examine each concept in detail as well as ask you to engage in an exercise and read an illustration. But first we invite you to imagine yourself in a group of five or six men—whether a sports group, work group, neighbors, or old friends. If you talked to them about whether this was what they needed to know and learn, what do you think would happen? Be real, not politically correct. Unless you have a very aware, honest group of friends, what would ensue would be joking, embarrassment, jabbing, making fun, and diverting from serious discussion.

What if the group included spouses and girlfriends? We bet the women would be very involved in the discussion and, in fact, dominate it. This would probably turn into a male-bashing conversation about why men

Table 2.1 The 10 Things Men Need to Learn for Individual Sexual Health

1. Value the five purposes for sex in your life.
2. Integrate your sexuality into your personality.
3. Have positive, realistic expectations of your body's response.
4. Affirm that sexuality at its core is relational, not autonomous.
5. Value touch and pleasure as well as function.
6. Be wise in regulating and expressing your sexuality.
7. Be aware of the three styles of sexual arousal and choose how to integrate these into your couple sexual style.
8. Value your partner as your sexual friend and be an intimate team.
9. Integrate sex into your real life and your real life into your sex life.
10. Realize that Good-Enough Sex rather than settling for mediocre is genuine, satisfying, and high quality.

can't open up and be honest about their feelings and about sex in a relationship. This book is not about the battle between the sexes. We encourage men to be aware of and proud of their masculinity and sexuality. There is too much male-bashing, and we need to challenge it. It is destructive for men, women, sex, and relationships. We advocate concepts that will help you as an individual man to be sexually confident.

Healthy sex is a positive, integral part of being a man. Sex can serve a number of positive functions in your life, from pleasure, self-assurance, intimate bonding, stress reduction, and reproduction. Contrary to the porn model (which defines sex as power over women, illicit, perfect performance, and visual focus), the essence of healthy male sexuality is giving and receiving both intense and relaxing pleasurable touch that integrates intimacy and eroticism. Real-life sex fits into your preferences, feelings, and relationship—it is positive and real, not an ideal, perfect performance. The most important, and also the most controversial learning, is to accept that 5–15% of sexual encounters will be dissatisfying or dysfunctional for you, her, or for both of you. Can that really be true? Absolutely. Most men would never admit to friends or even their partner that it's true, but it is.

Illustration 2.1: Craig

Thirty-six-year-old Craig is a sexually healthy man. He had no formal sex education but has learned to use relevant, trusted resources (books and Web sites) and processes sexual feelings, preferences, and experiences with his wife of 9 years, Ann. He'd been a finance major in college, and his career focused on arranging financial backing for start-up technology and health services companies. Craig is a good

(Continued)

(*Continued*)

judge of both business and people, mixing technical expertise with good interpersonal skills.

Craig's developmental sexual learnings were common for his generation. He'd had his first orgasmic experience with masturbation at age 13, his first orgasmic experience with partner manual stimulation at age 16, and, in the context of a serious dating relationship, his first intercourse at age 19. Craig had six serious dating relationships before meeting Ann at age 25 and marrying 21 months later. Although Craig had several disappointing and confusing relational/ sexual experiences, he was proud that he'd not had any sexually transmitted diseases or pregnancies. However, Craig was not judgmental when his best male friend contracted herpes and Craig urged him to view this as a health problem, not a moral failure. He urged his friend to be an informed, active patient and to learn his herpes cycle and what to do to reduce frequency of outbreaks.

Craig learned in his 20s what most men don't learn until their 40s or 50s (some, in fact, never do). Sex is more satisfying when it is mutual, pleasure oriented, and variable. Even as a young man, Craig did not view intercourse sex as the ultimate pass–fail test of masculinity. In addition to intercourse, he enjoyed giving oral sex as well as one-way erotic scenarios when he was manually pleasured to orgasm. Craig especially enjoyed highly erotic, focused, 5-minute intercourse scenarios.

Craig and Ann's typical lovemaking scenario involved about 40 minutes of kissing and touching in the den with clothes on, then going upstairs and getting nude and doing cunnilingus (Ann was multiorgasmic with oral stimulation), followed by intercourse in Craig's favorite sitting–kneeling position, which usually lasted 5 to 8 minutes before his orgasm; they very much enjoyed their non-verbal afterplay before drifting off to sleep. Of course, this was not their only lovemaking scenario. Although Ann really valued this scenario, Craig valued variability and unpredictability even more. Theirs was primarily a partner interaction arousal scenario, but when Ann wasn't in a sexual mood, Craig particularly enjoyed arousal where she would give to him and he could relax and take in all the pleasurable and erotic sensations (self-entrancement arousal). Most men Craig's age are only open to penile stimulation when they are already erect, but Craig was open to interactive stimulation as a way to develop arousal and erection. He knew Ann valued the fact that she could help him get in the mood and erect. Craig typically did

(*Continued*)

(*Continued*)

not view sex as a tension reducer but realized that Ann did and was responsive to that scenario.

Probably the most important learning for Craig, which would serve him well as he aged, was accepting that 5–15% of their encounters just didn't work. Craig's favorite story was about being in the middle of sex and saying to Ann, "I want you to really enjoy this, it's for you," and she stopped and said, "I'm not getting into sex at all; I was doing this for you." They were able to laugh it off, cuddle, and agree to try again the next day when they were awake, alive, and sexually receptive. With these attitudes and psychosexual skills, it is likely that Craig and Ann will have a healthy, satisfying sexual life into their 70s and 80s.

Think Independently

Whether in your 20s or 60s, married or unmarried, holding an advanced degree or a high school dropout, we all learned a core sexual lesson—"A real man never has questions or doubts about sex." In fact, most men learn the opposite lesson—"A real man is ready and able to have sex with any woman at any time and any place." These are very powerful cultural learnings, and men who question them are vulnerable to being labeled "wimps," "gays," or "girly men."

Does this constitute healthy thinking about male sexuality? Absolutely not. It takes personal courage to stand up to the cultural messages that trap men in a competitive, perfect performance approach to sex.

A striking example is that three out of four men fear that their penis is smaller than average. Other than being statistically impossible, it illustrates the competitive dilemma. Traditionally, men lie and one-up each other about sex, so there is a "feeding frenzy" about everything sexual—how many partners you've had, how often you have sex, how long you last during intercourse, how many orgasms you give your partner. Of course, you would never admit to losing an erection, not feeling interested in sex, experiencing premature ejaculation or ejaculatory inhibition, or having questions or concerns about what is normal. Such image management and the "blind leading the blind" subverts real-life, healthy male and couple sex.

Exercise 2.2: Enhancing Healthy Thinking and Confronting Poisonous Thinking

Men are not encouraged to think and talk about sex in a healthy manner. This exercise confronts that trap. It will require courage on

(*Continued*)

(*Continued*)

your part because we are asking you to engage in this small group discussion with men you know, respect, and trust. We suggest a minimum of two other men and a maximum of seven. You can be the group facilitator. We suggest two guidelines. First, try to be as honest, clear, and specific as possible about sexual attitudes, experiences, and feelings. Second, no one-upping, bragging stories, and no put-downs of other group members or women.

Here are some suggested topics/questions:

How did you learn about sex as a child? Who talked to you? What did you learn? If no one talked to you, where did you get sex information?

Whether from parents, school, church, or friends, what was your best, most helpful sex education experience?

When did you first experience orgasm/ejaculation? Nocturnal emission ("wet dream"), masturbation, partner sex, or fooling around with other boys? Was it a positive or anxiety-provoking experience?

When did you first hear about couple (marital) sex? Did it excite or repel you?

What was your first contact with pornography—*Playboy*, Internet, or sex stories? Was it exciting, shameful, erotic, guilt-inducing?

How old were you at your first partner sexual experience? Was it with a girlfriend, hook-up, prostitute? Did it involve manual or oral sex, rubbing, or intercourse? Was it a good or bad experience?

How did you react to negative sexual experiences—contracting an STD, getting a woman pregnant, being sexually abused, being sexually humiliated, being rejected, getting caught masturbating, having an unsuccessful first intercourse? Did you deny it happened, lie about it, or tell no one? In retrospect, how has this negative experience(s) affected you sexually?

What was your most positive premarital sexual experience? What was the quality of the relationship and the quality of the sex? What were your most positive learnings from this relationship about yourself, women, and sex?

What was your most negative premarital experience? How long did it last and how did it end? Are there legacies from this experience that subvert your sexual life in terms of self-esteem, view of women, view of sex, or view of relationships?

(*Continued*)

(*Continued*)

> When was sex the most vital and satisfying in your present relationship? What did you most value about it? If it is different now, what can you do to revitalize sex in your relationship?
>
> What questions do you have of your male friends that will increase your understanding of yourself and sexuality? Especially important are present questions or concerns about sex, women, and relationships.
>
> As you and your friends engage in this discussion, stay focused on the goals of sharing information, attitudes, experiences, feelings and learnings in a helpful, honest, cooperative manner—not competition or put-downs. Knowledge is power. Traditionally, men have not shared knowledge or experiences in a supportive or helpful manner. Hopefully, this exercise will facilitate your doing so and establish a base for healthy thinking about male sexuality.

What if you can't do this exercise? If this exercise is more than you can arrange, ask yourself some questions for your own learning: What prevents you from arranging and conducting this discussion? Is it that you don't feel you have buddies you can confide with? Are you afraid of rejection if you're honest? Are you ashamed of your honest sexual feelings or past?

What are ways for you to enhance your sexual health other than this men's discussion group exercise? Could you respond to the 11 questions in your personal journal? Could you talk with your partner and openly share your experiences, feelings, and learnings with her?

Context for Understanding the 10 Sexual Health Learnings

To cultivate the 10 learnings for sexual health, you'll need some context because the learnings involve knowing how to organize your thinking (cognitions), understand your feelings (emotions), and wisely manage your actions (behaviors). This will enable you to understand what we mean by integrating your thoughts, feelings, and behaviors for sexual health. The cognitive–behavioral–emotional (CBE) model is a way to organize these dimensions and learn male sexual health.

The CBE Model

The CBE model recognizes that each individual is composed of cognitions, or thoughts; behaviors, or actions; and emotions, or feelings (Figure 2.1).

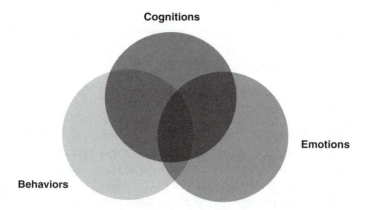

Figure 2.1 The C-B-E Model: Cognitive-Behavioral-Emotional.

These dimensions interact almost automatically—thoughts influencing feelings, feelings influencing behaviors, and behaviors prompting thoughts and feelings. In the integrative CBE model, each component is valued and promotes sexual health. Without appreciating that thoughts, feelings, and behaviors interact, yet are distinct, our experience of sex can be confusing and conflicted. Your insight will be strengthened by understanding the integrated role of cognitions, behaviors, and emotions in sexual health.

Cognitions or Thoughts

Cognitions involve ideas, beliefs, observations, interpretations, and reasoning. Epstein and Baucom (2002) describe five distinct cognitions that affect your sexuality: assumptions, standards and beliefs, perceptions, attributions (explanations of cause and effect), and expectancies (predictions). These are unique to each man. Cognitions are beneficial or detrimental depending on their effects on your feelings and actions. Our cognitions are the way we think about sex, our self-talk. When it comes to sex, we want to think accurately, positively, reasonably. When we don't, we set ourselves up for unrealistic expectations and frustration. Be aware; be deliberate. Think smart.

Behaviors or Actions

We act (or not) based upon our thoughts and feelings. Action is always a choice (decision). The freedom to choose your behavior is mitigated by thoughts and feelings, but responsible and mature living mandates accountability for your behavior. Whereas feelings are not viewed as ethical (that is, not judged to be good or bad), behaviors are. Behaviors may be constructive or destructive depending on their effect on each individual and the relationship. When sexually healthy, we act positively, passionately, cooperatively, joyfully about sex—and with self-discipline. We regulate sexuality to control impulses, as well as to be able to let go emotionally and experience sexual passion.

Emotions or Feelings

Emotions are chemical–electrical energy events in your body. You label this energy according to how you experience these physical sensations: fear, sadness, loneliness, panic, satisfaction, anger, worry, contentment, frustration, pleasure, irritability, excitement, anxiety, wonderment, confusion, shame, guilt, comfort, embarrassment, resentment, safety. Feelings are motivators that prompt, penalize, or reward action. Feelings are not themselves good or bad, right or wrong. Feelings influence the thoughts we have and the actions we take. Emotions can be positive or negative depending on how you subjectively experience them and how they influence your behavior. Understanding your feelings is crucial to prevent "emotional sexualization." You can manage your impulses as well as invest your feelings in an intimate relationship.

CBE Skills

A Cognitive Skill: Question Popular Culture's Messages About Male Sexuality

It is important as a man to be engaged and comfortable in our society but to also think for yourself. An important challenge is to find a balance between your solidarity with other men (and women) and your individual autonomy and independence. When we fail to think realistically and be grounded in accurate information, we set ourselves up for cognitive errors. Cognitive errors inevitably set us up to feel inadequate, a failure, and inept. Such feelings cause us to behave poorly. Think realistically. Think courageously. Think for yourself.

An Emotional Skill: Understand the Value of Your Feelings

Because your emotions are indispensable for achieving sexual health, it is crucial that you be aware of and be comfortable with your emotions. Everyone who has a body has feelings, but we differ in our level of awareness and comfort. Some men are very aware of their body's sensations and feelings and have elaborate words to express them. Others are aware of their feelings but have few words to describe them or have learned not to express emotions out of shame, fear, or sensitivity. Still other men ignore their feelings, believing emotions interfere with their masculinity.

What Are Feelings?

Feelings can be confusing, distracting, irritating, or frustrating unless you understand what they are about. Because many people—especially men—rely more on reason than emotion for direction in life, feelings are often viewed as irritants, distractions, or even enemies. At their base, feelings are biochemical energies in your body in response to various situations, influenced by your past experiences and current thoughts. Feelings (including sexual feelings) are not enemies; they offer you important information that your reason might overlook. Feelings offer data about yourself, your experiences, and your situation that are not available to you from logic or thinking alone.

A Metaphor for Your Feelings

Consider a metaphor that a number of men have told us helped them appreciate the value of their emotions.

Illustration 2.2: "Lifelong, loyal friends"

A way to appreciate your feelings is to consider them to be your "buddies"—lifelong, loyal friends. They have been with you through all of your life's experiences—from childhood to now. They remember your experiences even before you were old enough to remember, or now when you forget. Each feeling, then, is a savvy veteran of experience who will alert or protect you from situations that could distress you. Your friends vigilantly look after you. They will not lie to you, bullshit you, abandon you, or be silent when concerned that you may forget or be misled by your logic. A good buddy will take you aside, counsel you, and even argue with you when he thinks you could be making a mistake or overlooking potential trouble. You may not like the counsel, thinking your emotional friends overprotect (or underprotect) or make things worse, but they are just doing their job. When you are feeling tentative or conflicted about your sexual health, your "emotional buddies" (loyal friends) let you know—anxiety, shame, frustration. Your loyal buddies get your attention; "cover your back." On the other hand, when you are engaged in mutually healthy couple sex, they reward you with emotional self-assurance and satisfaction.

Feelings Can Be Complicated

Often we have mixed feelings—we feel two or more things at the same time. For example, you may worry that a disagreement with your partner is impossible to resolve, feel hurt and irritated at yourself or your partner, and feel shame that you have failed to find a resolution—simultaneously.

You may focus on only one dimension of the energy (feeling) in your body, ignoring the other feelings. For example, focusing only on frustration, you may miss feelings of hurt and worry.

One feeling can be converted to another. A person who is taught to not feel anger may convert feelings of anger to shame. A person who is taught that anger is okay but fear isn't may feel angry when afraid or threatened.

Feelings Are Useful

People tend to think of feelings as positive or negative depending on whether they agitate (like fear, anger, and guilt) or encourage (like pleasure, joy, contentment, and satisfaction). Our approach to understanding feelings is to think of them as guides, or loyal friends, trying to get your attention so you'll consider factors other than logic in your response to a situation. Feelings try to help you respond to different situations. Every feeling is good in terms of its purpose to serve you, protect you, and guide you. Your feelings offer honest information. Listening for feelings is an important skill. Considering them offers you more data to incorporate into your choices about action (behavior).

Exercise 2.1: Listening for Your Feelings

Alone, provide yourself a quiet, relaxing atmosphere. Focus your attention on relaxing your body until you feel calm, centered, and comfortable. Then imagine that you are a miniature explorer traveling around inside your body, searching for different energies or feelings.

> Where in your body do you experience joyful feelings? In your face, eyes, mouth? In your chest or legs?
> Where in your body do you experience feelings of anxiety or fear? In your stomach? In your chest? In your cold hands?
> Where in your body do you experience anger? In your hot cheeks or ears? In your throat or neck? In your stomach?
> Where in your body do you experience feelings of sadness?
> Where in your body do you experience feelings of confusion, indecisiveness, ambivalence?
> Where in your body do you experience feelings of sensuality and sexual desire?

Write down what you observe. Be specific about each feeling's "location" in your body. What are you learning?

Are You Free to Feel?

Your feelings are valuable sources of personal information, but don't let them run your life. It is not always a good idea to act on them—especially impulsive sexual feelings. Whether and how to act are ethical choices that you need to make. For example, a feeling of anger offers personal information to you about your situation, usually one in which you feel frustrated, treated unfairly, misinterpreted, hurt, threatened, or blocked. These feelings get your attention by agitating your body so you recognize the problem. What you do with this information is the issue.

The guiding principle is to accept your feelings and judge your behaviors. When you make this distinction between feelings and behaviors, you are free to feel. You can feel frustration and choose not to express this feeling to your partner. Rather, you can choose a more positive course by pausing to calm your body (feelings) and then asking your partner for a few moments to cooperatively discuss the matter. You want to learn from your feelings but not let them dictate to you. You want to listen to your feelings, consider their counsel, and then decide how to respond in a constructive, effective fashion. Integrating your feelings and reason gives you a more complete picture of your life, relationship, and sexuality.

Different Ways of Expressing Feelings

There are many direct and indirect ways to express feelings. The words to describe feelings are learned. Some words directly describe emotions: "I feel sad," "I feel close," "I feel frustrated." Others express feelings indirectly. You might say, "Isn't it a nice day?" to express "I feel good today" or "All you do is spend money" to mean "I am worried about money." The more directly you express your feelings, the more likely it is that your partner will understand and interpret your meaning correctly.

You and your partner have your own emotional language, nonverbal (a smile, a glance away) as well as verbal. How do you express your feelings? How does your partner? How have you expressed feelings about sexual concerns? How has your partner? Verbally? Nonverbally? Negatively? Positively? Calmly? Dramatically? Developing healthier ways to share feelings is important and will deepen your intimacy. Learning to "read" your partner's words and actions is part of the uniqueness of intimacy. It takes months and years of sharing experiences, explaining your thoughts and feelings, to develop a mutual emotional language.

Communicating emotions is an important skill in an intimate relationship. For most men and women, it is difficult to feel close without sharing verbally what and how you feel. Love involves sharing warm, positive, romantic feelings but also involves sharing difficult, negative feelings even when that may lead to conflict. Communicating negative feelings in a positive, constructive way can lead to emotional closeness. You can still feel loved and valued even if you are down, anxious, or had a failure experience. Love tries to provide that safe harbor amidst the storms of life.

Vulnerability Within Emotional and Sexual Intimacy

Sharing feelings is important to deepening your long-term sexual relationship. Emotional openness and the nakedness of sex are the two most vulnerable and tender aspects of committed love. During these experiences, we are most exposed. When you give and receive empathy while you are vulnerable emotionally and sexually, you communicate powerful acceptance and comfort and generate trust and love.

A Crucial Emotional Skill: Empathy

In intimate relationships, an important ideal is to feel emotionally valued and accepted without conditions, to feel unconditional positive regard from and for each other. Empathy, the skill of affirming feelings, is the glue of a deep relationship. It feels good to have your successes and strengths acknowledged, but you feel especially loved and respected when your vulnerabilities and weaknesses are accepted. To empathize with your partner, imagine for a moment that you are her. Imagine that you think and feel as she does, that you experience her reality. When you are empathic with your lover (although you may not agree with her), you offer the greatest gift: acceptance, nurturance, warmth, respect, reassurance, validation, care, patience, and appreciation. These are wonderful qualities to take into the bedroom.

Understanding your emotions is a crucial skill for sexual health in two important ways. First, recognition of your emotions will help you avoid emotional sexualization, which is a major source of sexual impulsivity as well as compulsivity. Second, recognition of your feelings is a valuable awareness to constructively invest in your relationship for emotional and sexual intimacy.

A Behavioral Skill: Self-Discipline

Some "drives" to act (behavior) are prompted by our body (e.g., testosterone affects sex drive), but we need to appreciate that our cognitions and emotions also are profound motivators for our behaviors. When we do not appreciate the "tag team" of biological, cognitive, emotional, and behavioral factors, we can feel and act in sexually impulsive, even compulsive ways. Men who get into sexual trouble (affairs, Internet porn abuse, prostitutes) later confess that they felt out of control, driven and confused, chiding themselves, "What was I thinking?"

Sexual health requires self-discipline. Often we think of self-discipline as mortification, punishment, or castigation. A healthier concept of discipline is physical, cognitive, emotional, and behavioral skills training. When we understand that discipline is beneficial and resourceful, it no longer is an enemy. Self-discipline is a personal strength. The athlete's "no pain, no gain" axiom applies here. It may be difficult, painful at times, but the gain is that self-discipline become easier over time. Repeated, consistent self-discipline builds skill, a learned way of thinking, feeling, and acting that we've trained into ourselves until it becomes second nature. The professional athlete trains his thoughts, feelings, and behaviors through analyzing "game film" (cognitive learning), workouts in a strength-building program, and repetitive practice to be at the top of his game. To promote your sexual health, you benefit from disciplining your sexual thoughts, feelings, and behaviors. Self-discipline is your friend, making the healthy regulation of your sexual impulses and behavior easier. Ironically, this self-disciplined skill enhances your ability to let go and enjoy sexual pleasure when you choose to. So become a well-disciplined sexual man for your own pleasure and satisfaction.

Sexual self-regulation includes arousal regulation as well as emotional regulation. This involves management of emotions like anxiety, loneliness, fear, frustration, and sadness. It also includes physical regulation of sleep, exercise, and food.

Sexuality is a good example of how your cognitions, emotions, and behaviors interact and blend. How you think about sex directly influences how you feel, which sets up behavioral patterns. Your sexual actions and feelings influence how you think, and the interplay continues. Recognizing this interplay offers you powerful, healthy options to manage your sexual thoughts, feelings, and behaviors and provides self-understanding that results in enhanced emotional and sexual satisfaction.

The 10 Things Men Need to Learn for Individual Sexual Health

1. Value the Five Purposes for Sex in Your Life

The more aware you are as a sexual man the better. Realize that there are five prime purposes (reasons) for sex (Table 2.2). Depending on your state in life and goals, these will vary (for you as well as your partner).

All five purposes may be suitable at different times for you and your relationship. It is the norm that sex has different roles and meanings and can serve several purposes at the same time. Most of the time, pleasure is the basic function of sex, especially in long-term relationships. Sex energizes and makes your bond special. You feel desired and desirable, which boosts self-esteem and confidence. Boosting self-esteem is a major function of sex in new relationships. Intimacy and relationship satisfaction is a

Table 2.2 The Prime Reasons for Sex

Shared pleasure and enjoyment.
A means to deepen and reinforce intimacy and satisfaction.
A tension reducer to deal with the stresses of a shared life.
A means to reinforce self-esteem and confidence.
The traditional biological function of procreation.

core component especially in serious, ongoing relationships. This is most likely to occur before (pleasuring) or after (afterplay) a sexual experience rather than during intercourse and orgasm. Tension reduction is probably the least talked about purpose of healthy sex, but that is a mistake. Sex as a refuge or port in a storm is a core element of healthy male sexuality. Some reasons may be to reenergize after a difficult time parenting a teenager or after a stressful trip, to rejoin after an argument, or to feel worth and energy after a professional rejection. The biological function for sex is procreation. Although reproduction is the natural purpose of sex, this is a choice, not a mandate. You do not have to conceive a child to justify being sexual or to prove you are a man.

2. Integrate Your Sexuality Into Your Personality

Sex is more than your penis, intercourse, and ejaculation. Your sexuality is a positive, integral part of who you are as a man and your attitudes, behaviors, and feelings (your personality). Many men act as though sex is a totally split-off personality part rather than a special facet of their personalities. So if in other areas of your life you are considerate and gentle, that would be part of your sexual style. If you are a funny guy or an adventurous guy, that too can be an aspect of your sexual style. If you are a spiritual/religious person, that can be integrated into your sexual person. Integrate your personality into your sexual life.

3. Have Positive, Realistic Expectations of Your Body's Response

Men who are realistic in other parts of their lives—work, equipment, sports—often do not transfer these lessons to their sexual bodies. For example, the porn image is of an enormous penis that is 100% reliable, hard as steel, and goes all night. Porn sex is about fantasy, having nothing to do with reality. The key element in understanding and accepting your body is that sexual response is based on realistic expectations of your sexual body. The three physiological systems that most affect sexual response are vascular, neurological, and hormonal. Sexual response is primarily a vascular response, involving increased blood flow to your penis and genitals. A crucial learning is that anything that interferes with your physical health will subvert your sexual health. For many men, a prime motivator to stop smoking is because it interferes with your vascular system.

You need to treat your body, especially your penis, in a healthy manner. Physical factors that interfere sexually include fatigue, poor conditioning, alcohol and drug abuse, poor eating habits, obesity, illness, side effects of medications, not maintaining good diabetic control, and a sedentary lifestyle.

4. Affirm That Sexuality at Its Core Is Relational, Not Autonomous

Teenage males learn that they can function autonomously (experience desire, arousal, and orgasm) without needing anything from their partner. This learning does not serve men well in their 30s and beyond, especially men in serious, ongoing relationships. Healthy male sexuality is an interpersonal experience, not an autonomous one.

Sex does not exist in a vacuum, but in the context of a relationship— whether a sexual friendship or an intimate marriage. Even if you are not in a relationship at the moment, you are relating to a "virtual" partner in your mind, a past partner or an imaginary future one. Ultimately, men and women want similar benefits from sex—emotional connection and sexual satisfaction. They traditionally seek this through different avenues. Young men traditionally pursue emotional connection through sex while women commonly pursue sex through emotional intimacy. Contrary to the cultural myth of a war between the sexes these are complementary, not oppositional, approaches. Sexuality for both men and women involves desire, pleasure, and satisfaction. You can be intimate, erotic friends who share pleasure and enhanced couple satisfaction.

5. Value Touch and Pleasure as Well as Function

Is the sole focus of sex intercourse and orgasm? We are strong advocates for intercourse and orgasm, but if that is your only focus, your sexuality is too narrow and ultimately vulnerable to dysfunction. If sex becomes intercourse or nothing, eventually nothing wins out. Pressure for perfect sexual performance (sex on demand) is ultimately a poisonous feature that subverts healthy sexuality. A good example of this is that four out of five men who have to follow an infertility protocol with the demand for intercourse controlled by the woman's ovulation develop either erectile dysfunction or inhibited sexual desire. He falls into the trap of anticipatory anxiety, pass–fail intercourse, and increasing frustration and embarrassment.

What is the antidote? It is enjoying the cycle of touch—affectionate, sensual, playful, erotic, and intercourse (Figure 2.2). The focus is sharing pleasurable touch. Intercourse is best understood as a natural extension of the pleasure/eroticism process. We prefer the term *function* to *performance* because we want to emphasize the essential importance of the natural response to touch and pleasure rather than the pass–fail approach to intercourse.

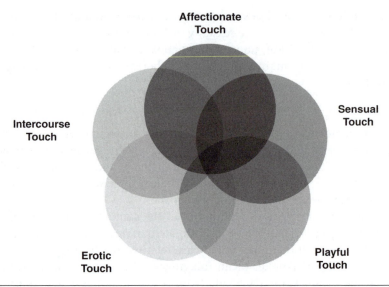

Figure 2.2 The 5 Kinds of Touch.

6. Be Wise in Regulating and Expressing Your Sexuality

Sex is not a mandate, it's a choice. You want to express your sexuality so it enhances your life and relationship. The traditional male charge of "be ready to have sex with any woman at any time and any situation" or "always take what you can get," is crazy-making and destructive. It seems like heresy for men to say "no" to sex, but you can't say "yes" to healthy, integrated sexuality unless you can say "no" to high-risk, destructive sex. In addition to the obvious issues of unwanted pregnancy, STD/HIV, and illegal sexual activity like exhibitionism and child sexual abuse, unregulated sexuality includes using sex compulsively to reduce anxiety (i.e., masturbate not for pleasure or stress reduction but as a way to avoid dealing with work issues or relationship frustrations) or to prove something to yourself or someone else (i.e., watching more porn than anyone in your group of friends), going to strip clubs or massage parlors when lonely, feeling that you have to have 14 orgasms a week or you will lose your masculine vitality, or needing to use riskier, more dangerous erotic scenarios and fantasies to feel turned on.

Remember, sex is a balance of pleasure, self-acceptance, partner intimacy, energizing your relationship, and personal and relational satisfaction. Sex is a positive, integral part of masculinity, but it is not the definition of being a man or the most important part of masculinity. Express your sexuality so that it enhances your self-esteem and relationship.

7. Be Aware of the Three Styles of Sexual Arousal and Choose
How to Integrate These Into Your Couple Sexual Style

Realizing that there are three sexual arousal styles (Figure 2.3) can help you (and your partner) find the right blend of arousal that will serve you well in your relationship.

The three styles of arousal (by frequency of use) are (a) partner interaction arousal, (b) self-entrancement arousal, and (c) role enactment arousal. The styles are distinguished by the focus of sexual attention—partner, physical relaxation and sexual sensations, or fantasy and erotic scenarios.

Partner interaction arousal focuses on partner touch and visual stimulation. This is the type of sex seen in movies and experienced early in the relationship. It utilizes two sexual guidelines—the "give to get" pleasure principle and that an involved, aroused partner is the major aphrodisiac. The man is active, eyes open, giving and receiving genital stimulation, talkative (erotic or romantic), and energetic. Each partner's arousal plays off the other's.

Self-entrancement arousal focuses on relaxing your body and being receptive and responsive to touch. He closes his eyes, is passive and takes in stimulation, and often relies on systematic and stylized touch as he becomes responsive and aroused.

Role enactment arousal is focused externally—on role play, variety, experimentation, unpredictability. The focus is on eroticism, not intimacy or pleasure. Examples include the woman dressing in sexy lingerie; role-playing being "sexually tough" or "virgin–prostitute"; having sex in new, risky places; using sexual toys like a vibrator or erotic video; and playing out erotic scenarios.

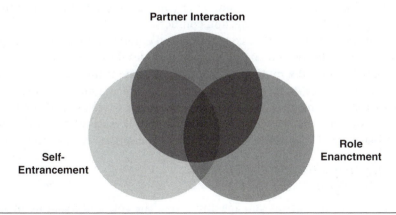

Figure 2.3 The 3 Styles of Sexual Arousal.

Some men utilize all three arousal styles and others only two. The most common pattern is a sequence of partner interaction and self-entrancement. Find the sexual arousal style that fits your situation.

The Common Male Worry—Sexual Boredom

Understanding these arousal styles helps you address a common male concern—sexual familiarity. You worry that sex with the same partner will become too familiar and arousal will become more difficult. If sex becomes too predictable, monotonous, boring, routine, the fear is that it will result in sexual dysfunction. Pornography producers understand this fear, which is why traditional magazines like *Playboy* or *Penthouse* are not one-time publications but monthly editions and why Internet sites have endless variety. Men who are burdened with this fear of boredom futilely demand excessive sexual variety from their partner or turn to pornography or sexual acting out.

The mistake is to believe that sexual arousal is solely dependent on variety and freshness. This reflects an overreliance on partner interaction arousal. When a man learns that sexual function with his partner is easier and more reliable with sensual self-entrancement and this can be supplemented with role-enactment arousal, his worry of sexual boredom and dysfunction is calmed. Healthy sexuality blends the multiple purposes for sex and multiple arousal styles.

8. Value Your Partner as Your Sexual Friend and Be an Intimate Team

In a one-night stand or a paid sexual encounter, the focus is on erotic sexuality; intimacy can interfere with sexual response. However, in a sexual friendship, serious relationship, or marriage, sex is part of an intimate relationship. Sex exists in the context of your real life activities, including dealing with chores, parenting, and conflicts.

Men traditionally pursue connection and emotional intimacy through sex. Sexuality for both men and women includes desire, arousal, orgasm, and satisfaction. At a minimum, being an intimate team means not treating sex as a power struggle or being coercive. Ideally, it means seeing your partner as your intimate and erotic friend, where touching and sexuality can serve a number of positive emotional and physical roles, and where you share positive as well as disappointing experiences without blaming.

9. Integrate Sex Into Your Real Life and
Your Real Life Into Your Sex Life

Your sex life changes as you age and grow. The role and meaning of sex is very different when you are a 15-year-old living at home, a 25-year-old young adult on your own, a 35-year-old man intent on conceiving his second child, a 45-year-old man feeling burdened with responsibility, a 55-year-old man who has launched his last child into college, a newly retired 65-year-old man, a 75-year-old man who is intent on beating the odds and maintaining physical health and sexual vitality, and an 85-year-old man who is enjoying a broad-based, flexible sexuality. The integration of varying life events into lovemaking recognizes the multiple purposes of sex. This can involve sex for anxiety release through orgasm, for emotional healing, for romance and emotional intimacy, and as a spiritual experience while sharing sadness about a parent's death. Sexuality has many roles and meanings in a man's life.

10. Realize That Good-Enough Sex Rather Than Settling for Mediocrity Is Genuine, Satisfying, and High Quality

This is such a central concept that we have devoted an entire chapter to it. Men worry that accepting Good-Enough Sex will somehow feminize them or means settling for second best. What nonsense. Theoretically, clinically, and personally we believe that the Good-Enough Sex model is the healthy, freeing, and realistic approach to male and couple sexuality. You are a sexual man, not a sexual robot/machine. Physically, emotionally, and relationally accepting sexual variability and flexibility is much superior to clinging to the traditional male model of perfect intercourse performance.

Closing Thoughts

It is crucial to establish a solid foundation for healthy male sexuality based on core concepts from the latest scientific findings and clinically relevant guidelines. Most of these new findings contradict the traditional macho sex role and perfect performance norm. Being a wise, confident, and strong sexual man entails awareness of healthy male (and couple) sexuality and adopting positive, realistic sexual expectations. You want to learn and adopt healthy thinking for healthy sexuality as a man.

CHAPTER 3

Boys to Men

What Is Normal and Healthy?

Your sexual growth is developmental and lifelong. Your sexuality as a boy, of course, is very different from that as an adult man. Yet there is a continuity between your childhood, adolescence, young manhood, and adulthood. You learn and grow through each developmental stage. Sexuality over the life cycle is a vital aspect of your personality, ripe for new learnings and personal growth; vulnerable to worries, hurts, and disappointments; and open to enhanced pleasure and intimacy whatever your age. In this chapter, we describe sexual behavior of boys, adolescents, and young adults. The facts—based in science—about what boys and young men do sexually can serve as reference points for understanding normal male sexual behavior as well as help you to determine what is healthy for you. We hope this will help you put your sexual development in a positive perspective and encourage you to be a healthy sex educator and model for your children.

Point of Reference #1: How We Learn About Sex

Boys and girls develop sexual health in similar and different ways. It is difficult to accurately understand these developmental features because of the limited amount of research on the sexuality of children, but scientific data do offer perspective. Otherwise, given the silence about children's sexuality, we are left to our own concept of what is normal or our observation of our own and others kids' experiences. Research about childhood sexual experiences can help you gain perspective on your experiences and what is healthy for you.

Boys' Childhood Sexual Experiences

First let's review what we know about the sexual experiences of boys and adolescents. One hundred years ago, Sigmund Freud explained that young children are sexual (although not in an adult way; e.g., intercourse), but the current cultural climate in the United States is quite polarized. The prevailing belief is that children are not sexual. What most of us remember from our own experiences as children, as well as what sexual research tells us, is that children are sexual persons—curious, inquisitive about our own body (penis) and others' bodies (penis, vagina), and experimental about pleasure (including penile and anal stimulation) and other kids' bodies. This inquisitiveness is the normal way children develop healthy sexuality.

How Boys Learn About Sex

How and what you learned about sex as a boy is likely similar to other boys of your generation. Because of the confusing sources of sex information, the variability in information, and the attitude accompanying the information, the quality of your learning will vary. The primary sex educators are parents; church, synagogue, or mosque; schools; the media; and other kids.

Parents as Sex Educators. The majority of parents (surveys suggest about 60%) do not say anything directly to their sons (or daughters) about sexuality. While this is unfortunate, it is very understandable, because most parents themselves did not receive any education from their own parents. For those who did receive parental sex education, it was often quite brief, in many cases, one-liners such as "Don't get into trouble," "Don't do anything you should not do," "Don't get her pregnant," or "Be sure to use condoms." From the surveys conducted in the United States, as well as our impressions from sexual history interviews we've had with thousands of men and women, it is clear that detailed, accurate, and healthy sex education messages and values from parents was sadly lacking. Some parents did offer their children books about sex, yet often the timing was several years late in terms of what might be useful. It seems that parents hope that schools, religious groups, or entertainment media will provide sex education instead.

Schools as Sex Educators. Most schools offer some form of sex education, although because of the public debates about sex education in schools, fueled by the 3–5% of ultraconservative parents who oppose it, the information is often watered down and limited to anatomy, sexual abuse, and STDs (sexually transmitted diseases). Some schools do attempt to discuss healthy relationships and future marriage. Others insert fundamentalist religious morality, which is often viewed as propaganda and turns young people off. People do benefit from human sexuality courses that are offered at colleges and universities. In addition, young people and adults find helpful, accurate, and positive books and other educational media through bookstores and reliable Web sites.

Religious Groups as Sex Educators. Several studies suggest that the best quality sex education is provided by moderate and liberal synagogues and mainline churches. They provide accurate information and positive sex values communicated from a religious perspective. This is different from approaches that present human sexuality outside of marriage as suspect, evil or sinful, warranting condemnation. In faith communities, sexuality can be valued as God created, positive ("God doesn't create junk"), and blessed when age appropriate and realistic.

Studies evaluating sex education programs that focus on a "say no" or abstinence standpoint without comprehensive and accurate sex information, wherein younger people pledge to be virgins until they wed find that, although well intentioned, they are not helpful to young people. Virginity pledges misguide young people and set them up to fail with unrealistic, simplistic notions that dishonor adolescent males and females who are trying to integrate healthy, realistic sexuality into their young lives. Studies of virginity pledges report that more that 85% of people violate their pledges, setting up guilt and shame as well as leading to STDs, unwanted pregnancies, and a sense of failure.

We think it is a wiser, more realistic, and healthier approach to provide young people with accurate, balanced, open information about sexuality from a positive perspective within the parents' religious or personal value systems. When fully informed about sex, young people are found to be more responsible, protective (from pregnancy and STDs), and more self-regulating of sexual impulses and behaviors. Studies find that fully informed young people make wiser choices and are more likely to delay sexual behaviors until the person feels personally ready—which may be marriage (although less than 10% of men wait until marriage to have intercourse). The United States has the highest unwanted youth pregnancy rate in the developed world. This is the result of sexual ignorance and naïveté, including virginity pledges that fail and sex that is unprotected in terms of pregnancy and STDs.

The Media as Sex Educators. Unfortunately, most young people are educated by the media—television, music, the Internet, and movies. Young people may not be savvy enough to understand that sex can be used to grab their attention in order to market a commercial product such as a CD, clothes, or movies. The information communicated through these media may not only be exaggerated but in most cases promote myths and distortions. Part of being a healthy sexual man is understanding the role of the advertising media not as an agent to accurately inform but rather to sell products. Without accurate information about your body, feelings, and growth, unreasonable expectations and distorted beliefs will result.

Common Negative Messages That Boys Learn About Sex

As a boy, what was your impression of sex? You were probably well aware of sex on television and in advertisements, cheerleaders at sporting events, girls at dances, Victoria's Secret, and *Playboy*. How comprehensive and accurate was the information you received? Many men remember growing up with an avoidance of sex or a great silence from the important people in their lives—parents, teachers, role models. Perhaps silence is better than negative messages, warnings, scare tactics, or condemnations. Yet, avoidance has its own message. Negative messages can be very harmful, but at least they are blunt, and a young person can question whether they are fair, honest, accurate, and meant to be helpful. When nothing is said about sex, youth receive a message that sex is so shameful that we cannot, should not, talk of it. Covert negative emotional information is a source of sexual shame and may be unhealthier than negative information.

The paradox is that as a boy there are many mixed messages. Sexual aspects of youthful life—seeing girls, curiosity about bodies, sexual interests, feelings of excitement, spontaneous (and, yes, embarrassing) erections in situations you don't want, like an erection on the bus or classroom—are amusing in retrospect. Yet, there is learned shame about such things—but there was no one to openly talk to about these confusing messages and experiences.

Mixed Messages. The confusion boys experience about sex is not surprising. Our society, with its great diversity, has mixed, confusing, and competing messages about sex. "Don't do anything…" versus "Whatever you can get…" or "Anything goes." Suppression competes with opportunism. Condemnation versus celebration. In some cases, condemnation exists together with sexually acting out. You recognize the hypocrisy of these situations and develop cynicism and mistrust of authority figures as credible guides for sexual health.

Messages to Regulate Sex. One paradox that we recognize in our clinical practice with adult men, especially those whose sexuality has gotten them into trouble—affairs, compulsive sex, harassment—is that they don't remember ever learning from an important, credible adult man (or woman) that sexual feelings are healthy but, like other human feelings, must be regulated. On the other hand, a good number of adult men received the opposite message—sex must be controlled like a slave camp. The irony is that both underregulation and overregulation can handicap a man and become a barrier to balanced, healthy, male sexuality. Underregulation encourages a man to sexually act out, and overregulation robs him of sexual enjoyment and intimate bonding.

Male Bravado. Men have a problem with being open with each other. We cannot be honest and open about our actual sexual thoughts and feelings or we run the risk of teasing, ridicule, or even harassment. Locker rooms do not tolerate genuine communication about sex. Rather, the competitiveness encourages bravado, hyperbole, and exaggeration: "Hey, John; Aaron scored with your girl last night…"

Negative Impressions of the Sexual Behavior of Adult Men. As boys, we also took in messages about men and sex by the events and issues that were in our family or the community media. Perhaps it was a cousin, who was only 16 when she became pregnant—"What is wrong with that girl?" Or your mother fighting with your father and accusing him of infidelity. Or, the unmarried couple next door were such nice neighbors, but it didn't seem conceivable that they had sex because they were so kind and respectful. You remember the news stories about the little girl in New Jersey who was abducted by a man and the victim of a "lust crime." Or, your mother laments that uncle Jerry is gay so he won't have a "normal" life, and that is "so sad." Or, you were caught masturbating, and the shame washed over you like a tidal wave. Yet aunt Jodi and uncle Steve were fondling on the couch one evening when you walked in on them and they seemed happy; but then they were embarrassed that you discovered them. And the movie star couple that your mother thought was so cute got a divorce because the guy picked up a prostitute. You heard about the clergyman who was arrested for sex abuse of a young girl or the lawyer who went to jail for having child pornography on his computer.

Such events carry messages for many boys and young men that are internalized as confusing and shameful messages about male sexuality. Men's sexuality can be bad; dangerous; troubled; criminal; harmful. And where were the positive images, events, messages? Can you imagine the TV news reporting that the president and the first lady have a healthy sex life? Or that the pope has proclaimed male sexuality as one of God's greatest gifts to humanity?

Duplicity, Ambivalence, Confusion. The result of such experiences growing up creates a lack of accurate information, confusion about the powerful sexual energy in your body, shame about sexual feelings, and compulsion instead of sexual energy regulation. Regulation difficulty is an important male sexual health issue, whether one of overly controlled sexual impulses (difficulty letting go and enjoying sex in a committed relationship) or undercontrolled sexual impulses (difficulty managing sexual impulses such as pornography misuse or exhibitionism).

Illustration 3.1: The Different Sex Educations of Steve, Brian, and Todd

Steve

Steve's childhood sexual learnings illustrate a young man who received little adult guidance and lived a lonely life in his family. Steve grew up in a very loose ("hands-free") family. Parents and siblings went about their own business and did as they pleased. It was a sort of "official" family, pit-stopping for supplies. Steve grew up with an absence of comforting touch and affection. As Steve grew older, he realized that his family felt "cold," emotionally detached from each other. He often felt lonely. The family expectation was for him to take care of himself and do well in school. He received no information about sex from his parents, who were often absent and avoided personal matters. Without any guidance from his parents about sex, he learned about sex on the streets and from music and visual media. Pornography was easy to come by and gave him the impression that sex was about fun and orgasm and a way to feel less lonely. There were no boundaries—"Anything goes." From the age of 12, he became sexually promiscuous, impulsively seeking sex. He sought to fill the emotional void of his family life through sex. By 17, he had had multiple sexual partners and an STD. His sexual health was on an unfortunate, misguided path.

Brian

Brian illustrates a young man from a strict and repressive family. His needs for touch, hugging, consolation, and affection were poorly met by his mother, who was depressed, and his father, who believe corporal punishment made "good kids." When he was 6 years old, his mother caught him with a 6-year-old neighbor girl comparing genitals and he was told never to do that again or his mother would spank his penis with a spoon. Brian received instruction that sex was bad and relationships with girls were dangerous. "You stay out of a girl's pants or I'll beat the shit out of you," his father had warned; and "Girls are trouble, so stay away from them," his mother advised.

(Continued)

(Continued)

He was only allowed to socialize with boys or in large groups of boys and girls. When he was found with two girls and one other boy, he was grounded for a month.

Sex education in school consisted of a class on reproduction and sexually transmitted diseases. While Brian was at times aware of having strong sexual desires, he quickly denied them and told himself that he was not a very sexual man. Sex became a threat to him although he at times longed for the touch he so wanted as a child but did not receive. He felt little sexual desire, thought of himself as asexual, and trained himself to be sexless by excessive commitment to school and video games.

Todd

Todd illustrates a positive developmental experience. He grew up in a family where physical holding as an infant brought him a sense of security and attachment. Hugging and touching were common throughout his childhood. While his parents said little about sex per se, they talked naturally about his having a penis, girls having vaginas, and sex as part of being an adult. Touch was about affection and comfort, and as a child he was soothed by both his mother and his father when injured or hurt. At 5, he learned sexual privacy when his mother discovered him touching his penis in the living room, and she used the situation to teach that his penis is a source of pleasure but only in private. At school he learned about sexual anatomy, reproduction, and STDs. His parents encouraged him in day-to-day and matter-of-fact ways to respect others and value friendships with both boys and girls. He was given several sex-positive books when he was 9 and 12 that were age appropriate. His parents were responsive to the questions he asked over the years of his childhood and puberty. All in all, he socialized with his friends, talked with his mother to learn to handle his hurt feelings when a girl he liked in eighth grade "dumped him," and gradually learned to understand and negotiate his sexual feelings in relationships. He learned about his sexual desires in a progressive way. He "played doctor" with two other children at age 6, went to dances as an adolescent, hugged, held hands, kissed a girl, fondled her clothed breasts, became erect as his girlfriend fondled his penis through his pants, progressively experienced sexual pleasure with a girlfriend, and practiced contraception and STD prevention when he first had intercourse at age 19.

These three brief examples of sex education in the family demonstrate the variability in the quality of touch and the attitudes toward the body and sex. Our view is that regardless of what training you received—the "anything goes" of Steve, the severe repression of Brian, or the more positive learnings of Todd—your sexual health is now under your control. You need to learn to value and express your sexuality so that it enhances your life and relationship.

Exercise 3.1: How and What Did You Learn About Sexuality as a Child?

Directions: Try to remember different learnings about touch, your body, and sex at different ages in your life. For example, remember the comfort you felt when scared as a 4-year-old you were cradled by your mom, or your father talked to you about girls, or you were touching your penis as a child and your mother saw this. In the space below, write a brief summary of several experiences, and what you thought and felt. Then indicate whether the experience for you was + (positive), − (negative), or +/− (ambivalent).

Age	Description of the experience:	Your thoughts and impressions. The message:	Your feelings	Positive vs. negative

Point of Reference #2: Scientific Learnings About Childhood Sex Behaviors

Ages 2–5 Years Old

Child psychologists tell us that children are very sexually interested and curious. Childhood sexuality involves learning about your body, other kids' bodies, sensual feelings of touch, as well as guidance from adults about what is appropriate. Childhood sexuality is much broader than adult notions of sex, which are focused on arousal and intercourse. Children may role-play intercourse or having a baby, but the explorations are almost always about age-appropriate touch, physical exploration, and play. The reality is that healthy children are sexual people, and children explore and act in sexual ways.

A respected child psychologist, Dr. William Friedrich, has studied boys and girls' sexual behaviors in the United States at different ages using his Childhood Sex Behavior Index (CSBI; 1997). This index measures what adults (usually parents or teachers) observe a child doing. Some of the behaviors he has studied—and some behaviors you may remember doing as a boy—are listed in Table 3.1.

Dr. Friedrich' s research indicates that (a) children are curious, sexual beings and will exhibit a broad range of sexual behaviors. Some adults may

Table 3.1 Observed Childhood Sexual Behaviors

Touches genitals when in public places
Masturbates with hand
Draws genitals when drawing pictures of people
Touches or tries to touch women's breasts (e.g., mother, aunt)
Masturbates with toy or object (blanket, pillow, plastic toy)
Touches another child's genitals
Touches genitals at home
Touches animal's genitals or nipples
Makes sexual sounds (sighs, moans, heavy breathing, etc.)
Rubs body or genitals against people or furniture
Tries to look at people when they are nude or undressing
Pretends that dolls or stuffed animals are having sex
Shows genitals to adults
Dresses like the opposite sex
Stands too close to people
Tries to look at pictures of nude or partially dressed people
Talks about genitals
Kisses and hugs other children they do not know well
Shows genitals to other children
Is very interested in the opposite sex
Puts his mouth on mother's or other women's breasts

Note. Selected items from the Childhood Sexual Behavior Inventory, W. Friedrich, 1997.

overreact and make the mistake of viewing child experiences as automatic indications that children have been sexually abused, but these behaviors are common among children; (b) sexual behavior is ubiquitous in preteen children; (c) younger children had higher (more frequent) scores on sexual behavior than older children because as children develop, they learn to set boundaries and regulate their behaviors in public; and (d) almost all sexual behaviors in children are nonpathologic, follow a developmental course, and can be quite varied (Friedrich, 2003).

The Importance of Adult Reactions

Because so much of childhood sexual behavior is normal exploration, an important dimension of learning sexual health as a boy is the reaction of important adults to the sex behavior. In your life, do you remember parents reacting in a positive but direct way when you were publicly touching your penis? Did they calmly teach you, "Touching yourself feels good, doesn't it, but you should only do this at home, in private." Or did they react with shock and disgust? "Oh! Don't ever do that again!" When adults are positive, calm, and clear about sexual boundaries, kids learn healthy messages and boundaries. If this positive approach was your prominent experience growing up, appreciate your parents' wisdom. If not, it is now your job as a man to develop healthier beliefs, feelings, and behaviors—and to be a sex educator with your own children.

Sex Behaviors of 2- to 5-Year-Old Boys

The commonly reported sexual behaviors of boys aged 2–5 are (a) touching his penis or anus at home (60%); (b) touching or trying to touch his mother's or another woman's breasts (42%); (c) standing too close to people (29%); (d) touching his penis or anus in public places (27%); and (e) trying to look at people when they are nude or undressing (27%). By comparison, the reported behaviors of girls aged 2–5 are: (a) touching her vagina or anus at home (44%); (b) touching or trying to touch her mother's or another woman's breasts (44%); (c) trying to look at people when they are nude or undressing (27%); and (d) standing too close to people (26%). Interestingly, the sexual behaviors of young boys and girls are similar. Differences are that boys engage in more frequent sexual behaviors than girls, and the girls are observed to touch their genitals less in public.

Sex Behaviors of 6- to 12-Year-Old Boys

For boys aged 6–12 years old, overt sexual behaviors decline from young childhood. Between the ages of 6 and 9, the common sexual behaviors are: (a) touching his penis or anus at home (40%) and (b) trying to look at people when they are nude or undressing (20%). During the ages of 10–12 years old, boys ceased public sexual behaviors (they learned the boundary) other than acting interested in the opposite sex (24%).

Similar to boys, girls' overt sexual behaviors decline. Girls aged 6–9 (a) touched their vagina or anus at home (21%) as well as (b) tried to look at people when they were nude or undressing (21%). When 10–12 years old, they, like the boys, were observed to be very interested in the opposite sex (29%).

These data show that boys and girls are sexual individuals, that their public sexual behaviors decline from toddlerhood to puberty, and that during these years, children are learning the values and boundaries of the family and community.

Studies of children 0–11 years old in Europe also confirm the sexual curiosity and behaviors of boys and girls. Perhaps because some European societies are more sexually open and accepting, studies report more sexual behaviors than in the United States. For example, "touching breasts" is reported for 42% of U.S. boys (and girls); in Spain, 63% (Lopez Sanchez, Del Campo, & Guijo, 2002); in Sweden, 68% (Larsson & Svedin, 2002); and in the Netherlands, 74% (Sandfort & Cohen-Kettenis, 2000).

What Is Natural and Healthy Sexual Behavior for Children?

Children are curious, exploratory, and mimic adults. While some adults want to believe that children are not sexual—that is, curious about their bodies, genitals, physical pleasure, other kids and their bodies, adults and their bodies—the research data indicate that children are sexual (although not with an intercourse focus). Boys (and girls) are progressively learning about their bodies, how they work, and anticipating becoming sexual adults. Parents may remember their childhood sexual explorations and experiences but, because of sexual shame, avoid appreciating what their own children may be doing. Parents are frequently confused about what is healthy childhood behavior. Parents want their kids to grow up well but the societal silence, superficiality, and social shame make it difficult to know what is sexually healthy.

How to Evaluate the Health of Your Childhood Sexual Behaviors

How do you know if your sexual behaviors as a boy were normal? Was your sex play typical, or was it peculiar or extreme? Because the range of sexual behaviors is broad and what motivates the sexual behavior can be so complex, this is not an easy question to answer.

Understanding your sexual behaviors as a boy is important because your childhood learnings influence your sexual health now—your thoughts and feelings about yourself. To evaluate your childhood sexual behaviors, consider (a) your age at the time; (b) whether your primary motivation was curiosity or to be provocative, and (c) the level of hostility or rebelliousness against parental boundaries.

If your childhood sexual behaviors reflected age-appropriate curiosity, and you respected boundaries that you were taught, you likely had adults in your life who were promoting sexual health. On the other hand, if your childhood sex behaviors were provocative, hostile, repetitive (you kept doing the same provocative behaviors), and you did not have instruction from parents or other adults about sexual boundaries, you probably learned unhealthy attitudes and feelings that impeded sexual growth. Remember that the vast majority of childhood sexual behaviors are exploratory and age appropriate, so do not make the mistake of labeling them sick or deviant unless (a) you clearly see them as provocative or hostile/angry and (b) you did not outgrow the stage.

As you recall your childhood sexual experiences, consider your placement on the sexual behavior health continuum (Figure 3.1). Here are some factors to consider:

- Use the results of studies of childhood sexual behaviors as a starting point for getting your bearings on what children do. These studies probably underreport what children actually do because parents and teachers do not see or know about every behavior of their kids. Use these data as a reference point for understanding your own experiences.
- Remember and accept that age-appropriate childhood sexual experiences with peers is normal, but not with adults or adolescents

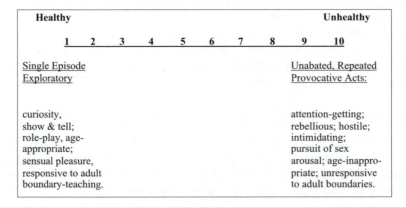

Figure 3.1 The Childhood Sexual Behavior Health Continuum.

5 years older. Children may be curious and even provocative, but it is the adult's responsibility to set clear physical and emotional boundaries with a child. For example, when a child asks to touch an adult's breasts or penis, the adult needs to calmly say no. When adults appropriately handle such experiences, kids learn healthy sexual boundaries.

- Exploratory sexual behaviors vary by age and are healthy when age appropriate. Sexual behaviors that do not fit the child's age are questionable and can be problematic.
- Consider the purpose of your childhood sex behavior. Was it exploratory—"show and tell"—or provocative or attention getting? Was there a rebellious quality to it? To what extent was it seeking sensual pleasure or sexual arousal? Was the behavior motivated by other than sexual feelings (loneliness, frustration, anxiety, anger)? This reflects the issue of emotional sexualization. To what extent was a boundary breached repetitively, especially after a parent or other adult told you that the behavior was not age or socially appropriate? A single event of innocent exploration (curiosity) by a 4-year-old who responds to the parents boundary-teaching is normal and healthy, whereas a 4-year-old who cruelly hits another boy's penis and, even after parental instruction, repeats the behavior rebelliously, raises serious psychological and sexual concerns.
- Identify the level of sexual health that occurred in your childhood and adolescence. If you feel confused or concerned, consult a psychologist who specializes in sexual therapy to assess your thoughts, behaviors, and feelings. Also, if you viewed your experiences as being sexually abusive, humiliating, or traumatic, using therapy to help you understand and process this will enhance your adult sexual health.

Point of Reference #3: Sex Is a Learned Behavior

We learn appropriate sexual behaviors and comfort gradually over years. We take in information and learn attitudes toward our and other persons' bodies and about pleasurable feelings with touch. We learn as infants and children that touching and being held feels comforting and enhances feelings of safety. We learn that parts of our bodies—our penis, testicles, or anus—bring special pleasure. Our curiosity about our bodies and others' bodies leads us to examine and experiment. A feature of the healthy step-by-step exploratory process is when children and adolescents progress at their own pace, guided by their own curiosity and comfort level. In fact, one of the destructive features of child sex abuse is that the abusive behaviors interrupt—even destroy—the spontaneous and natural self-determining sequence of this growth process. Sex, like other aspects of life, is learned when we are ready to learn. Child psychologists refer to this as *developmental readiness*.

There is an imprecise sequence to growth in sexual health. Individual boys have their own pace of comfort and readiness. Touch and affection as infants and children, curious explorations of touch, and information-seeking about genitals and gender differences are healthy. Age-appropriate explanations are received from parents, and boundaries are learned from patient, understanding adults. For example, a 4-year-old learns "Yes, it feels good to touch your penis, but you do that only when you are alone in your room or the bathroom. It's private." There is a respect for the child's readiness when adults offer matter-of-fact acceptance and teaching about your body, honesty about sensual feelings, and help in managing sexual feelings.

Healthy Step-by-Step Progressive Sexual Learnings

Gradually, children gain more experience and grow because of their curiosity about others, learn words for sexual body parts, discover self-touch, examine other children's bodies, learn boundaries acceptable to the adult world, and gradually progress in the level of sensual–sexual experiences.

To grow from playfully holding hands with a girl at age 3 or 4 to "playing doctor" with a neighbor kid as a 6- or 7-year-old, to holding hands and kissing as a 10- or 12-year-old, to experimenting with breast fondling and genital touching as a 12- to 15-year-old reflects a natural progression that is guided by the individual's level of curiosity and comfort. When this progression proceeds with the self-determined readiness and age-appropriate spontaneity of the child and adolescent, sexual health is facilitated (Brady & Levitt, 1965). Should this sequence be interrupted or experienced out of sequence (such as in childhood sex abuse), a boy's sexual development can be disrupted, fueled by internal sexual conflicts and broken trust in adults.

Prevalence of Self-Reported Childhood Sexual Experience with Peers

Studies that ask adults to remember their own childhood experiences report childhood sexual experiences with peers ranging from 39 to 87% depending on age. Reynolds, Herbenick, and Bancroft (2003) found that 87% of adult males and 84% of adult females remembered having sexual experiences with peers prior to starting high school. Among very young children this may involve helping each other wipe after using the toilet, asking to touch the other's genitals, kissing while pretending to be married, or swapping stories about adult sexual talk. U.S. studies report that about 66% of boys (57% girls) play doctor (Greenwald & Leitenberg, 1988; Haugaard, 1996), and 64% of boys (59% of girls; Goldman & Goldman, 1988) in Australia do; in Spain, 94% (boys and girls; Lopez Sanchez et al., 2002), and in Sweden, 76% (74% of girls; Larsson & Svedin, 2002). Late grade-school and middle-school children frequently engage in kissing and light fondling and sometimes direct genital stimulation.

Forty-three percent of males and 30% of females reported that there was erotica or pornography in their home, and many more—80% of males and 49% of females—reported having access to pornographic materials outside of the home during childhood.

What If You Did Not Have Healthy Sexual Experiences and Learnings?

While parents, teachers, policy-makers, and others worry about childhood sexual experiences with peers, it is important to understand that age-appropriate sexual exploration is healthy and part of sexual growth. In fact, the question is "What happens to children who have no childhood sexual experiences with other kids?" Several studies (Rutter, 1982; Greenwald & Leitenberg, 1988) indicate that without age-appropriate childhood sexual experiences, men actually found it more difficult in their 30s to become sexual, to experience sexual well-being, and to be free from sexual problems. This reinforces the beneficial effects of graduated and sequential sexual experiences.

Comfort and skills are learned step-by-step, over years of experience. Think how stressful and strange a job interview would be had you not interacted with adults at school, given talks in class, or filled out forms throughout school years. Similarly, experiences with touching, kissing, hugging, fondling through clothes, fondling with clothes partially removed, laying together on a sofa or a towel on the beach, and learning what such experiences involve and how they feel are healthy when you are ready and it is welcomed, comfortable, and acceptable for both the boy and the girl.

Exercise 3.2: Sexual Health and Your Peer Sexual Experiences

Experiences with peers are the way we learn and grow sexually. Sexual experiences as a young boy helped establish your feelings about your body and your sexuality. In retrospect, how do you feel about your childhood sexual experiences with peers?

Did you have sexual exploratory experiences with peers—meaning with children within 1 year of your age when you were 2–5 years old? Within 1–2 years when you were 6–12?

What types of sexual experiences with much older or younger kids did you have? How did you feel then about the experience? How do you feel now? Was there a power difference involving intimidation or coercion?

How ready were you for these different sexual experiences? How did your readiness influence your feeling of comfort or anxiety? How did you feel about the behavior at the time? Now?

(Continued)

(*Continued*)

What motivated you to engage in sexual exploration—Curiosity? Hostility? Rebelliousness? Fear of rejection? Loneliness?

To what extent were you prodded or forced into sexual experiences by peers?

To what extent did you prod or coerce peers into sexual experiences? What motivated you? Curiosity? Hostility? Rebelliousness? Demand for acceptance? Loneliness?

Adolescent Sexual Behavior

Try to remember what you felt like as a 13-, 15-, or 17-year-old. Those years move quickly for most boys. Often 13- or 14-year-old boys feel deep shyness and mask it with bravado. Learning what it means to be a man as a 13-year-old is challenging! The "toughness" message is dominant: "Men don't cry"; it's crucial to act confident and strong; masculinity is grounded on competitiveness; or sex is automatic and autonomous.

Learning to Masturbate

How did you learn about masturbation? Boys typically learn from the talk of other boys and experimentation. Your age when you first masturbated to ejaculation is an important marker in your development to manhood. Boys typically first ejaculate with masturbation between 12 and 14, the age when voice change and pubic hair development begin (Bancroft, Herbenick, & Reynolds, 2003).

The myths about the dangers of masturbation are not as great as in the past but are still reflected in the difficulty in discussing this behavior. Masturbation in the past 150 years is an interesting study in erroneous thinking even within the medical community (Michael, Gagnon, Laumann, & Kolata, 1994). Before the American Revolution, many physicians believed that masturbation was the cause of illnesses like tuberculosis and neuroses. While we understand now that fears of masturbation are unfounded, fueled by myth and preserved by the shame and silence around accurate discussions of sexuality, these myths are slow to die. Integrating positive attitudes toward masturbation even today amidst such myths illustrate the barriers to male sexual health. In truth, masturbation is a healthy, developmental sexual behavior.

First Intercourse

Over the past 50 years, sexual activity has started at progressively younger ages (Guttenmacher Institute, 1998). However, in recent years, the proportion of males between 15 and 17 who have intercourse has decreased

Table 3.2 Reasons Reported for Having Intercourse the First Time

Reason	Men (%)	Women (%)
Curiosity/ready for sex	51	24
Affection for partner	25	48
Physical pleasure	12	3
Wedding night	7	21
Peer pressure	4	3
Wanted to have a baby	0	1

Note. From *The social organization of sexuality: Sexual practices in the United States*, by E. O. Laumann, J. H. Gagnon, R. T. Michael, and S Michaels (1994). Chicago: University of Chicago Press. Table 9.3, p. 329.

significantly, and condom use has become more frequent (Bancroft, 2003). Yet, 25% of sexually active teenagers become infected with a sexually transmitted disease each year (Bancroft, 2003).

Four out of five young males have had intercourse before they reach age 21. Reasons for first intercourse are summarized in Table 3.2. Laumann, Gagnon, Michael, and Michaels (1994) found that peer pressure is now more of a factor and that there are more opportunities for younger people to initiate intercourse than in the past. When first intercourse occurs and a young man (or young woman) is not ready or does not want it, peer pressure is an important influence (29% of men and 25% of women), as well as the influence of alcohol or drugs (3% of men and 7% of women).

Do Media Presentations of Male Sexuality Help Sexual Growth?

The abundance of sex in the media causes a great deal of pressure to keep up. Using sexual moods to market multiple products directly targets youth. Young men easily identify with the Bud Light beer commercial model of male sexuality. Beer commercials show young people as physical and partying. The message is that drinking and unbridled sex go together. The focus on the female body, breasts (wet T-shirts), or the male's muscles and genital bulge suggests that the objective is to drink beer and "score."

In R-rated films sex is always short, intense, nonverbal, perfect, and, most important, the man is always turned on before they even begin. Interestingly, marital sex is rarely portrayed in movies; rather, it is premarital sex or an extramarital affair. Pornography videos present an even more unrealistic model. The porn star always has a firm erection no matter what, and the crazier the woman and the more bizarre the situation, the more erotic it is. The message could not be simpler—male sexuality is youthful, illicit, wild, easy, and requires no intimacy, cooperation, or pleasuring.

These presentations make great fantasy but are unrealistic. Sexually healthy men clearly know the difference.

Exercise 3.3: Your Sexual History

Take time to remember your own sensual/sexual experiences as a boy and adolescent. Use the columns to help you recall what you did (e.g., play doctor) your feelings then, what you thought about it at the time, and your feelings and sense of meaning now.

Age	Sexual experience	Feelings then	Thoughts then	Feelings and meaning now
Example: 8 years old...	Played doctor with neighbor girl	Curious, fascinated, yet afraid of discovery by adults	Perplexed at my interest and curiosity. What is this about?	Accepting of my childhood curiosity and sad at the secrecy and shame around sex as a boy
2–5 years old				
5–8 years old				
9–11 years old				
12–15 years old				
15–18 years old				
19–25 years old				

Young Adult Sexual Practices

The sexual behaviors and experiences of young men are quite varied. Studies of young adult sex practices provide yet another reference point for what men and women do, but be careful to not use these data as a standard for your sexual health. Data give averages, including healthy and unhealthy men, healthy and unhealthy motivations. Nevertheless, the numbers can give you a reference point for understanding your own sexual experiences.

Men have an average of 6 sexual partners in their lifetime; the range is zero to hundreds of partners. What do you think is healthy? Do you think it is healthy to have one sex partner in a lifetime? 6? 20? Is it healthy to have hundreds?

Sexual frequency for men is about 1–2 times a week. Again, this is an average with a range from rare (less than monthly is considered a sexless relationship) to three times a day (among new young couples). About one third have partner sex at least twice a week, a third have partner sex several times a month, and the other third have partner sex a few times a year or have no sex partner. Remember, sexual satisfaction is a function of sharing pleasure and being an intimate team rather than sexual frequency.

Experiencing a sexual dysfunction (like premature ejaculation) is statistically normal—most young men will begin as premature ejaculators or on occasion do not get an erection. The issue is how you deal with a sexual problem. If you panic and overreact, you will unintentionally set up subsequent performance pressures that will make the sexual problem more severe and chronic.

Physically healthy men will enjoy lifelong sexual function.

Sexual Identity and Orientation

You've probably experienced thoughts, feelings, or fantasies about men and felt confused by these. While sexual orientation—heterosexual, homosexual, bisexual, transgender—is talked about in either–or (straight or gay) labels—in reality, orientation is more about qualities of your sexuality than a state. Your orientation identity (see Figure 3.2) is best described as the composite of five features:

1. your sexual attraction,
2. sexual behavior,
3. fantasy arousal,
4. social preferences (e.g., friends), and
5. emotional preferences (the gender you feel most emotionally comfortable with).

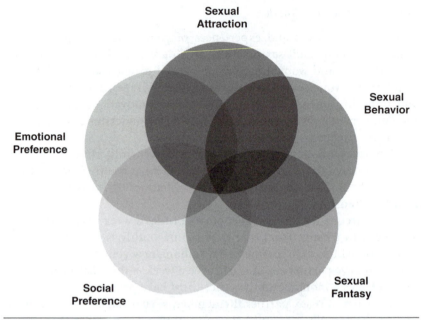

Figure 3.2 The 5 Features of Orientation Identity.

The NHSL study reported that 6% of men were attracted to other men, 5% had engaged in same-sex behavior since turning 18, and 2% had engaged in same-sex behavior in the prior year. Nine percent said they had engaged in same-sex behavior since puberty and of these, 40% reported their same-sex behavior occurred before they were 18 (Laumann et al., 1994). In regard to one's identity as homosexual (combining the 5 features), 3% of men defined themselves so, although other research suggests that the figure is between 4 and 6%. Fear of homosexuality is almost universal among boys and adolescents (who worry about being normal), which adds to the prejudice about gay men.

Point of Reference #4: Common Male Worries About Sex at Different Ages

The hallmark of male sexual health is feeling comfortable with your sexuality. This simple but reliable standard of sexual health can be your measure at any age as long as you do not "bullshit" yourself. Feeling a level of comfort with your body, regulation of your sexual fantasies and behaviors, your relationship, sexual function, level of intimacy with your partner, and your place in the larger community is a reliable mark of your sexual health.

Throughout our lives there are a variety of sexual worries or self-doubts we experience. Review them—not to accentuate your anxiety but to remind yourself that most men share these concerns (although we don't share them openly with each other) and that we can and do grow through them. You can increase your comfort and enhance your sexual health.

Childhood—Confusion and Uncertainty

We are naturally curious as boys, and we explore our bodies from infancy. Touch is one of the basic needs of every person. We experiment by touching our penis, testicles, anus, and other body parts as we learn about our own sensuality. As we grow through childhood, we may wonder about other children's bodies, how girls are different, what it might feel like to touch another person's genitals, and whether other kids feel some of the same feelings. In the process of learning boundaries, we may be confused about why adults seem anxious about sexuality and what is expected of us. Boys feel confused about the negative messages they receive about their bodies and curiosity. Perhaps the most common worry for boys is how to integrate their natural curiosity with mixed or absent messages about what is appropriate sexual behavior.

Teenage Years—"Am I Normal?"

The overriding concern of teenagers is normalcy. With the myths and hiddenness about sex, it is difficult for an adolescent to compare his personal experiences and observations of his body with the distorted and inaccurate impressions he receives from others and the media. Concern about his normalcy, anxiety about the uncertainties of becoming a sexual man, and conflicts between his feelings and the public portrayal of men and sex present major worries for many adolescents.

Teen boys have a number of worries, many about their body and how it works. Is masturbation okay? Is it normal to have wet dreams? Is my penis normal? Am I attractive? Why do I have spontaneous erections? What does my curiosity and interest in other boys mean? Am I gay? How am I supposed to perform sexually? What am I supposed to do? What about sexually transmitted diseases? Should I be more sexually involved than I am? Is it okay to feel uncertain and scared about sex matters? Will I find acceptance with a girl? What's a girl's body all about? What does she like/want? Will I become a good lover?

Your Sexual Road Map

The road from infancy through childhood, boyhood, adolescence, and young adulthood to healthy adult sexuality travels through literally thousands of formative experiences involving comfort versus discomfort with touch, body acceptance, curiosity about your genitals, the sexuality of others, exploring your body and its pleasures, masturbation, hugging and kissing, questions about your sexual being and fantasies, confusion about the powerful sexual urges in your body, emotions of fear and shame, anxiety about your curious explorations, strong feelings and urges about a girlfriend, depression over whether your sexual urges are "sick," feeling the awkwardness of sexual experimentation, enjoying the pleasures of sexual fondling ("petting"), questions about normalcy, loneliness, confusion, and worry. Also, it is difficult if there is no trusted person to ask for accurate information about sex.

This road has brought you to your current level of sexual health. If you feel you've only been a passenger on this trip of sexual growth, now is a good time to become the driver. You're now in charge of your sexual health. The rest of your life offers plenty of room for new growth. In the chapters ahead, we offer you a road map and guidance for increasing your sexual and relationship health. Make the decision to build your confidence, pleasure, and satisfaction as a man and to be a good sexual role model and educator for your own children.

CHAPTER 4

Vive le Difference

His Sexuality and Her Sexuality

Men and women—when it comes to sex are we really so different that we come from different planets? Or are we more similar? In offering our perspective on gender and sex, we explore (a) learnings from history; (b) the biological and physiological makeup of men and women; (c) what science tells us about men and women's sexual attitudes, behaviors, and feelings; (d) new information about the development of sex and love for men and women and how sexual drive and desires are similar yet different; (e) the importance and value of men regulating their sex drive; (f) thoughts about the "hot potato" issue between men and women—pornography; and finally (g) how similar men and women are when it comes to the ultimate sexual goal—emotional and sexual satisfaction. These issues are important for sexual health because they help you develop realistic expectations about yourself as a sexual man, your relationship, and how to cooperate and share as an intimate team.

Reflect on the sexual stereotypes about men and women. People believe that women are very complex in terms of sexuality, while men are very simple. Others (those who favor political correctness) believe that there are absolutely no differences between the sexes. Still others suggest that men and women engage in "the war between the sexes," have for centuries, and always will.

To understand the sexuality of men and women, the optimal model is a multidimensional, integrated, biopsychosocial approach. Sexuality is a lifelong developmental process, grounded in the body, profoundly enriched through psychological growth, and culminating in interpersonal integration. The history of men and women's sexuality in Western culture (as well as other cultures) demonstrates this developmental process. Traditionally, beliefs centered on understanding biological sexuality. Until about 1500 B.C., human beings did not understand that pregnancy was the result of sexual intercourse. The myths that culture designed to explain the meaning and significance of sex and fertility seem naïve and grandiose from our historical vantage point, but they were honest efforts to comprehend sexuality. The integration of the biological, psychological, and interpersonal aspects of sexuality in a scientific manner is new thinking in the last hundred years.

Point of Reference #1: Learnings From History

Men's sexual health has a fascinating history. Most of us have limited information about the variety and richness of sexuality in history and in cultures other than our own. We have a myopic (near-sighted) view about the powerful energy of sex in culture. In a macroview of history, human sexuality has experienced its own maturing process from a biological to a biopsychosocial understanding. People struggled for biological understanding—sexual impulses, penis, erection, vagina, intercourse—for centuries. Spiritual, theological, and religious perspectives—and superstitions—brought meaning in the absence of verifiable observations of science and medicine. Scientific—objective, observable, empirical, tangible, and physical—knowledge gradually emerged to help validate, integrate, and offer meaning to the realities of sex.

Variations in Sexual Behaviors

Throughout history, there is evidence of a variety of sexual behaviors but with a wide range of societal acceptance or condemnation. For example, monogamy was often the norm, yet in other phases, polygamy was not uncommon. Similarly, same-sex relationships have long been condemned, but at times have been tolerated, and in some societies were considered important for male bonding. Societies and periods fluctuate in acceptance of fidelity and condemnation of affairs. Prostitution is consistently part of societies, varying in acceptance or condemnation. Multiple-partner sex has occurred in most eras. Sex between adult and child is almost always condemned, although there are periods where it was common. Until relatively recently, children's sex education occurred by living life in the family, observing animals, and sleeping in a one-room house with parents and siblings. From the earliest records of humanity, there are cave drawings of humans and animals having sex (zoophilia). Other variant sexual behaviors are also evident in different cultures—exhibitionism, voyeurism, sadomasochism.

The message from human history is that (a) sexual behaviors are prevalent, extensive, and variable; (b) amidst this variety is evidence that societies struggled to make sense of and regulate sexual behaviors; (c) many periods idealized the male and female body (Greek statuary, Hindu mystics, Roman gods, medieval paintings, contemporary models); (d) gender differences ranged from romantic idealization to resentful conflict; and (e) there are fluctuating periods of sexual repression and sexual openness (for example, the openness of the 1960s–1980s in the United States compared with current conservative trends). One consistent societal theme is that sex is a fundamental and powerful human energy, at times viewed as dangerous or even demonic (the medieval Inquisition) and at other times as joyful and spiritual energy (the Christian mystics; the Bible's Song of Songs, and Hindu mysticism [Kama Sutra]).

Throughout human history, there has been an indisputable association of sex with life's meaning. For example, the Egyptian mythology of Nut and Ged (earth and sky) have sex to create the firmament. Sexuality permeates man's cosmology and spirituality—fertility cults, the deities seducing and progenating new gods, the sexual imbued with sacred meaning.

Society's Understanding of Sex

A society's understanding of sex is influenced by its level of logical and scientific thinking. There has been a fascinating mix of superstitions, ignorance, and sloppy science surrounding sexuality throughout the centuries. For example, Greeks worshipped the male penis as an icon for protection, fertility, and power and even built a 15-foot erect phallus out of stone on a fancy pedestal on the Isle of Delos. To protect their property, Romans marked it with statues of the Trickster, a devious little charm with a major erection. In the Spring, young nubile girls would dance around a maypole to invoke nature's fertility. And how to explain women's sexual attractiveness to men? During the Inquisition in Europe, attractive women were viewed as possessed by the devil, given their power over men. A scientific, legal evaluation of the time was to weigh the suspected woman's breasts in the evening and then in the morning, and if they weighed less, she was thought to have had sex during the night with the devil.

When mentally ill people were hospitalized in Europe in the mid-1850s, the frequency of boys and young men masturbating was misinterpreted by the doctors as the cause of mental illness or mental retardation. Devices were invented in the mistaken effort to prevent what we now know to be healthy nocturnal erections and wet dreams. One device placed electrical wires around the penis to ring a bell in case of erection. The wires made contact in order to awaken him and thereby prevent erection or wet dreams. A less humane device involved a leather strap with needles embedded that would prick the penis when it swelled. One can only imagine the harm caused to young boys by these misguided, unhealthy practices. Yet we should be humble in our judgments of those cultures and professionals. Some of our current sloppy sexual science likely will not stand the test of time.

The Relationships of Men and Women in History

Throughout history, men and women have shown remarkable cooperation and achievement. At the same time, history shows a tension surrounding gender roles, love–hate relationships, and evidence of a war between the sexes. Our view is that throughout time and cultures, men and women have been melded by humanity yet seen as different in personal qualities. These gender differences have been valued to varying degrees by different cultures. Anthropologists label cultures as *matriarchal* (female prioritized) or *patriarchal* (male prioritized). Evolutionary psychologists view gender as nature's brilliance to ensure the procreative functions required for survival.

Contemporary sexual science struggles to balance knowledge amidst social biases, psychological fears, political pressures, and past (and present) scientific sloppiness. Contemporary sexual science endeavors to provide an objective perspective on human sexual development and behavior.

The science of sex (sexology) is complicated. While sexology tries to be objective, it too is susceptible to social biases and political pressures because sexuality is such a powerful energy and value-laden part of life. Sexual science attempts to pursue the facts as we find them (Table 4.1).

Table 4.1 Learnings From the History of Sex

There is wide diversity of sexual behaviors, and the variety of sexual activity is ever present, although it may be socially denied or hidden from public discussion.

There are remarkable variations in what is, or is not, openly acknowledged, discussed, and officially sanctioned.

Pubic acceptance of different sexual behaviors has varied. There appears to be a cyclic pattern to public expression or condemnation of various sexual behaviors.

The history of the knowledge of sexuality itself appears to model an interactive, developmental process; that is, learning evolves with increasingly accurate understanding of the body, the psychological meaning of sex, and relationship growth and intimacy.

Sexual science pursues objective evidence. Accurate sexual information promotes reasonable sexual expectations.

History varies in its respect for men and women but is constant in showing that men and women share an ongoing cooperation as well as tension in roles, preferences, and sexual meaning.

Accurate information about sex can help us get our bearings and understand reasonable sexual expectations. A major motivation for our writing this book is to provide the most reliable, trusted, and accurate information—a balanced picture of male sexual health. Our Good-Enough Sex model of male and couple sexuality is based on both sexual science and clinical experience to help men and women develop positive, realistic sexual expectations and enjoy sexual satisfaction.

Point of Reference #2: Men & Women's Sexual Anatomy and Physiology

Physiology Is the Foundation

The body is the foundation on which you build your sexual "house"—including your psychological and relationship health. Accurate knowledge of how your body functions is the underpinning for realistic expectations. Poor health habits, illness and medications, misunderstandings, or unrealistic expectations of your or your partner's body can cause disappointment, frustration, and sexual dysfunction.

Men and women's sexual function is a lifelong ability. Your sexuality matures and grows, increases in quality, and continues lifelong unless there are severe physical, emotional, or relationship barriers.

Healthy Men and Women Respect Each Other

Men and women are similar and different. The question of whether men and women are more alike or more different has been argued for ages—but is not a "yes" or "no" reality. Physically, men and women are very much alike and also very much different. We'd like it to be a simple yes or no, but real life is complex, multicausal, and multidimensional. Healthy men and women appreciate this complexity, respect it, celebrate and enjoy the differences they experience, while recognizing and valuing the similarities in the depth of being a person, a man, a woman, a couple. As adolescents and young adults there are major differences in male and female sexual function and socialization. However, sexual development does not stop at 25. As men and women age, and especially as their sexual relationship becomes more mature, there are more similarities than differences.

Physiological Differentiation of the Sexes

The body itself demonstrates gender similarities and differences. Consider the sex differentiation that occurs before we are born. The physiological foundation for both men and women is the same in utero. For the first 4 to 8 weeks, we are sexually undifferentiated—that means, physically you couldn't tell whether we're male or female. Technically, if nothing was introduced (androgens, the male hormones), we would all end up female. But with androgens triggered by the genetic structure (male XY, or female XX), a male fetus emerges. It's interesting to realize that the undifferentiated embryo has similar anatomical and neurological structures. We looked female anatomically, having a genital opening that becomes the vagina in females or is "sewn shut" in the male. When you examine your testicles, look for the seam down the middle of the sac that holds your testicles. Consider, too, that your penis is actually a much enlarged clitoris.

Understanding the common anatomical structures of men and women can help in understanding similarities and differences in sexual pleasure and arousal. The sensitivity of your penis's tip corresponds to the sensitivity of her clitoris. Some women find too vigorous, direct touch to her clitoris to be irritating or even painful; you can relate to this by noticing that as you ejaculate, intense direct stimulation to the head of your penis can be too much—even painful.

Also appreciate that your testicles and her ovaries come from the same gonadal tissues. While her gonads developed into ovaries and remained inside her torso, your gonads became testicles and descended into the scrotal sac before you were born. In rare cases, a boy's testes don't descend, and a doctor will surgically help the testes to descend to prevent sterility.

The breasts and nipples of men and women are frequently sensuously pleasing and erotic. At times, her breasts may be more sensitive depending on her hormones. Don't take it personally when she asks you to leave her nipples alone or be exquisitely gentle—this is due to her body's hormonal fluctuations. Remember, a woman's sensuality fluctuates more than a man's. In healthy individuals, body and sexual awareness is progressively enhanced with psychological and social learnings.

How Your Sexual Body "Works"

Understanding how your sexual body works can help you practice good physical care and improve your sexual self-confidence through accurate information and realistic expectations. Physiologically, this means understanding the role and function of your vascular, neurological, and hormonal systems and having positive, realistic expectations of your sexual body.

Your Penis   Erection is a natural physiological response. Even before you were born, you had spontaneous reflexogenic erections. A newborn male baby has his first erection within a few minutes of delivery. And to this day, every night while you sleep, whether sexually active or not, you typically have a 10- to 20-minute natural, physiological erection approximately every 60 to 90 minutes, thus having three to five erections a night. These erections occur during REM sleep (REM means *rapid eye movement*).

Physiologically, nighttime erections are a way for your body to oxygenate the tissues of your penis to maintain healthy function. Laboratory studies have been done on 90-year-old men in good health who have erections. Truly, you are a sexual person from the day you're born to the day you die.

Getting to Know Your Body and Your Penis. Sex is more than your penis, intercourse, and orgasm. Sexuality is an integral part of who you are as a man—your body, attitudes, experiences, and feelings. From the moment babies are born they are fascinated by their bodies. Within the first year, you experience pleasurable sensations by rubbing and stroking your genitals—sexual awareness is born. In childhood, boys and girls examine and compare genitals, playing "house" or "doctor." Looking, touching, and exploring are a part of normal development and promote healthy attitudes toward your body and sexuality.

Sexual Realism: The Human Sexual Response Cycle. Your body is remarkable. Do not base your sexual expectations on a fantasy model of male sexual performance but on a positive, realistic understanding of sexual function. We want you to understand your partner's body and sexual responsivity. There are many similarities, but also some differences, that help you to be sexually positive and realistic in your expectatins of your sexual body.

Masters and Johnson's research (1966) revolutionized the field of human sexuality by describing the physiological sexual response cycle divided into excitement, plateau, orgasm, and resolution components. Kaplan (1974) broadened the model to include a critical initial stage: sexual desire. The complete sexual response cycle consists of five phases; desire, excitement (arousal), plateau, orgasm, and resolution (satisfaction). These physiological patterns are true for both men and women, although the psychological pattern does differ.

- Desire: Desire is the core component of healthy sexuality. The desire phase involves sexual anticipation, fantasy, and yearning, as well as a sense of deserving for sex to be good for you and your relationship. This includes both physical and emotional openness to sexuality. On the other hand, fear and shame can cause inhibited sexual desire. Using sex compulsively or to sexualize emotions can result in a self-defeating, hyperactive sexual desire.
- Excitement: During the excitement phase, in addition to a subjective sense of pleasure and feeling turned on, you experience erection and a few droplets of "precum" are secreted from the tip of your penis. Women experience increased blood flow to the

genitals, vaginal lubrication, breast swelling, and vaginal changes to increase receptivity to intercourse.

- Plateau: The plateau phase is when your body's arousal maintains a high level of pleasure. If you are physically relaxed, you will experience pleasurable arousal without quickly moving to orgasm. During the plateau phase your body "settles in" (becomes saturated with pleasure). Unless there is continual gentle penile stimulation, it is normal for your erection to subside, to take a break. Not understanding that this is normal, men unnecessarily panic, thinking they have lost their erection and it will never come back. This panic is a huge distraction that disrupts the plateau phase and erotic flow, instead creating anxiety that makes arousal and erection difficult to regain. With calm relaxation and trust in your body, all that is required is direct gentle touch to the penis and your erection will easily return. This is your sexual body's normal wax-and-wane erection process. This also occurs with female sexual excitement and lubrication.

- Orgasm: Sexual pleasure peaks during the orgasm phase and is accompanied by rhythmic contractions of the pelvic muscles and the release of sexual tension. A sensation of ejaculatory inevitability precedes the contractions that result in ejaculation. This is the beginning of the orgasm experience for men. Orgasm is similar for women but more variable and complex. She might be nonorgasmic, singly orgasmic, or multiorgasmic which can occur in the pleasuring phase, during intercourse, or through afterplay. Most men experience one orgasm, which occurs during intercourse.

- Satisfaction: During the afterplay phase, your body gradually returns to the nonaroused state. Both the man and woman experience a pleasant afterglow, feeling relaxed and sexually satisfied. While you may feel "wasted" after you ejaculate, your body only needs 1–3 minutes to rest and will recover interest so you can talk, gently fondle, and enjoy the afterplay process. This can be a time of special emotional bonding and seals the couple's relationship satisfaction.

Understanding How Your Penis Works: Basic Physiology

What happens when you have an erection is a remarkable and complicated process. We want you to appreciate your body and how it functions, ensure that your expectations are reasonable, and understand the rationale for some strategies that we suggest in the Good-Enough Sex model (e.g., physiological relaxation to promote reliable and easy erections).

The Vascular System. A problem with the penile vascular system is the most common physiological cause of erectile dysfunction (ED). When you are relaxed and open to mental and physical stimulation, blood flow increases to your genitals; specifically, to your penis. A number of physical, psychological, relational, and situational factors can interfere with this natural functioning. Common physical causes of ED include—in the order of frequency—high blood pressure, side effects of some medications, vascular disease, high blood sugar (poorly controlled diabetes), and vascular injuries.

Psychological and relationship stresses can impact your body and cause or sustain a sexual dysfunction like ED. Common psychological factors are anticipatory or performance anxiety, distraction, antierotic thoughts, being a passive spectator, and depression. Relational factors that subvert erectile function include emotional alienation, miscommunication, unresolved conflict, lack of attraction or desire, coercion or intimidation, anger, frustration, worry about your partner's anxiety or sexual discomfort, not feeling subjectively turned on, shyness, or inhibition. Situational factors that cause dysfunction include lack of privacy, trying to have intercourse when minimally aroused, and fatigue. Appreciate that these same factors can impede your partner's arousal, excitement, and orgasm.

The Physiology of Erection. Erection occurs when nerve impulses from the brain (psychogenic erection) and from genital stimulation (reflexogenic erection) combine to cause blood to flow faster into than out of the penis. Your penis is a sophisticated hydraulic system. There are three sponge-like cylindrical bodies that run the length of your penis, which are fed blood from small branches of the penile artery into the spongy tissue. These three tubes swell with blood to cause an erection. Two of these tubes, the corpora cavernosa, lay side by side along the shaft of your penis, and the third is the corpus spongiosum, which lies underneath. Together these three cylinders make up the shaft of your penis. An erection happens by relaxing the microscopic muscles that surround the arteries in the penis, causing dilation of the arteries. Blood rushes into the spongy tissues, creating a hydraulic elevation of your penis. Simultaneously, muscles near the base of your penis contract, preventing blood from leaving your penis.

When your erection subsides, those microscopic muscles surrounding the arteries constrict (the opposite of relaxation), and the blood in the three cylinders is carried away by the veins that surround them. Most men (and women) are surprised to learn that an erection occurs by physiological relaxation.

The Chemistry of Erection. Complex chemistry processes manage all this activity. Erection occurs when nitric oxide acts on the smooth muscles surrounding the penile arteries, acts on an enzyme, which then relaxes the smooth muscles, and an erection begins. The enzyme called phosphodiesterase type 5 (PDE-5) blocks muscle relaxation. So the way a pro-erection medication like Viagra works is to inhibit PDE-5 so that it does not block relaxation. This enhances (prolongs) the effect of vascular relaxation, which encourages blood flow, producing and maintaining an erection. Accept the complexity of your sexual response and appreciate that it is relaxation (not performance demands) that facilitates erection. So now you understand why pelvic muscle relaxation is important for good erections.

The Neurologic System. Your nervous system responds to both mental and physical stimulation to enhance arousal, penile firmness, and orgasm. Common neurological problems include disorders like multiple sclerosis, effects of diabetes and other untreated or poorly controlled illnesses, medication side effects, alcohol and drug abuse, and physical injury to the penis. Psychological, relational, and situational factors can also inhibit neurological function.

The nerves involved in this process connect the lower spine to the penis via the pelvic nerve, which branches into the cavernous nerve that manages the three spongy cylinders of the penis. The importance of these nerves is evident when damage occurs during prostate or rectal surgeries, causing postsurgery neurologic injury.

An erection is a neurological reflex involving the spinal cord and brain. The spinal reflex causes relaxation of the penile smooth muscle, causing dilation of the penile arteries, resulting in an erection. Higher central nervous system areas in the brain (e.g., hypothalamus and amygdala) are involved in obtaining and maintaining erections as well as triggering ejaculation and the pleasure of orgasm.

The Hormonal System. The hormonal system influences desire and erections by such hormones as testosterone, leutinizing hormone, and prolactin. Very low levels of testosterone can disrupt sexual desire and sexual functioning. Possible causes include a systemic hormonal problem, fatigue and stress, alcohol and drug abuse, or a pituitary tumor.

Exercise 4.1: Exploring Your Sexual Body

Increase your sexual awareness by engaging in an exploration of your body, especially of your genital area. Find a time when you have at least 30 minutes of privacy—perhaps the next time you take

(Continued)

(Continued)

a shower or bath. A full-length mirror will be helpful, along with a hand mirror. You may feel awkward at first, but relax and put aside any thought that this is unnatural. Take a good look. What are you proud of? Uncomfortable about? Appreciate that it is your body and it is a good one.

Start with your testicles ("balls"). Hold them in your hand, using a hand mirror to examine them from all sides. Be aware of their weight and shape. Don't be afraid of hurting them; your testicles are amazingly resilient. The testicles are the principal male sex glands and house the seminiferous tubules where sperm are manufactured. In addition, the testicles manufacture the hormone testosterone, which affects male physical characteristics (like hair and beard growth) as well as sexual desire. So efficient are the testicles that if one is removed (for example, testicular cancer), the remaining testicle is adequate for sexual and reproductive function.

Sperm are created by the millions in your testicles. Sperm travel through the epididymis tubes inside the testicles, where they become mature. Sperm leave the testicles by way of the vas deferens, two soft, thin tubes. The vas deferens lead into the seminal vesicles (storage chambers for the sperm) and then into the prostate. It is in the prostate that the sperm are mixed with seminal fluid called semen, the whitish alkaline liquid that spurts from your penis during ejaculation. Sperm are extremely tiny, contributing only slightly to the total volume of the ejaculate, the major portion (97%) of which consists of semen. When the vas deferens is severed during a vasectomy (sterilization), only sperm are left out of the mix. After a vasectomy, you continue to ejaculate semen as before, with no decrease in force, amount, or pleasure.

The testicles are housed in a bag of loose, wrinkled skin called the scrotum. One testicle usually hangs lower than the other. The scrotum can contract or relax, at times allowing your testicles to dangle freely against your thighs, at other times drawing up into a neat, tight package. Notice the seam made when the tissue was closed in utero to form your scrotal sac. This is the same tissue that forms part of the lips of the woman's vagina. The scrotal muscles come into play during sexual excitement. When aroused, your testicles rise in your scrotum and increase in size. If arousal does not culminate in ejaculation, the swelling remains, causing an uncomfortable sensation of prolonged vasocongestion popularly known as blue balls. This is temporary and causes no damage.

(Continued)

(*Continued*)

Emerging just above the scrotum is the base of your penis. The shaft of your penis is the "barrel" and extends from the base to its top or "head." The head of your penis is called the glans. This is the most sensuous, erotic part of your penis, containing an extremely high concentration of nerve endings. A particularly sensitive area of the glans is the ridge at its base, called the corona. Areas of greater sensitivity vary according to your experiences and feelings. Some men find the penile shaft particularly responsive to stimulation. Some find anal stimulation pleasurable; others do not.

Most men have thought about and handled their penis, exploring the sensations. It is the focus of intense emotions; few men regard their penis dispassionately. You may be proud of it, ashamed of it, anxious about it, even afraid of it. Part of sexual health is developing a positive, "friendly" relationship with your penis—and your entire body.

Clear your mind of preconceived notions and look at your penis as if you have not seen it before. The erotic stimulus for your erection may come from your brain via sexual thoughts and fantasies or from direct physical touch. The first kind of erection, called psychogenic, spontaneous, or automatic, is common in younger men. As you become older—about 35 or 40—erection usually requires direct stimulation to your penis. This is not an indication of a problem but is a natural change that occurs with aging and can enhance sensation and pleasure.

Now that you have taken time to explore your penis, have a good talk with your partner. What do you feel about your penis? Proud? Anxious? Shy? Embarrassed? Confident? "Cocky?" Do you appreciate your penis or take it for granted? Then reflect about feelings you've had about your penis if there are sexual concerns or problems. Confused? Disappointed? Numb? Angry? Frustrated? How can you and your penis become friends (again)?

The Myth of Penis Size and Female Anatomy

One reason to get your facts straight about male sexual anatomy and physiology is that this has been so dominated by superstition and misinformation. Men stubbornly perpetuate penis myths because they are afraid to challenge self-defeating sexual folklore of what it means to be a "real man." A destructive myth that continues to exert a powerful negative influence in spite of scientifically established fact concerns penis size. Penis size differences (or, more precisely, perceived differences) are the basis of an enormous amount of male anxiety. It is true that there are differences in the flaccid size of the penis, but that has little to do with penis size or sexual functioning in the erect state. The average penis is from two and a half to four inches in the flaccid state and from five and a half to six and a half inches when erect. The diameter is about one inch flaccid and one and a half inches when erect. It is more meaningful to say a normal penis is of proper size to function during intercourse. This definition includes almost all men.

Interestingly, three out of four men believe that their penises are smaller than average, which illustrates how the performance machine model dominates male sexuality, leaving men to feel anxious and insecure. Psychological and relational health is promoted by adopting a positive body image, which includes accepting your penis. Remember, solid scientific evidence demonstrates that there is no relationship between penis size and sexual desire or response for either the man or the woman. Most women say it is not the size but how you make love that is important.

A related myth is that a large penis results in the woman being orgasmic during intercourse. This is based on the mistaken belief that the vagina is the woman's major sex organ. In truth, the woman's most sensitive genital organ is her clitoris—a small, cylindrical organ located at the top of the vaginal opening where it joins with the labia ("lips" of the vagina). The clitoris has a multitude of nerve endings—like the glans of your penis, only concentrated in a much smaller area. It is the focal point of her physical sexual pleasure. Most women prefer indirect clitoral stimulation, whether with your hand, tongue, or penis.

During intercourse, the clitoris is stimulated by the pulling and rubbing action caused by pelvic thrusting—stimulation that is independent of penis size. The vagina, which is in contact with the penis, has fewer nerve endings, most of which are in the outer third. Moreover, the vagina is an active rather than a passive organ, which means that the vagina swells and expands with a woman's arousal to engage the penis and can adjust to the penis whatever its size. It usually takes 10 to 20 minutes of pleasuring (foreplay) for the vagina to fully expand. If a couple is rushing to intercourse, the man mistakenly thinks that his penis is too small because the vagina does not feel snug. The remedy is enjoying pleasurable touch and genital stimulation before intercourse to allow her body and vagina to reach the plateau stage of arousal. Sexual incompatibility based on the couple's genitals is, with extremely rare exceptions, a myth.

Responsive Sexual Desire: A New Model of Female Sexuality

Both men and women follow a similar physiological arousal sequence, although the psychological and relationship factors are somewhat different. Basson (2002) has found that in committed, long-term relationships, women's sexual desire becomes more integrated into her psychological system. In the beginning phase of a new relationship, romantic love and passionate sex lead to easy sexual response for many women, but in a long-term relationship (after one or more years), increased distractions and fatigue lead to a different kind of sexual desire pattern.

In this model of female desire and sexual response, women have a lower biological urge for the release of sexual tension than men. Orgasm is not necessary for satisfaction and does not need to occur at each sexual encounter. Basson proposes that women's sexual desire is often a responsive rather than a spontaneous event, greatly influenced by subjective psychological excitement. While a man's sexual desire may be energized by physical drive, typically a woman's sexual desire develops from her receptivity to gentle, relaxed sensual touching and/or playful, teasing touching. This touching leads to sexual desire and continues to emotional closeness, sensuality, genital stimulation, arousal, and eroticism. Sexual desire develops after initial sensual contact.

Healthy female sexual response in an established relationship often begins in sexual neutrality, but sensing an opportunity to be sexual, the partner's desire, or an awareness of potential benefits that are important to her and their relationship (emotional closeness, bonding, love, affection, healing, acceptance, commitment), she elects to seek sensual contact and stimulation. With beginning arousal, she may become aware at that time of a desire to continue the experience for sexual reasons and experience heightened arousal, which may or may not include wanting orgasm. This brings her a sense of physical well-being with added benefits such as emotional closeness, love, affection, and acceptance. This model acknowledges that for men sexual desire may be more biologically driven, whereas for women it is more psychological and relational. Advertising appreciates this: consider the billboard ad for a five-star hotel that shows an attractive couple smiling at each other over dinner with the caption: "Gentlemen: We do for her what lingerie does for you." Too often, men mistakenly believe that sexual performance is more important than emotional intimacy for women. Most women in fact value your presence, touch, and shared closeness.

Learning to Be a Lover

Understanding your and your partner's sexual bodies reminds you that lovers are made, not born. Your ability to enjoy sex and make sex enjoyable for your partner is dependent on your confidence, comfort, awareness, psychosexual skills, sensitivity, imagination, and ability to communicate—all of which are a matter of learning and experience. You can increase your potential as a lover and learn how truly satisfying sex can be if you transform performance-oriented sex to pleasure-oriented sex. Sexuality integrates feelings about you as a man—including your body image, physical well-being, attitudes, emotions, behavior, values, and—most important—your relationship. Base your sexual expectations solidly on knowledge about your body while remembering that, at its essence, sexuality is an interpersonal process.

Point of Reference #3: What Science Tells Us About Men and Women's Sexual Behaviors

Sex research gives us perspective on the similarities and differences between men and women. Be careful about information available in the media and on the Internet, as it is usually not based on reliable scientific research. Remember that we live in a commercial society where selling something as a problem and a product to fix it are common.

Surveys of particular groups like readers of *Playboy* or *Glamour* do not give the full picture of the entire community. A representative survey is scientifically structured to gain data from the entire community. Consider that readers of *Penthouse* may answer differently than readers of the *Christian Science Monitor.* So rely on scientific studies for accurate information.

The National Health and Social Life (NHSL) (Laumann et al., 1994) data surveyed a large representative U.S. sample that includes different ages, racial, ethnic, religious, and geographic areas. Compare these scientific data with what you have heard on TV or read in magazines about the use of fantasy, erotic materials, the frequency of sex, number of partners, and behaviors such as oral sex, masturbation, and orgasm.

Sexual Thoughts (Fantasy) and Use of Erotic Materials

A major disparity between men and women is the level of sexual fantasy and their different use of erotic materials. Men have more frequent fantasies and make greater use of erotic materials than do women. The NHSL survey reported that 54% of men and 19% of women enjoyed fantasies at least "everyday" or "several times a day" while 43% of men and 67% of women reported "a few times a week" or "a few times a month." Only 4% of men and 14% of women reported having sexual fantasies "less than once a month" or "never." The percentages of men and women's use of various erotic materials are listed in Table 4.2.

Comparisons that focus on visual erotica are uncertain because women's erotica is less visual and more emotional, such as sexual stories with romantic content, romance novels, or movies like *Gone with the Wind, Sleepless in Seattle,* or *Three Weddings and a Funeral.* Romance movies and novels are sometimes described as "women's pornography." This is a healthy use of sexual fantasies as bridges to desire and/or bridges to high arousal and orgasm.

Table 4.2 Erotic Materials Men and Women Use

Erotic material	Percentage of men who use	Percentage of women who use
Any form of erotic materials	41	16
X-rated movies or videos	23	11
Strip bar or club with nude/ semi-nude dancers	22	4
Sexually explicit books or magazines	16	4

Note. From *The social organization of sexuality: Sexual practices in the United States*, by E. O. Laumann et al. (1994). Chicago: University of Chicago Press. Adapted from Table 3.9, p. 135.

Frequency and Duration of Sex

The best scientific data regarding couple sex—contrary to common media presentations—show that adults do not have a secret life of abundant sex. Among Americans between the ages of 18 and 59, one third have sex as often as twice a week, one third a few times a month, and one third a few times a year. The average frequency of intercourse is 6–7 times a month. There is a slight decline in frequency with aging, and yet sexual satisfaction increases with age, especially among serious and married couples. For 70% of couples, their sexual encounters (not just intercourse) last between 15 minutes and 1 hour each time.

Lovemaking Activities and Appeal

There is a very wide range of sexual behaviors. NHSL reported that three quarters of American couples enjoyed oral sex (receiving, men = 79%, women = 73%; giving, men = 77%, women = 68%). About one half of couples had engaged in anal intercourse at some time in their sexual lives (men = 45%, women = 55%) and about 10% in the past year. Table 4.3 summarizes the NHSL data about the appeal of various sexual activities.

Adult Masturbation

Men grow up learning negative or confusing messages about masturbation and believe that it is second best, bad, wrong, or even sick. If we view masturbation as behavior that can have a wide range of positive and negative functions and meanings, then it is important for men and women to learn to regulate their sex drive (including masturbation frequency) so that it supports sexual and relationship health. Many men and women masturbate (Table 4.4).

While in truth adult masturbation is normal and healthy, half of adults report that they feel guilty about masturbating. Approximately 57% of

Table 4.3 The Appeal of Sexual Practices to Men and Women

	Men (%)	Women (%)
Vaginal intercourse	95	96
Watching partner undress	93	74
Receiving oral	79	73
Giving oral	77	68
Group sex	46	7
Lifetime occurrence anal intercourse (heterosexual)	45	55
Watching others do sexual things	40	17
Stimulating partner's anus with your fingers	26	15
Using vibrator/dildo	23	17
Anus stimulated by partner's fingers	22	18

Note. Adapted from *Sex in America: A definitive study*, by R. T. Michael et al. (1994). New York: Warner Books.Table 12, pp. 146–147.

Table 4.4 Men and Women's Frequency of Masturbation

	Men (%)	Women (%)
Single who masturbate	68	48
Married who masturbate	57	37
Masturbate at least 1 time per week	27	8
"Always" or "Usually" orgasm with masturbation	82	61
Masturbation during the past year by education level		
Graduate degree	80	60
Did not complete high school	45	25

Note. Adapted from *The social organization of sexuality: Sexual practices in the United States*, by E. O. Laumann et al. (1994). Chicago: University of Chicago Press. Table 3.1, p. 82.

married men and 37% of married women masturbate occasionally—often when the partner is not available, ill, or away. The level of education influences the percentage of individuals who masturbate (better educated individuals are more likely to masturbate). Men and women are very similar in their reasons for masturbating. The most common reason is tension relief (Table 4.5).

Number of Sex Partners

There is a wide range in number of sexual partners that individuals have during their lifetime, with a range from none to several hundred; the average is about six. There are three social trends that influence why people have more lifelong sexual partners now than 50 years ago: earlier first intercourse, marrying later, and more frequent divorce (Bancroft, 2003).

Table 4.5 Reasons to Masturbate (by rank) and Percent Who Feel Guilty

Purposes	Men (%)	Women (%)
Relieve anxiety/sex tension	73	63
Physical pleasure	40	42
Partner unavailable	32	32
To relax	26	32
Go to sleep	16	12
Partner doesn't want sex	16	6
Boredom	11	5
Percent who feel guilty about masturbating	54	47

Note. Adapted from *The social organization of sexuality: Sexual practices in the United States*, by E. O. Laumann et al. (1994). Chicago: University of Chicago Press. Table 3.3, p. 86 and table 3.1, p. 82.

Sexual Fidelity

Although the popular media report that most men and women are sexually unfaithful, over three quarters of men and women are sexually faithful to their committed partner throughout life. The scientific data report that about 20–25% of men and 10–15% of women are ever sexually disloyal (extrarelationship affair; Allen et al., 2005).

Orgasm

The frequency of orgasm during partner sex is 95% for men and 71% for women irrespective of age. And while the frequency of sex may gradually lessen with age, the frequency of orgasm during sex remains fairly constant.

Summary

This information from the best sexual science may fit your impressions or challenge them. The data suggest that men and women are similar yet have several notable differences such as in the use of fantasy and erotic materials, the regularity of orgasm, and the sources of sexual desire. On the other hand, men and women are very similar in reasons for masturbation, sexual loyalty, lovemaking preferences, sexual frequency, and desire for sexual intimacy and satisfaction.

Point of Reference #4: Sex and Love Are Developmental

Sexual health involves a commitment to integrating your maturing sexuality into your life and relationship. At whatever age, appreciate that your sexuality is a vital aspect of your personality, ripe for learning, growth, and enhanced intimacy. This includes valuing your own passion for sex, the richness of increasing understanding of your partner's sexual feelings,

Table 4.6 Three Forms of "Love"

Lust, sex desire, drive, passion	The craving for sexual gratification; associated primarily with testosterone and related brain pathways in both sexes
Romantic love, infatuation	Characterized by ecstasy, heightened energy, focused attention on a preferred mating partner, attraction, obsessive thinking and craving; associated with elevated activity of dopamine and probably also with low levels of serotonin
Attachment, pair-bonding/union/parenting	Feelings of calm and emotional union with a long-term partner; associated with oxytocin and vasopressin and their neural circuits

Note. Adapted from *Why we love: The nature and chemistry of romantic love*, by H. E. Fisher (2005). New York: Henry Holt.

and learning to enjoy and share the entire sexual experience: intimacy, pleasure, playfulness, arousal, eroticism, intercourse, afterplay.

This developmental process is demonstrated by what anthropologist Helen Fisher and other scientists (Fisher et al., 2002) describe as the three forms of love—lust, romance, and attachment (Table 4.6). These three basic drives influence aspects of courtship, mating (reproduction), and parenting and have differing biological mechanisms. There are similarities and differences between men and women in the role of their sex drive. The essential point is that the biopsychosocial system guarantees our species' survival with some grace and style, although you don't have to procreate in order to justify being sexual.

Sex Drive

The drive for sex is a powerful human motivation and healthy men and women throughout history have had a profound respect for it. Sex drive is understood as libido, lust, or the craving for sexual gratification. The drive is associated primarily with androgens (testosterone) and related brain pathways effecting motivation in both sexes.

Male sex drive is stimulated to a greater degree by visual stimuli than the female sex drive (Hamann, S., Herman, R.A., Nolan, C. L. & Wallen, K., 2004). Women are more sexually aroused by romantic words, images, and themes in films and stories (Ellis & Symons, 1990). Fisher suggests that the evolutional function of this difference is for the man to find a partner to procreate, so he will size a woman up for youth, health, and her ability to bear a child. Complementarily, women size up a man by her mood integration, feelings, and memory recall. Also, novelty attracts a man by increasing dopamine, which influences sex drive. Pornographers have long understood this. Magazines like *Playboy* are monthly magazines, not annuals. Internet promoters are constantly changing the variety of sexual stimuli to play on this interest in novelty.

Male sex drive is focused more directly on copulation, whereas the female sex drive is embedded in a wider range of stimuli (Fisher, Aron, Mashek, Li, & Brown, 2002). Female sexual desire is often a responsive rather than a biological or spontaneous event, greatly influenced by subjective psychological excitement. Male sex drive is more constant, whereas the female sex drive is more variable and flexible but can be more intense.

Romantic Love

Romantic love involves attraction, characterized by ecstasy, heightened energy, obsessive attention, infatuation, constant craving for the partner, and passionate feelings. Its function is to motivate individuals to select among potential partners and focus their courtship on an appropriate individual. Both sexes express romantic love with approximately the same intensity.

Both men and women are attracted to partners who are dependable, mature, kind, healthy, smart, educated, sociable, and interested in home and family (Buss, 1995). There are differences in what men and women find attractive in a mate: men tend to be more attracted to a partner's physical appearance, particularly beauty and health. Evolutionary psychologists have observed that women are more inclined to be attracted to men with money, education, and/or position (Buss, 1995). These are initial influences and become less important as individuals develop a serious relationship.

Attachment

Attachment is the feeling of calm, comfort, and emotional union with a long-term partner. Its function is to motivate individuals to sustain connections at least long enough to complete parental duties. Attachment is associated with the neuropeptides oxytocin and vasopressin and their neural circuits. Oxytocin is associated with stress reduction, calming, and soothing (e.g., the feeling post-orgasm) as well as memory and learning. Separation anxiety is associated with a lack of oxytocin; it occurs when there is a break in pair-bonding. Men are more likely to define emotional closeness (intimacy) as doing things side by side. Women more often view emotional closeness as talking face to face.

The systems of sexual drive, romantic love, and attachment are often linked. For example, when you fall in love, you also feel intense sexual drive for your beloved—perhaps because dopamine can trigger testosterone. It is very important to be aware that these three brain systems are not always connected. You can feel deep attachment for a long-term partner while you feel romantic passion for someone else, and lust for still others. These physiologic influences can be in conflict. Better understanding of the different drives can help you appreciate potential conflicts, help set realistic expectations, and develop wise strategies to encourage your sexual and relationship health.

Point of Reference #5: The Importance and Value of Regulating "Lust"

For men, lust is not a stage. If you are in good physical and emotional health, sexual drive continues your entire life. Lust is the drive to copulate, the urge for intercourse. For sexual health, however, men (and women) learn to balance sex drive (lust) through several regulatory learning tasks: (a) respecting and managing the biological imperative; (b) balancing sexual objectification versus personalization; and (c) differentiating sexual feelings from other emotions—that is, managing emotional sexualization (Table 4.7).

Sexual Health Learning Task #1: Libido, Drive, and Lust Require Self-Regulation

It is sheer naïveté for a man not to appreciate the power of sexual energy in his body and that sexual "objects" attract a man. Men's and women's bodies have a biological imperative, or "urge to merge." Healthy men and women accept and respect the power of these urges. Because the sex drive in men is more specific and object focused than in women, men have a special responsibility to regulate and manage their sex drive wisely, like anything else, such as food, sleep, and exercise. One of the most interesting factors in therapy with men who have gotten into trouble sexually (compulsive sex, affairs, sexual harassment in the workplace, compulsive use of Internet pornography)

Table 4.7 The Big Three Sexual Health Learnings

Task #1	Accept the male biological imperative, or lust. Respect its power and the need for self-regulation. Regulate this drive with physically healthy habits, exercise, and self-discipline.
Task #2	Accept the male biological tendency to objectify external sexual stimuli. Accept the requirement to regulate this tendency toward sexual objectification by self-discipline of cognitive focus and place conscious priority on personalization of your sexual relationship.
Task #3	Realize the male tendency for emotional reductionism; that is, to overlook emotions such as loneliness, frustration, sadness, resentment, anxiety, irritability, or obsessiveness, and to misinterpret and transform these to sexual feelings. Sexual health involves developing an emotional sophistication about your feelings and direct, healthy ways of emotional management.

is that these men were not aware that their sex drive needed to be regulated. As youth, they needed a parent, clergyman or rabbi, doctor, friend, sex education teacher, or book to give a clear message: "Your sexual health requires balanced regulation of your sex drive." When this regulation is in balance, your lust does not create problems for you and you can freely enjoy sex with your appropriate partner. When unregulated, sex drive can cause a variety of personal, sexual, and relationship problems by compulsively acting out or conversely, depriving you of healthy lust and passionate pleasure.

Sexual Health Learning Task #2: Regulating Sexual "Objectification"

This natural biological imperative promotes sexual objectification (vs. personalization). The male body—notably in teenagers and young adult men—appears to be biologically programmed and arousal is dependent on external sexual stimuli, especially visual stimuli. Compulsive use of pornography, infidelity, and sexual abuse are manifestations of extreme objectification. When objectification is predominant, it renders sex mechanical, performance focused, and depersonalized. Men's predisposition to focus on physical characteristics of women and sexual novelty is something that healthy men respect as natural, and they can enjoy their propensity to objectify a woman's body—breasts, butt, shape, vagina, legs, eyes, hair. At the same time, healthy men learn to carefully regulate this energy and balance it with personal respect for women.

It helps to understand the different styles of sexual arousal, especially that overobjectification of a woman's body can lead to overdependence on partner-interaction arousal. Men fear sexual failure (e.g., erectile dysfunction) and feel sexually inadequate in the absence of novel sexual stimuli. Without understanding that there are other styles of sexual arousal, they will do what has worked in the past—objectify the female body and seek novelty. This sets off a dysfunctional pattern that demands constantly raising the ante of more and more objectification and novelty. Men are blinded to this pattern as they focus on the impulsivity of sexual excitement. Unchecked, this pattern can harm your intimate relationship. When the man has learned to regulate objectification and balance his arousal, it can bring spice as well as comfort to the couple. One way to regulate the tendency to sexually objectify is to utilize self-entrancement arousal or role-enactment arousal and enhance attachment feelings with your intimate partner.

Sexual Health Learning Task #3: Managing the Tendency to Sexualize Emotions

One manifestation of a problem with sex drive regulation is emotional sexualization. Because of the power of sex, it is common to misinterpret other emotions and feel them as sexual feelings or add them to sex drive to produce what feels like a compulsive urge to be sexual, that is, have sex or mastrubate. Men (and women) commonly masturbate for tension release. This is a normal, healthy function for masturbation. The problem with emotional sexualization is that anxiety, depression, worry, loneliness, sadness, irritability, and obsessiveness can be misunderstood as sex drive. Men "funnel" a range of emotions to sex: anxiety, hurt, depression, low self-esteem, rejection, inadequacy, low self-confidence, fear, loneliness, anger, sadness, obsessiveness, shame. When these emotions are transformed to a sexual impulse, men compulsively rely on sex to seek emotional relief. When you have non-sexual feelings but transform them into sexuality, you feel like a sexual idiot, or sexually out of control. Compulsive use of pornography, strip bars, Internet sex, and prostitutes is an extreme manifestation of emotional sexualization.

A healthier strategy is to be aware that sexual feelings may be powered by nonsexual feelings such as frustration about work. You can manage the feelings with strategies that directly address the issue (consider and plan your options at work; exercise) and/or intentionally seek tension relief through sex with your partner. Because you are aware that you have options, you will not make it an intense, either–or sex demand on your partner, which can create conflict. If sex is inconvenient, you can make a date for sex later, sleep on it, or masturbate. You understand your energy and your feelings, so you can handle them well.

Emotional awareness and arousal regulation is at the core of male sexual health. A healthy man develops an emotional sophistication, an awareness of the need to regulate sex drive, and a deep acceptance and respect for emotional and sexual cooperation with his partner (Exercise 4.2).

Exercise 4.2: Distinguishing Sexual Emotions From Other Emotions

In the column "Label for the feeling," write down several general feelings you commonly have. For example, sadness, worry, frustration. In the next column, write a description of the feeling. What characterizes the feeling for you? Then identify where you feel this in your body. For example, worry: "in my stomach" or "tension in my neck." When you've identified several feelings and their location, rank them by level of intensity. Finally, estimate the percentage of your sex drive (the last time you masturbated or had sex with your partner) that you think was driven by each nonsexual feeling.

(Continued)

(*Continued*)

Label for the feeling	Description of the feeling	Location of feeling in your body	Rank	Percentage of your sex drive energized by this feeling

What percentage of your sex drive is for pleasure and intimacy? To resolve other emotional concerns? Ideally, healthy sexual desire for pleasure and intimacy fuels over 75% of your sexual experiences. If other emotions account for more than 25%, address your tendency to sexualize other emotions and consider options to directly deal with these emotions. Otherwise, the buildup of feelings could press you to make excessive sexual demands of your partner or increase your vulnerability to anti-intimate sexual behaviors such as compulsive masturbation, pornography misuse, or an affair.

Point of Reference #6: The Use and Misuse of Erotic Materials and Pornography

Erotica and pornography are not the same thing. Figure 4.1 will help you understand the range of pornography and its role for the man and couple. While it is clear that a *Playboy* centerfold photo is dramatically different from a violent snuff film that depicts rape and murder, among far-right political groups, sex-negative religious groups, radical feminists, and others with sex-negative agendas, even nudity, classical art, and erotica are labeled as pornography and vilified. Healthy men (and women) respect the complexity of sexuality and do not fall victim to simplistic thinking. The range of erotica and the variability in its impact and role in couple sexuality is understood so the man and couple can make choices between healthy and detrimental uses.

Visual Pornography Continuum				

1	2	3	4	5
Sensual Erotica	Nudity, explicit sex	Mutual sex acts	Dominant sex acts	Violent sex acts

Examples:

Sensual Art	Playboy	Penthouse, Screw	S & M	rape video, "snuff"

Pro-Intimate ◄ - ► *Anti-Intimate*

Figure 4.1 Visual Pornography Continuum

To evaluate the role of erotica for your individual and relationship health, consider the following dimensions:

Exercise: 4.3: Features to Consider in Evaluating the Role of Erotica in Your Life and Relationship

What is the context of the erotic material? Does it portray sex in a context that is distant from your life or is it possible (i.e., portrays the girl next door or sex with a coworker)? The closer to your real life, the more risk there is of evolving from fantasy to reality.

Consider the following:

1 The content itself: are the stories or images clearly fantasy and sex positive?
2 What is the function of the erotic materials for you? For your relationship?
3 What is the meaning of the material for your relationship? How will it or does it impact your evolving sexual intimacy, emotional cohesion, and relationship identity?
4 Does the erotic material benefit or harm your relationship comfort, harmony, and intimacy?

To most men, discriminate use of pornography is not infidelity, whereas for many women, any use of pornography is viewed as infidelity. The important outcome is that the couple blends and integrates the use and meaning of erotic materials in their individual lives and in their relationship in a fashion that respects individual autonomy and relationship cohesion. At a minimum, the couple reaches an agreement both can live with, optimally one that is mutually satisfying, comfortable, and enriching.

Point of Reference #7: The Ultimate Objective Is Emotional and Sexual Satisfaction

While there are differences between men and women, what unifies the couple is the common desire and ultimate purpose for sex—emotional and sexual satisfaction. The avenues to get to satisfaction may differ, but not the purpose. It seems that men often misread a woman's pathway to sexual intimacy through emotional intimacy, while women often misread a man's pathway to emotional intimacy through sexual intimacy. When a woman disregards the man's prominent pathway ("John, all you want is sex. You're compulsive!" or "You only think with your penis…") or the man disregards the woman's primary pathway ("Mary, you're so emotionally needy…" or "Stop demanding I talk about my feelings…"), each unwittingly blocks the very intimacy they want by refusing to provide the intimacy the other wants.

What is important to understand is that men and women want and need both. Men without emotional intimacy facilitated through a satisfying sex life feel lonely and press for more sex (Figure 4.2). Unfortunately, this can easily appear to be mechanical and impersonal and a disregard of her desires for nonsexual emotional intimacy. It is important for men to appreciate that women don't pursue intimacy solely through the sexual pathway and for women to appreciate that men don't pursue intimacy primarily through the emotional pathway. These pathways are tendencies, not rigid rules. Ideally, men and women learn to pursue emotional and sexual satisfaction on both pathways. Relationship intimacy works best when both the man and the woman value, nurture, and pursue both emotional intimacy and erotic intimacy.

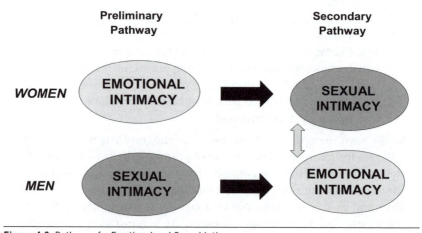

Figure 4.2 Pathways for Emotional and Sexual Intimacy.

What If Your Partner Is Not on the Same Page?

Women, like men, are not all alike. What if your partner wants performance from you, has an "I deserve an orgasm, so give it to me" or a "do me" attitude? What if she does not value Good-Enough Sex? Consider that your impression may be inaccurate. For example, you may interpret her words in a way that she does not intend. For example, she may be trying to turn you on with sexual challenges or her sexual anxieties may surface in this way. What if she has difficulty reaching orgasm, and she is frustrated, wishing you could magically rescue her? A healthy strategy is to respectfully and gently talk with her about your concerns—that you feel pressure and confusion about what she means. You can work together as a team for mutual pleasure. If your efforts are ineffective, it is wise to seek a good couple sex therapist to help with the difficulty.

Closing Thoughts

Appreciating the complexity of men and women's sexuality is an important factor in your sexual health. Adopting realistic expectations of yourself, your body, your masculine feelings, sex, love, and your similarities and differences with the woman in your life can serve a strong, positive role in cooperation with your partner both in and out of the bedroom.

CHAPTER 5

The Mantra of Healthy Sexuality
Intimacy, Pleasuring, Eroticism, and Satisfaction

The traditional mantra for male sexuality has been frequent and perfect intercourse performance. The extreme of this is that "A real man is willing and able to have sex with any woman, any time, any place." Maybe this is okay for single men in their 20s (although we doubt it), but it is a terrible approach for men in their 30s and beyond, especially those in a serious relationship or married. Why? Because it creates unrealistic pressures to be a sexual machine, which, paradoxically, is the perfect setup for causing sexual performance problems.

What is the new mantra for healthy male sexuality? It is to enhance (a) intimacy (b) pleasuring, and (c) eroticism for (d) mutual satisfaction. Let's carefully examine each component in the context of healthy lifelong male and couple sexuality.

Intimacy

Intimacy is very different from the Hollywood romantic love idealization or the new image of ideal sex with your soul mate. We advocate developing a mutually comfortable level of emotional intimacy that promotes feeling genuinely connected to your mate while giving you the space to see her as an erotic woman. The challenge for all couples is to find a balance of emotional intimacy and eroticism that facilitates feeling safe, connected, desirous, and erotic. In paid sex or a sexual hook-up, intimacy is neither necessary nor valued, and in fact can interfere with sex. However, in an ongoing relationship, intimacy is not only necessary, but the healthy man

Table 5.1 The New Mantra for Healthy Male Sexuality

Enhancement by means of:
Emotional and sexual intimacy
Pleasuring as well as sexual function
Integrated eroticism
Mutual emotional and sexual satisfaction

values genuine emotional and sexual intimacy. Intimacy is important, but it does not have to be serious all the time. Intimacy is about feeling sexually connected to and playfully involved with your mate.

Pleasuring

The concept of nondemand pleasuring is the component most at odds with traditional male sexual socialization. Affection and sensuality (foreplay) have been viewed as the woman's domain, something he does for her. For most men (and some women), the idea of mutual affection, sensuality, and playfulness (all dimensions of nondemand pleasuring) as valuable is almost an alien concept. Yet, this enhancement—expanding and valuing pleasuring and mutuality—will dramatically increase enjoyment of your own and couple sexuality. Men can value affection, sensuality, and playfulness. This is a human experience, not just a female experience. Men fear feminizing their sexuality, impeding sexual vitality, or settling for a second-class sexuality. Such thinking is anti-male and ultimately impedes male and couple growth and sexual satisfaction. In truth, being open to receiving and giving nondemand pleasuring is a major component of healthy male sexuality. It will not only serve you well at this time but will inoculate you from sexual problems (e.g., erectile dysfunction), especially after age 50. A key concept for healthy male sexuality is to value a variable, flexible couple sexual style. Nondemand pleasuring is the foundation for this style.

Integrated Eroticism

When men think of eroticism, the image is of porn magazines and videos. This approach to eroticism emphasizes raw and wild sex, carnal feelings, powerful erections, and perfect performance. The wilder the situation and the crazier the woman, the more erotic. Not surprisingly, we take a very different approach to integrated eroticism. Eroticism is a healthy part of you as a man and your couple sexual scenario. If you think of arousal being on a 10-point scale (where 0 = *neutral*, 3 = *sensual*, 5 = *arousal signified by the beginning of an erection*, 8 = *high arousal*, and 10 = *orgasm*), erotic stimulation ranges from 6 to 10. Intimacy and pleasuring are a solid basis for sexual arousal, but high arousal and orgasm involve genital stimulation and erotic scenarios and techniques.

We emphasize the concept of erotic flow, allowing yourself to go from 7 to 9 where the feelings, sensations, and the erotic experience combine in a positive, synergistic manner. A key factor in erotic flow is allowing yourself to piggyback your arousal on your partner's arousal. Truly, the major erotic stimulus (aphrodisiac) is an involved, aroused partner. Key elements of eroticism are unpredictability and allowing yourself to let go and enjoy intense erotic feelings. The key to integrated eroticism is respecting, valuing, and owning your body's sexuality, not viewing it as a porn scenario. An ordinary erotic technique is to use fantasies that serve as a bridge to greater arousal in partner sex.

Genuine Satisfaction

The vital component is a sense of genuine satisfaction. In traditional sex therapy the focus has been on performance—erection, intercourse, and orgasm (ejaculation). The new mantra in sex therapy is mutual intimacy, pleasure, eroticism, and satisfaction. Satisfaction certainly includes erection, intercourse, and orgasm, but it is not limited to that. Satisfaction involves emotional, sexual, and couple factors. In Hollywood movies, sex is always perfect—both people are turned on before they even begin touching, the sex is impulsive, short, intense, and nonverbal, both are easily orgasmic, and satisfaction is mutual and total. It's a wonderful image but harmful to real-life men and couples. In truth, if you have Hollywood type sex once a month you are more fortunate than 90% of men. In sexually happy couples, if half of their experiences involve both being desirous, aroused, and orgasmic they are fortunate. Often, the sex is better for the man than his partner, but she enjoys him, his pleasure, and the encounter. Sometimes, the sex is unremarkable, functional, but not special or satisfying. The most important factor in terms of positive, realistic expectations is that 5–15% of sexual encounters are unsatisfying or outright dysfunctional. Rather than panicking or apologizing, the man (and woman) is better to shrug it off and accept this experience as normal sexual variability (especially after age 40). A healthy couple approach is to talk together briefly about an alternative scenario or take a rain check. Try to reconnect in the next one to three days when you feel receptive and responsive so you don't let anticipatory sexual anxiety build. The essence of satisfaction is sharing and enjoying sensual and sexual pleasure (Exercise 5.1). You feel better about yourself and energized about your relationship after a sexual experience.

Exercise 5.1: Assessing and Changing Your Sexual Response

The focus of this exercise is to realistically assess these four essential components: intimacy, pleasuring, eroticism, and satisfaction. Make changes where needed, and maintain positive, realistic expectations of sexuality in your life and relationship.

Rather than falling into the traditional male trap of exaggerating and bragging about sexual prowess, think clearly about each component. Be honest with yourself (and your partner) rather than giving either the supermacho response or the politically correct one.

Part I: Your Preferences

What degree of intimacy/closeness facilitates feelings of sexual desire and allows you to experience eroticism with your mate? Some men find that holding hands and gazing into her eyes is a sexual turn-on, others experience it as a turn-off. What kind of physical and emotional connection allows you to feel desire and eroticism?

How much do you value affectionate touch and pleasuring? Do you prefer hugging, kissing, holding hands? Do you value sensual pleasure? Playful touch, both genital and non-genital? Do you prefer mutual touch or taking turns? Do you like one type of touch at a time or multiple stimulation?

What about eroticism? Is your preference a predictable sexual scenario or do you enjoy unpredictability? Is eroticism just between the two of you or do you like to use external stimuli like videos, music, candles, or sex toys? Do you use erotic fantasies to heighten arousal and serve as a bridge to increase your response? Erotic fantasies are almost never about your mate and seldom are socially acceptable—remember, fantasies are totally different from real-life behavior. Is your preferred arousal pattern partner interaction arousal, self-entrancement arousal, or role-enactment arousal?

Satisfaction is the most challenging component to honestly assess. Traditionally, men have equated satisfaction with orgasm, a simple pass–fail test. Obviously, we are strong advocates for orgasm but believe that satisfaction is much more than orgasm. Do you feel better about yourself and your relationship after a sexual encounter? This is the core issue in satisfaction. What physical, emotional, and relational aspects of the experience allow you to feel the most satisfaction? Most men value their partner's orgasm but also realize that only a minority of women are orgasmic at each sexual opportunity. Again, stick to expectations that are both realistic and positive. Is it possible for a man to be sexually satisfied if he's not orgasmic? Most

(Continued)

(*Continued*)

20-year-olds would say no, but sexually sophisticated 60-year-olds would say yes. What is the truth for you?

Once you have completed this assessment, we suggest that you share this material with your partner. Her observations, perceptions, and understanding can be of great value for you, especially in formulating a change plan.

Part II: Targets for Improvement

The next step is to decide whether you want to change any of the four components. Which component (intimacy, pleasuring, eroticism, satisfaction) do you feel most satisfied with? Is there any component you are concerned about or want to modify? If so, choose one component (or two at the most) and develop a realistic change plan. If most of the components are problematic, this is an indication of the need for professional help. Seeking therapy for a sexual problem is an indication of good judgment and a smart approach to growing as a man and couple.

Most men prefer to first try to change a problem on their own (with the support and active involvement of their partner). Choose one or two areas that you would like to significantly change or at least modify and improve. Make sure that you have a specific goal and plan for the change process. Major enemies of change are settling for good intentions (you need an active change plan) or setting a perfectionist goal. Perfectionism is an enemy of change because it is unrealistic. A successful change plan involves a commitment to making a significant (not perfect) change, having a specific goal, being willing to learn a new psychosexual skill(s), enlisting your partner for support, viewing this as an intimate team challenge, and staying disciplined and motivated until you achieve your realistic enrichment goal.

The following are illustrations of change plans for each component.

A. Intimacy:
1. Discussing sexual issues over the kitchen table or on walks
2. Saying "I love you" on a daily basis
3. Lying in bed and sharing emotions once or twice a week; just sharing, no fixing
4. Making one or two emotional or sexual requests of your partner
5. Talking about the value of both intimacy and eroticism in your relationship

B. Nondemand pleasuring:
1. Setting aside time for a sensual, non-genital pleasuring date

(*Continued*)

(*Continued*)

    2. Trying a new sensual lotion to enhance pleasurable sensations

    3. Spending time on the sofa "making out" and valuing that for itself

    4. For a couple who always do mutual, simultaneous touching, try taking turns

    5. The woman setting the pace and sequence of the pleasuring scenario

C. Eroticism:

    1. Starting a scenario in front of the fireplace and instead of going to the bedroom, playing out the scenario there

    2. Trying one-way sex to orgasm with the giving partner enjoying without expecting anything back (perhaps at a different time switching roles)

    3. Experimenting with switching intercourse positions two or three times during an encounter

    4. Each partner experimenting with introducing an external stimulus (R- or X-rated video, music, candles, reading a section of an erotic story or erotic scene from a novel) that your partner is receptive to

    5. Expanding your sexual repertoire to enhance erotic flow so that you do not transition to intercourse until your partner has an orgasm and your arousal is at least an 8

D. Satisfaction:

    1. Experimenting with three or four afterplay scenarios and find at least one that is special for you

    2. Before a sexual encounter, talking to your partner about what you would like to try to enhance the experience

    3. Listening to your partner's feelings and requests; her pleasure will enhance your satisfaction

    4. Planning a special date that integrates intimacy and eroticism

    5. Planning a date after a sexual encounter that shows appreciation for your pleasure at being a sexual couple and reinforces your relationship bond

As you proceed with this exercise, remember that the focus is not performance but sharing intimacy, pleasuring, and eroticism.

Understand that these four components are not either–or deals but that healthy, satisfying sexuality is a progression, an upgrading of your enjoyment at each stage of your life as a man and as a couple. Sex and life are more satisfying as you learn and grow.

The Core of Male and Couple Sexuality

What is the essence of male sexuality? Your penis? The centrality of intercourse? Sexual autonomy? Testosterone? Being proud of and never apologizing for your sexuality? Are you afraid if you give up the emphasis on male sexual autonomy and intercourse performance that you will turn into a second-class sexual citizen? A wimp?

Healthy male sexuality integrates your biological drive, attitudes, behavior, and feelings within your interpersonal experience. The mantra for sexual satisfaction includes intimacy, pleasuring, and eroticism. The challenge for most men is to learn to value nondemand pleasuring and intimacy. Does that mean diluting your sexuality so that it is not so testosterone driven? This is a major fear men have—that being person based and adopting an integrated approach will somehow feminize their sexuality. Is there an answer to the conflict between testosterone (i.e., "having balls") and being a politically correct man? Like most dichotomies—that is, an either–or way of thinking—this is false. Rather, think of healthy male sexuality as a blending of psychobiosocial dimensions, with a range of intimacy and erotic options.

Take the Best and Leave the Rest

Integration means merging the best from the traditional male role, discarding the worst, and incorporating new, healthy components. The best of traditional male sexuality is the positive association between masculinity and sexuality, feeling proud as a man, valuing sex, enjoying arousal, erection, intercourse, and orgasm and not feeling guilty or apologetic about sex—whether masturbation or partner sex. The worst of traditional male sexuality, which needs to be confronted and discarded, is the rigid emphasis on perfect performance; the shame of asking questions or feeling uncertain; autonomous sex vs. intimate, interactive sexuality; perfect control vs. enjoying a variable, flexible couple sexuality; and one-dimensional sexual performance vs. understanding sex as a process of sexual intimacy, pleasure, and eroticism. The key in formulating a new model of healthy and strong male sexuality is to value both intimacy and eroticism and to view the woman as a sexual friend to share with rather than perform for. Rather than giving up a core element of testosterone or pride in erection and intercourse, the new healthy male sexuality broadens that base, integrates intimacy and pleasuring with eroticism and intercourse, and focuses on sexual satisfaction as an interpersonal process, not an autonomous one.

Champion the Good-Enough Sex Model

The most difficult but most crucial issue is the incorporation of the Good-Enough Sex versus the perfect intercourse performance approach to male and couple sexuality. In our competitive society, saying you should not strive to win (perform) every time—especially sexually—sounds like heresy. Men want to win, not settle for a winning record. You want to win the Super Bowl or World Series, not just make it to the playoffs. Certainly, traditional men ask how can you be satisfied without intercourse and orgasm each time? Is Good-Enough Sex—which might include inter-course and orgasm 85% of the time—really satisfying? Or is that just for men after 70? In truth, if you learn to value erotic non-intercourse sex and interpersonal intimacy in your 30s, you will discover new dimensions of sensuality, pleasure, and eroticism, and inoculate yourself against sexual problems in your 40s, 50s, 60s, 70s, and even 80s. Your sex life will feel more accepting, and you'll experience greater self-confidence, content-ment, and satisfaction.

The Key to Lifelong Sexual Satisfaction

Good-Enough male and couple sexuality is not only normal for satisfied and happy couples; it's a key to lifelong sexual satisfaction for both the man and the couple. When couples stop being sexual, whether at 40, 60, or 80, it is almost always the man's decision, made unilaterally and conveyed non-verbally. He can no longer guarantee perfect erection and intercourse so he is at first anxious, then embarrassed; then experiences inhibited sexual desire and, ultimately, avoidance of all sensual or sexual touch because he doesn't want to start something he can't finish. The healthy cycle of intimacy, positive anticipation, pleasuring, eroticism, intercourse, orgasm, and satisfaction has been overthrown by anticipatory anxiety, perfor-mance-oriented intercourse which increasingly fails, and then forfeits intimacy, pleasuring, or eroticism.

Probably 90% of men by age 40 have had at least one experience of erectile failure. By 50, half of men report at least mild erectile anxiety. Contrary to advertising and marketing campaigns, relying on Viagra to return you to 100% perfect intercourse performance is not the answer, although for many men pro-erection medications are a valuable resource. The answer is adopting a broad-based, flexible approach to sexuality that involves intimacy, physical vitality, pleasuring, eroticism, and seeing your partner as your sexual friend, mixed with positive, realistic expectations of Good-Enough Sex.

Illustration 5.1: Nick

Nick considered himself a "man's man." He was a very active, athletic, guy who loved the outdoors and team sports—both competing and viewing. He believed that his sexual attitudes and behavior were normal and masculine—Nick began masturbating at 12, first orgasm with a partner at 16, first intercourse at 18. Nick could enjoy both "hook-up" sex as well as sex with his girlfriend. He prided himself in always using a condom and had easy, predictable erections. Nick graduated high school, was in the Navy for 4 years, and then finished an apprenticeship as an electrician. He is now a master electrician who runs his own successful business.

Nick married at 22 when his girlfriend became pregnant but soon realized it was a fatally flawed marriage, and they separated after 18 months. Nick felt he recovered well from the divorce. When he remarried at 27, it was a thoughtful, emotionally wise choice and Nick was committed to having a satisfying, stable marriage with Alicia. They established a strong, resilient marital bond of respect, trust, and intimacy and had their first child after 2½ years.

At 42, Nick valued his masculinity and sexuality but felt ready for a new quality of male sexuality. There were two impetuses for this. The first was his marriage and family. Nick and Alicia just celebrated their 15th wedding anniversary, and his children were 12 and 10. Nick also reestablished connection with his 19-year-old son from his first marriage. Nick hoped that his children would learn from his positive model and not repeat his mistakes. Nick's openness to Alicia's influence had clearly improved the quality of his life—this marriage has brought out the best in Nick. The second factor was events around him that made Nick more aware of the negative results of the supermacho role and he was determined not to allow that to happen to him. Nick's older brother had been diagnosed with adult-onset diabetes at age 43, caused in large part by poor health habits—he was overweight, drank too much, and didn't exercise. He heard through Alicia that his brother had developed erectile dysfunction, was depressed, and was not managing either his health or his life. An older electrician had a serious auto accident while driving drunk. Many of his friends were wasting their time and money on Internet porn, seduced by the message that this was a harmless entertainment with no consequences for their lives and relationship when in fact it was a compulsive behavior that interfered with their lives, relationships, and finances.

(Continued)

(*Continued*)

Nick was committed to a healthy life and healthy sexuality, which Alicia strongly supported. The most important health factor that Nick modified was his drinking habits, drinking socially but not alone. He was still active in team sports, although in a less competitive league. Instead of the traditional male approach to drinking, eating, and playing until something negative happened (a heart attack, major injury, surgery), Nick determined that he could still enjoy being an active man while moderating his behavior. Physically, Nick did not have to prove anything to himself or anyone else.

Sexually, Nick was learning to balance being a man's man with being a healthy, integrated new man. Nick liked sex, his penis, intercourse, and was proud to be a man. Just as important, Nick was learning to value intimacy, pleasuring, Alicia's sexuality, afterplay, sexuality as sharing pleasure—not performing—and realized that not every touching experience had to result in intercourse and orgasm. Alicia enjoyed sex with Nick much more now than in their first couple of years. The sex was less a physical performance and somewhat less frequent but was now more genuine, intimate, interactive, and varied. Nick felt more like a lover than a sexual athlete and was enjoying sexuality more. Nick had friends who joked that they wished they could be studs like they had been in their teens, but for Nick (and Alicia), this new variable, flexible male and couple sexuality was more real and satisfying.

Nick was aware that if sex was going to be a healthy part of his 50s, 60s, 70s, and 80s that what he was learning now would pay off then. The traditional man's man usually stops being sexual in his 50s or 60s because he is embarrassed that he can't perform with the total predictability and control he used to have. Nick realized that this integrated approach to intimacy, pleasuring, eroticism, and satisfaction would inoculate him against sexual problems with age. A real man can enjoy variable, flexible couple sexuality throughout his life.

Closing Thoughts

This is a great time to be a sexual man. New scientific and clinical information from psychology, medicine, and relationship science guides men in how to enjoy lifelong sexuality. There is not one right way to be sexual, but there are useful guidelines about how to integrate intimacy, pleasuring, and eroticism to promote satisfaction for the man and couple. This new information confronts the self-defeating, one-dimensional traditional male approach of sexual autonomy and striving for perfect intercourse performance. Incorporating the new, integrated Good-Enough Sex model for male and couple sexuality promotes lifelong, satisfying sex; values intimate, interactive sexual experiences; focuses on sharing pleasure; promotes integrated eroticism; and celebrates a variable, flexible approach to male and couple sexual satisfaction. Will you integrate this new sexual mantra for yourself and your relationship? This would be a wise move for you, whether you are 25, 45, or 75.

CHAPTER **6**

Good-Enough Male and Couple Sexuality

The Good-Enough Sex model of male and couple sexuality is the most challenging as well as most important concept in this book. The traditional male sex model has been all about a big, powerful penis and perfect intercourse performance to prove yourself to the woman and be competitive with male peers. Sexually, men were either winners or losers. Being thought of as a sexual loser is a controlling male fear. The essence of being a loser is not having a penis ready for action any time and any place. By that definition, the truth is that 95% of men are losers and the remaining 5% are afraid it would eventually happen to them. In the traditional perfect performance male model, you are always one failure away from devastating your sexual self-confidence.

The Good-Enough Sex model challenges that self-defeating performance criterion. Focus on enjoying pleasurable sex; you do not have to prove anything to yourself or anyone else. It is about acceptance, pleasure, and positive, realistic sexual and relationship expectations. This is an opportunity for you as a man, for your male friends, for couples, and for our culture to change the understanding and meaning for men's sexual health.

With the Good-Enough Sex model, intimacy and satisfaction are the ultimate purpose, with pleasure as important as function and mutual acceptance as the context. Sex is integrated into the man's and couple's daily life and daily life is integrated into your sex life to create a unique couple sexual style. Living daily life well as both a person and a couple—with its responsibilities, stresses, conflicts as well as joys, moments of pleasure, special erotic experiences, and emotional and sexual satisfaction—is vital.

Good-Enough Sex provides the opportunity to experience a range of sensual, playful, erotic, and intercourse experiences which will enhance your sexuality. The ultimate goal of couple sex is relationship intimacy and satisfaction.

The traditional criterion of male sexual confidence has been perfect control over erection, intercourse, and orgasm. Sex as a pass–fail test. This new approach emphasizes that the essence of sex is self-confidence grounded on giving and receiving pleasure-oriented touching and that 85% of the time this will flow to intercourse and orgasm. Touching has value in itself—whether affectionate touch, sensual touch, playful touch, erotic touch, or intercourse. Intercourse is a special pleasuring/erotic experience, not the pass–fail measure of sexual prowess. Touching experiences that do not result in intercourse can be normal and enjoyable, not viewed as a failure. The essence of sexual confidence is sharing pleasure, not perfect performance.

We anticipate that as you read about this new model for male sexual satisfaction you will wonder whether this is for real. Stick with us so we can explain how Good-Enough Sex can be great. Or maybe you're thinking, "Wait, isn't that what women want, not men?" Well, you're right about what most women want. Healthy women prefer our Good-Enough Sex model and wish more men understood how the old performance model burdens women as well as men. But even men with healthy thinking about sex who would like to adopt the Good-Enough Sex model wonder if this is what a woman really wants. Don't take our word for it. The way to find out is to discuss with your partner what you each want. The Good-Enough Sex model (Table 6.1) is a sexual lifestyle—with thoughts, behaviors, and feelings—that you both have to grow into (Metz & McCarthy, 2007). Consider what Good-Enough Sex can mean for you.

Let us examine each component in detail and make them personal and concrete for you. Remember, these are guidelines that you integrate with your partner to promote your sexual health and couple sexual satisfaction. Sex is a good element in life, an invaluable part of a man's and a couple's comfort, intimacy, pleasure, and confidence.

We live in a culture that gives very complex and mixed messages about sex and its value. On one hand, sex is the measure of masculinity and it is crucial to prove yourself sexually. On the other hand, a man's fears are wide ranging, including being afraid that his penis is too small, that he doesn't last long enough, that he's not as good in bed as his peers, that he masturbates too much, that his fantasies are abnormal, or even that if he can't get an erection on demand a woman will think he's gay and gossip to others, as well as fears of STDs and HIV or unwanted pregnancy.

Table 6.1 The Qualities of the Good-Enough Sex Model for Male & Couple Satisfaction

1. Sex is a good element in life, an invaluable part of the man's and couple's comfort, intimacy, pleasure, and confidence.
2. Relationship and sexual satisfaction are the ultimate developmental focus. The couple is an intimate team.
3. Realistic, age-appropriate sexual expectations are essential for couple sexual satisfaction.
4. Good physical health and healthy behavioral habits are vital for sexual health. The man values his own and his partner's sexual body.
5. Relaxation is the foundation for pleasure and function.
6. Pleasure is as important as function.
7. Valuing variable, flexible sexual experiences (the 85% approach) and abandoning the "need" for perfect performance inoculates the man and couple against sexual dysfunction by overcoming performance pressure, fears of failure, and rejection.
8. The five purposes for sex are integrated into the couple's sexual relationship.
9. The couple integrates and flexibly uses the three sexual arousal styles.
10. Gender differences and similarities are respectfully valued and mutually accepted.
11. Sex is integrated into the couple's real life and real life is integrated into their sexual relationship. Sexuality is developing, growing, and evolving throughout life.
12. Sexuality is personalized. Sex can be playful, spiritual, and special.

1. Sex Is a Good Element in Life

We want to present a clear, affirmative message. Sex is a good thing in life; your sexuality is a positive, integral part of your personality. The essential issue is how to express your sexuality so it enhances your life and relationship. You are sexual from the day you are born until the day you die. Sex can play a 15–20% beneficial role in your life and enhance relationship satisfaction, whether at age 20, 40, 60, or 80.

It is important that both you and your partner value sex as a positive energy in your lives. Sex encompasses how you use your bodies for touch, pleasure, fun, and play. Seeing sex as more than intercourse invites you both to utilize affection and soothing touches as a message of mutual acceptance, cohesion, support and closeness.

Accepting and affirming that your and your partner's sexuality is a good element in life and a core of your relationship is crucial. Your sexual relationship can enhance your self-esteem—enhance your deep-down inside-your-body feeling that you have self-worth as a man. Don't allow shame, anxiety, or embarrassment about male sexuality to diminish your sexual self-esteem.

Satisfying sex begins with your strong approval of your sexuality, appreciating your built-in personal drive for sex, and the contribution of sexual satisfaction for you and your relationship. Sexually satisfied men and couples value sex as inherently good and intentionally counter any negative judgments of sex. While sex—like any aspect of life—can be misused or abused, the drive for sex, the urge to connect with another, the longing for intimacy is respectable and vital energy for a man.

2. *Relationship and Sexual Satisfaction Is the Ultimate Developmental Focus. Relationship and Sexual Factors are Essentially Intertwined. The Couple Is an Intimate Team*

Teenage and young adult men learn sexual response as an autonomous function—he can experience desire, arousal, and orgasm, needing nothing from his partner. As you mature and are involved in a serious relationship, you learn to value sex as an intimate, interactive experience. Accepting the partner as your intimate, erotic friend is the key. In traditional sexual socialization, initiation and intercourse frequency were the man's domain, with affection and intimacy the woman's domain. You can break out of these rigid roles and realize that when both the man and woman value intimacy, pleasuring, and eroticism, it is a healthier and more satisfying relationship. The man and woman in an adult, healthy sexual relationship share more sexual similarities than differences. The emotional and sexual differences are usually complementary, not oppositional. The major similarity is that both want sexuality to play a 15–20% role in overall relationship satisfaction.

A core understanding is that your sexual satisfaction is essentially intertwined with your relationship satisfaction. The Good-Enough Sex model's axiom that you grow as an intimate team refers to cooperation both in and out of the bedroom. If your relationship outside the bedroom is divisive, your sexual satisfaction will be undermined. Remember that healthy sexuality does not exist in a vacuum but in your relationship. Sexual health and satisfaction are directly influenced by the quality of your entire relationship. Essential dimensions that comprise your overall relationship health include couple identity, conflict resolution, and emotional empathy. These relationship features are crucial to sexual health.

Understanding Core Dimensions of Your Relationship

The cognitive-emotional-behavioral (CBE) model can be extended to understanding your relationship (Figure 6.1) including your relationship identity (who you are as a couple), relationship cooperation (how well you work as a team to resolve your conflicts), and relationship intimacy (especially how well you empathize with each other's feelings).

Your relationship identity includes what you together believe a relationship should be like, how to act as an intimate couple, how you blend gender roles, and how you balance your needs for autonomy and cohesion. To understand your similarities and differences and integrate them requires

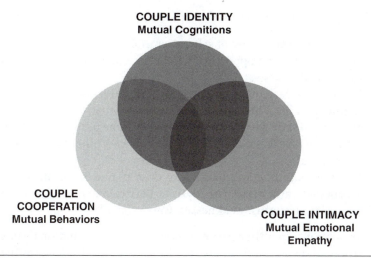

COUPLE IDENTITY
Mutual Cognitions

COUPLE COOPERATION
Mutual Behaviors

COUPLE INTIMACY
Mutual Emotional
Empathy

Figure 6.1 The C-B-E Dimensions of the Couple.

discussion and respect for your differences. You do not have to defend your beliefs, feelings, and needs as a man; but you do need to cooperatively integrate them with your partner's beliefs, feelings, and wants. Remember, you seek to be an intimate team.

Your relationship cooperation dimension accepts that differences and conflicts are inevitable because you are two persons with individual thoughts, feelings, and behaviors. Many men (and women) are afraid of conflict, believing that it will inevitably lead to destructive arguments and cause damage to intimate feelings. Such romantic notions are destructive when they lead you to avoid dealing with differences or withdraw when conflict occurs.

Think about your relationship conflicts as opportunities for increasing intimacy. Day-to-day conflicts are the ordinary way you increase intimacy because when you work cooperatively to resolve them, you avoid power struggles, come to understand each other's perspective, and figure out how to resolve disagreements in ways that feel good for each of you. It is this win–win resolution that is the criterion for constructive conflict resolution. Even when you can't resolve the conflict, you can reach an agreement to accept the situation so that it does not subvert loving feelings. So don't fight, but don't cave in either. Invest your thoughts, feelings, and wants in a relationship and respect those of your partner. This cooperation is an important factor to bring to the bedroom. Otherwise, what you bring to the bedroom can be irritations, harbored hurts, disappointments, bitterness, or distant feelings that undermine your sexual health and satisfaction.

When you work as a team and cooperatively resolve conflicts, you:

- Develop a greater sense of self-esteem.
- Give each other an opportunity to better understand and support the other's requests.
- Learn about each other's complexity and uniqueness.
- Reinforce respect and admiration for each other.
- Develop confidence that future conflict can be positively resolved.
- Create positive feelings and comfort with each other that facilitate your sexual desire.
- Feel that you have an honest relationship, one based on mutual acceptance rather than the myth of perfection. You each can be yourself—strengths, weaknesses, warts and all.

Your relationship intimacy dimension is about the emotional support, affirmation, and empathy you provide for each other. Understanding the importance of emotional intimacy is sometimes difficult for men because they tend to cue off of sexual intimacy to feel connected and try to demonstrate their love by problem-solving and action. When you love someone very much, it is romantic to feel that this love will make your partner happy. But when a woman is distressed or critical, a man can make the mistake of misinterpreting her problems as his failures to love her well enough. If he then tries to cheer her up or "fix her" by telling her to get over it, "it's not so bad," or defend himself with a logical debate about how he didn't mean to upset her, he blows it. Why? Neither strategy demonstrates the emotional understanding and empathy that men and women long for in their prized relationships. It is not the unconditional positive regard that is expected—albeit often unconsciously—in committed relationships.

Many men are reassured—even if amazed—that simply providing understanding, empathy, acceptance, and affirmation of a woman's distress (without debating the fairness or logic or expecting agreement) is usually all that's needed. Affirming her distress is usually more helpful (and less stressful for you) than problem-solving. Empathy is a good response to emotional distress, which is a plea for understanding. If this doesn't work, conflict resolution as an intimate team can often resolve the issue. The 10–20% of problems that are neither resolvable nor modifiable can be designated as differences to accept and tolerate in the interest of relationship intimacy.

These relationship dimensions—identity (e.g., balancing autonomy and cohesion), mutually satisfying conflict resolution, and reciprocal empathy—are features that bring confidence and positive feelings to the bedroom.

Illustration 6.1: Jon and Sonia

Sonia, a petite, 28-year-old trial lawyer, would sometimes come home to Jon, a 29-year-old Ph.D. candidate in mathematics, and complain—even in tears—about a horrible day in the courtroom. She would lament to Jon that the judge, a "sexist tyrant," would deny her objections to the opposing counsel's innuendoes and even personally insult her: "Stop these objections and sit down, Sweetie..." Jon at first felt protective and wanted to call the judge on the carpet but resisted this unreasonable strategy. In his love for Sonia, he would try to help by offering suggestions: "Ask the judge for a meeting in chambers to point out his rude behavior" or "File a complaint with the lawyers' bar."

As Jon continued to try to help, Sonia became even more upset with the horrible experience. Jon then tried even harder to handle Sonia's distress. When he finally said to her that "You're taking this all pretty hard, and I can't imagine it was that bad...." Sonia lost it and turned on Jon. He was stunned and hurt that his efforts to love and support her seemed so dramatically rejected. He walked out of the room, muttering under his breath "What a bitch!"

Not a good scene. So what happened? Sonia comes home to soothe her wounds. Jon tries mightily to take care of the woman he loves. How can their pro-intimacy intentions go so wrong?

In a nutshell, Jon blew an exceptional opportunity to provide empathy. He made the mistake of trying to be reasonable and logical when the situation called for empathy, not for rational problem-solving. What Sonia sought was a "safe harbor from the storm," where she wanted to be greeted with open arms and listened to so she could vent. Jon's trying to fix the problem not only missed the mark but made it worse by unintentionally criticizing Sonia. Think for a moment how it looks for a mathematician to be telling a trial lawyer how to handle the courtroom. Not a pretty picture! No wonder Sonia would get even more upset and then turn her anger toward Jon. This train wreck is sad because it was so unnecessary. A couple with good intentions is working against empathy.

Eventually Jon and Sonia calmed down and figured out what was happening. Jon learned that Sonia simply wanted a "Greek Chorus" (an amplification of her feelings, "You're really frustrated by all this") and validation ("What an ass the judge is"). Sonia learned that if Jon goofs and tries to problem-solve her feelings (a major error), she'd call time-out and ask for what she really wants; "Jon, please, I just want you to be my safe harbor...." Cooperation as an intimate team is good for both your general and sexual relationship.

3. Realistic, Age-Appropriate Sexual Expectations Are Essential for Sexual Satisfaction

As you age and your body changes, your sexuality also changes. Sex is different at age 20 than at 40 or 60 or 80, but aging itself does not mean an end to sex. You truly are a sexual person until you die.

The most important positive, realistic expectation is that you are aware of and accepting of your bodily changes rather than fighting against your body. As you age, your vascular and neurological systems become less efficient, so psychological, relational, and psychosexual skill factors become more important in sexual function and satisfaction. Contrary to popular mythology, there is not a dramatic change in testosterone levels with healthy aging. A key to healthy developmental sexuality is to confront the cultural myth that you are past your sexual prime by 22 (this refers to a very narrow definition of sexual ability as able to become aroused quickly after ejaculation). Your penis and orgasm are an integral part of your sexual body, but intimate intercourse is the key to healthy sex after 25. Enjoy being an adult sexual man. Sexual satisfaction at any age is grounded on realistic expectations of your body, emotional well-being, and relationship health.

4. Good Physical Health and Healthy Behavioral Habits Are Vital for Sexual Health. A Man Needs to Value His Own Body as well as his Partner's

Taking care of your physical health and body will enhance your sexual function and satisfaction. Anything that is detrimental to your vascular, neurological, or hormonal system is harmful for you sexually. An important example is smoking, which impairs your vascular system. Another crucial factor is drinking. Many young men learn to be sexual in the context of alcohol. Alcohol is a central nervous system depressant that negatively impacts sexual response. However, for young men, their sexual enthusiasm and more efficient vascular and neurological systems can override these effects. Alcohol also "greases social encounters" and can reduce self-consciousness. One or, at the most, two drinks can improve social confidence and put the man (and woman) in a passionate mood—this can be a legitimate use of drinking. The danger is when he needs alcohol as "liquid courage." A common trap occurs when sex and alcohol are strongly linked. Alcohol abuse is a very frequent cause of male sexual dysfunction, especially erectile dysfunction.

In contrast, men who don't smoke and have healthy sleep, exercise, eating, and drinking habits are protecting their sexual bodies and facilitating sexual response. This is of value throughout life, but especially after the mid-30s, because the vascular and neurological systems are less efficient and therefore sexual response is more vulnerable. Remember, healthy sexuality resides in a healthy body.

5 Relaxation Is the Foundation for Pleasure and Function

Whether induced by psychosexual skill relaxation techniques or a pro-erection medication, the foundation of sexual response is relaxation. Relaxing your body is best done by taking time and using the self-entrancement arousal approach. This means lying back (often with eyes closed) and focusing on being receptive to touch and comfortable, sensual feelings. Rather than stimulating your partner, using erotic fantasies, or getting turned on by her, you allow yourself to be passive, take in sensations and pleasure, and tune into the warm feelings in your body, feeling open and receptive to her non-genital, sensual touch. By removing barriers to healthy sexual function (performance anxiety, shame, and spectatoring), your body will relax and sexual function will follow a natural flow of comfort, pleasure, arousal, eroticism, and orgasm. As demonstrated by the physiological effects of pro-erection medications, you can naturally relax the musculature surrounding the arteries in the penis with entrancement arousal, which enables enhanced blood flow and erection. Although counterintuitive, relaxation is the vital and reliable foundation for arousal and erection.

6. Pleasure Is as Important as Function

The essence of sexuality is giving and receiving pleasure-oriented touching, which is the foundation of healthy sexual function. We prefer the term *function* to *performance*. Function means awareness of the natural sexual response of desire, arousal, orgasm, and satisfaction. Pleasure and function go together and are promoted by psychosexual skills that include feeling responsible for your own sexuality; accepting positive attitudes and feelings about your body and sexuality; enjoying both self-entrancement and partner-interaction arousal; viewing your partner as your intimate, erotic friend; enjoying "give to get" stimulation; and developing erotic scenarios and techniques.

In contrast, pressure for perfect sexual performance (sex on demand) can poison your sexual experience. A vivid example is of a couple dealing with infertility who have intercourse on a very rigid schedule in order to maximize their potential to conceive. Over time, the majority of men will develop erectile dysfunction, ejaculatory inhibition, or inhibited desire. The on-demand, pass–fail intercourse performance takes the fun out of sex. Sex becomes all about anticipatory anxiety, tense, performance-oriented intercourse, and frustration, embarrassment, and avoidance. The healthy cycle is positive sexual anticipation, pleasure-oriented sex, and a regular rhythm of desire, pleasure, and satisfaction.

When pleasure becomes as important as function, the crucial role of touch becomes clearer. While countless men believe that they have a need for sex, a major part of this feeling is the deep need for touch. In the 1950s–1960s, a number of studies documented the fact that our bodies actually experience "skin hunger," the craving for touch. Recent controlled studies suggest that touch reduces stress; diminishes irritation, frustration, and anger; consoles and comforts; and reassures or soothes fear. We have a profound need for touch, and sex is a common way men seek touching. Touching soothes loneliness. Touch can be pleasurable even if it is not sexualized. Appreciate the value of each kind and level of touching, balance the multiple kinds of touch, and blend touch desires with your partner. This Good-Enough Sex focus on pleasure adds a powerful dimension to your sexual relationship that is not a part of the old male performance standard. Enjoy.

7. *Valuing Variable Flexible Sexual Experiences (the 85% Approach) and Abandoning the Need for Perfect Performance Inoculates the Man and Couple Against Sexual Dysfunction by Overcoming Performance Pressure, Fears of Failure, and Rejection*

The reality for emotionally and sexually healthy couples is that the quality of sex varies. The male myth portrayed in the romantic love/passionate sex media (including R and X-rated videos) is that each sexual experience involves perfect performance. What nonsense. In truth, both scientific findings and clinical experience show that emotionally satisfied, sexually functional couples have a variable, flexible sexual response (Table 6.2). This means that about 35–45% of encounters are very satisfying for both partners, another 20–25% are better for one (usually the man) than the other, and 15–20% are okay but not remarkable. The most important information is that 5–15% of sexual encounters are unsatisfying or dysfunctional.

The Good-Enough Sex model accepts that among satisfied couples, up to 15% of the time their sexual encounters will not flow to intercourse. Rather than thinking of these as failures, accept them as part of normal variability. Instead of apologizing, you can transition to a backup scenario—either a warm, sensual scenario or an erotic, non-intercourse scenario leading to orgasm for you, her, or both. The Good-Enough Sex approach encourages relationship satisfaction with an acceptance of variability in the quality of sex grounded on positive, realistic expectations. This serves the man

Table 6.2 The Quality of Good-Enough Sex in Well-Functioning, Satisfied Married Couples

35–45%	Very Satisfying
20–25%	Good (at least 1 partner)
15–20%	Okay (not remarkable)
5–15%	Unsatisfying (dysfunctional)

Note. Adapted from Frequency of sexual dysfunction in normal couples, *by E. Frank, C. Anderson, and D. N. Rubinstein (1978). New England Journal of Medicine, 299; and The social organization of sexuality: Sexual practices in the United States,* by E. O. Laumann et al. (1994). Chicago: University of Chicago Press. Table 10.10, p. 374.

and couple well and inoculates them against sexual problems with aging. Accepting Good-Enough Sex is often easier for the woman than for the man, but it promotes sexual satisfaction for both.

Generous Sexual Cooperation

The Good-Enough Sex model focuses on what characterizes healthy and satisfying sex for a couple. One feature is mutual, cooperative generosity. This involves each partner giving pleasure to the other even when you are not in the mood. When both partners understand that in real life, they will not always be in the same mood or place, they can generously give to the other with the understanding their generosity will be reciprocated another time. With this "give to get" generosity, they balance pleasing each other, providing the physical interaction that each values, giving one time, getting another time, in a mutually cooperative, sexual relationship.

Illustration 6.2: Marcello and Maria

Marcello, 34, and Maria, 32, have two small children and busy, demanding jobs. As a dimension of Good-Enough Sex in their marriage, they accept realistic, cooperative sex that fits their daily lives. They know that sex will vary, ensure that they have opportunities for a variety of sexual experiences, and embrace the multiple purposes for sex. Because of the demands of work and family, their priority is to ensure that they have opportunities for extended lovemaking sessions, so they schedule a date night twice a month where they spend the evening out, come home, have 20 minutes to relax, and then make "slow love"—a special intimate, erotic encounter.

They also cooperate for day-in and day-out sex to fit their lives. They adapt sex to what is going on. Some days, when they have energy left, they have a 30- to 45-minute sexual encounter with energetic lovemaking. After a very busy, exhausting day when Maria is drained but Marcello is sexually energized, they briefly check in on what they are up for. They are not on the same sexual page; Maria is ready to get to sleep, and Marcello is "horny." To honestly fit their sexuality into this situation, they have a variety of flexible ways to honor each other's wants. What is important is that neither thinks or feels that the other is rejecting his or her desires or extorting sexual behavior.

Maria and Marcello do not let their sexual feelings ride on one night alone. They realize than their sexual life is a composite of their day-in and day-out cooperation for mutual pleasure and satisfaction. For example, one night Maria may be wasted and Marcello earnest

(Continued)

(*Continued*)

for sexual tension release. Each briefly lets the other know what they are honestly wanting ("I want to just go to sleep" and "I am really wanting sexual release") and are committed to find a way to mutually respect each other's place—not an either–or deal. They will often find a middle ground that is good enough for each. Maria might generously suggest that he touch her for his arousal and he accept her question "Is it okay to be a log tonight?"

Another time, when Maria is feeling stressed and wants to cuddle at bedtime, she wants to feel that Marcello will put her desires first. After she asks to simply hold and cuddle before falling asleep, Marcello generously agrees, holding back his own desire to do more, and relaxes his body to comfortably embrace and cuddle to please her. This self-discipline, he finds, is easier because they have regular sex (Maria ensures that they have some sexual experience at least twice a week) and Maria is flexible with him, inviting his "getting off" with her body when she is not in the mood in order to take care of his sexual needs. For his part, Marcello attends to what he has learned is Maria's desire for boundless nonsexual touch (skin hunger), holding and cradling. Maria and Marcello are a sexually cooperative intimate team.

Developing Flexible Scenarios

Enjoying flexible, variable couple sexuality includes intimate intercourse as well as erotic, non-intercourse and sensual, backup scenarios. Good-Enough Sex involves pleasuring that flows to intercourse in 85% of encounters. A core concept is that you want pleasuring/eroticism to move into an erotic flow (including your response to her arousal) and transitioning to intercourse at high levels of arousal. Avoid switching to intercourse as soon as you're erect.

Cooperate with your partner to maintain a regular sensual, playful, erotic, and intercourse connection. This makes it easy for you to accept that not every sexual experience needs to end in intercourse. Flexibility and variability will enhance your sexual desire, not inhibit it. Manual, oral, rubbing, and vibrator stimulation are excellent ways to experience high arousal and orgasm for one or both of you. In truth, the majority of women find it easier to be orgasmic with manual and oral stimulation. Orgasm reached through erotic, non-intercourse stimulation can be satisfying for your partner and for you.

A key to intimate sexuality is awareness that there are a number of ways to give and receive pleasure rather than feeling anxious, panicking, and trying to force your penis into her vagina. Stay actively involved in the sexual give and take. You can request oral stimulation to enhance erotic flow or focus on stimulating her so you can piggyback your arousal on hers. Feel free to take a break from intercourse and relax or talk together. Your erection may subside, but there is more than one erection in you if you stay relaxed. Don't panic, fearing that your erection is lost forever. Relax and refocus with gentle touch, and your erection will easily return.

Sometimes an encounter will not involve erotic response or intercourse. Rather than feeling frustrated or withdrawing, either of you can say that this will not be a sexual night, but that you want to feel warm, caring, and sensual. Ending the encounter in a genuine, positive, and close manner allows you to enjoy affectionate and sensual touching and intimacy (Exercise 6.1). This motivates you to have a sexual encounter in the next one to three days when you have the time and energy for an experience that integrates intimacy, pleasuring, and eroticism.

Illustration 6.3: Ivan and Dawn

Ivan had never thought much or talked much about sex in his 48 years. He was a microbiologist who viewed sex from a detached scientific framework. Sex was a basic life instinct that created his three children and a means of orgasm/tension reduction, nothing more or less. That simplistic view was challenged by Ivan's first experience of erectile problems at age 46 (he was not aware that erectile failure occurs in 90% of men by age 40). This experience resulted in an overwhelming sense of embarrassment and panic. Dawn's attempts to calm/reassure him backfired. Ivan felt even more deficient and self-conscious. Sex became an infrequent and unpredictable experience. At times, intercourse was as easy as in the past, but with increasing frequency Ivan lost his erection right before or after intromission. His reaction was silence and an internal sense of devastation. He turned away from Dawn, who had her own feelings of confusion, hurt, and frustration. Was it her fault, his fault, or was there something terribly wrong with them as a couple?

In his career, Ivan thought of himself as an excellent problem-solver. He had seen too many work projects become stalemated by the blame–counter blame dynamic. He didn't want that to happen between him and Dawn but feared "talking sex to death." Ivan's first attempt to get information and help was not beneficial—a for-profit male sex clinic where he was prescribed a pro-erection medication, an antidepressant, testosterone, and penile injections. Ivan decided to do careful research on the Internet and was surprised and confused by the very contradictory information and advice. Ivan

(Continued)

(*Continued*)

chose to undergo a complete physical. His internist was aware that erectile dysfunction can be a first symptom of a serious vascular or cardial condition so he was very thorough in his assessment. Happily, there were no major medical problems. He counseled Ivan that erectile problems are best understood and treated as a biopsychosocial problem. He prescribed Viagra but also suggested that Ivan and Dawn consult a certified couple sex therapist for guidance and counseling. Dawn was enthusiastic, but Ivan was reluctant. He wanted to see if the Viagra alone would be enough. After 3 weeks, Ivan realized the medication was helpful but was not a stand-alone intervention. In making the couple appointment, Ivan was clear that he didn't want long-term therapy but a focused intervention about regaining erectile confidence and couple sexuality. The therapist was both competent and flexible. He helped Ivan and Dawn to view the erectile problem as a challenge to build a new couple sexual style that would not only help them regain comfort and confidence with erections but inoculate them against sexual problems with aging. Ivan found this approach both intellectually and emotionally appealing.

The hardest concept to accept was the Good-Enough Sex model of variable, flexible sex with 85% of encounters flowing to intercourse. Dawn's enthusiasm for an intimate, interactive couple sexual style and realization that her sexual experience was congruent with the 85% guideline finally won Ivan over. He was not a perfectionist in the rest of his life, so why would being a sexual perfectionist help him? The single most important thing the therapist said was "Wise men learn to enjoy grow-up erections rather than show-up erections. When intercourse doesn't flow, they enjoy erotic, non-intercourse sex."

Exercise 6.1: Create Your Sexual Scenarios

Take a moment to think about three sexual scenarios you would enjoy. Ask your partner to do the same. Prod yourselves to be creative and flexible by allowing only one of the three to include intercourse. Then take turns sharing these scenarios, alternating one at a time. Be careful not to judge, but enjoy a variable, flexible, couple sexuality.

8. *The Five Purposes of Sex Are Integrated Into Your Couple Relationship*

It is not unusual for each partner to have different purposes (pleasure, intimacy, tension reduction, self-esteem, procreation) for an encounter. For example, a man may seek sex for orgasm and a tension reducer, whereas a woman might value sex for emotional connection and sense of desirability.

Realize and accept that people have sex for multiple and fluctuating purposes. Rather than getting into arguments and power struggles, this understanding will enhance partner cooperation and sexual satisfaction.

In addition, you and your partner may pursue different goals at different times. One day sex may be motivated primarily by testosterone and for relief of workday pressures and 3 days later for pleasure and closeness. Most men, but not all, pursue each of these five purposes at one time or another in their lives. Often, multiple purposes are pursued simultaneously.

The priority of one purpose over another can fluctuate significantly from time to time—even day to day. For example, you may engage in sex with 40% of the purpose to feel pleasure, 40% for loving feelings, and 20% for self-esteem. Five days later, sex may be 50% for stress reduction, 20% for love, 20% for pleasure, and 10% for self-esteem. Often your purposes are different from your partner's. Accepting that each person has sex for multiple and fluctuating purposes is a way to break the traditional male–female power struggle in which the woman thinks the man wants sex for selfish reasons and the man thinks the woman values affection but not sex. Clarifying the sexual agenda, developing partner congruence, and cooperation are important.

9. Integrate and Flexibly Use the Three Sexual Arousal Styles

Being aware and appreciating that there are three primary sexual arousal styles (by order of use: partner interaction, self-entrancement, and role enactment) is helpful to the man and the couple.

Partner-interaction arousal focuses on the partner. This is the sexual pattern seen in movies and celebrated in love songs and is the arousal style used by most young men. You are active, eyes open, looking at your partner, talkative (romantic or erotic), engaged, and energetic. In this sexual style, each partner's arousal plays off the other's.

Self-entrancement arousal focuses on your body and relaxation as the source of arousal. You close your eyes, go within, are quiet and receptive, and passively take in pleasure. Regular, stylized touch gradually builds arousal. The focus is on physical and emotional relaxation, being receptive and responsive to touch, feeling saturated with pleasure, and slowly building arousal.

Role-enactment arousal focuses on external stimuli—role-play, fantasy, experimentation, and unpredictability. Examples include being turned on by your partner's sexy lingerie, role-playing erotic scenarios like virgin–prostitute or first pick-up, acting out a scenario from a movie or erotic novel, having sex in new or high-risk places, using toys (vibrator, paddle, bondage), watching an X-rated video. The focus is on experimentation and novelty to build eroticism.

Contrary to traditional sexual socialization that partner interaction is for men, self-entrancement for women, and role enactment for "kinky" couples, the truth is that these are all legitimate paths to arousal for both men and women. Couples are capable of blending arousal styles for sexual variety and enhanced satisfaction in long-term relationships. You can choose and vary which arousal styles add to your sexual satisfaction.

10. Gender Differences Are Respectfully Valued and Similarities Are Mutually Accepted

Sexually men and women are not clones of each other. In serious relationships and with aging, similarities outnumber differences. Traditionally, men focus on sex as a way to connect emotionally and value feeling invited to be sexual. Traditionally, women focus on feeling connected emotionally and then sexually and enjoy feeling desired. Men focus on sexual function as the base of their confidence, whereas women focus on trust and feeling safe, attractive, and special. Couples do better sexually when they accept and celebrate different preferences as well as similarities. For example, the preference for a quickie is typically male. The preference for a sensual bath or a foot rub is typically female. Couple sex works best when both the man and woman value intimacy, pleasuring, and eroticism. It helps when a man is receptive to his partner's way of initiating, her sequence of pleasuring/eroticism, her leading the transition to intercourse, and her preferred afterplay scenario. You can be both intimate and erotic friends while maintaining individuality and sexual preferences.

11. Sex Is Integrated Into the Couple's Real Life and Real Life Is Integrated Into Their Sexual Relationship

Sexuality is developing, growing, and evolving throughout life. Your sexual experiences and the role of sexuality in your life will continue to evolve: sex as a college student, sex as you establish a new relationship, sex early in your marriage, sex while parenting young children, sex while balancing parenting and career, sex while parenting teenagers, sex after children leave home ("empty nest"), sex in retirement, sex during illness, sex in older age. Integrate sex into the reality of your life events to recognize the multiple roles and purposes for sex.

Sometimes sex is primarily about tension reduction, sometimes for affection and connection, another time for escape and fun, another for emotional healing, another to reinforce intimacy, and still another time as a spiritual experience as you share sadness and caring after the funeral of a friend. Sex can be integrated into your daily life and daily life can be integrated into your sexual life.

Sex plays all kinds of roles and can serve a multitude of meanings. For example, sex on vacation, to become pregnant, to heal after an argument, during times of career stress, to celebrate after a class reunion, as a haven to deal with life disappointments or a way to connect after traveling for a week, to reenergize as an "empty nest" couple, to adapt to changes with illness and medications, to enjoy increased time flexibility after retirement. Good-Enough Sex is congruent with your life and makes your relationship special (Exercise 6.2).

Exercise 6.2: Integrating Life Events and Couple Sex

Appreciate that events in your daily life may subtly yet distinctively personalize and enrich your sex life and your sex life can personalize and enrich your daily life.

Select an event that stands out in your life—work stress, fun with your children, resolving a couple conflict, illness of a friend, success at work—and write a brief description in the "Life Event" column. When you have sex with this event as context, note your purpose for having sex. Then write down the arousal style(s) you used during lovemaking. Finally, describe what the life event and the sexual experience meant for you. Don't expect dramatic or profound insights; keep it simple and look for subtle and personal meanings.

Life event	Purpose for sex	Arousal style	Description of its meaning
e.g., Ongoing problems at work	Stress reduction	Self-entrancement, then partner interaction	Soothing and affirming that my partner is so caring and helpful

12. Sexuality Is Personalized. Sex Can Be Playful, Spiritual, and Special

Satisfying sex is sometimes playful, other times highly erotic, and on occasion it can be spiritual. Playfulness is underutilized, but mature playfulness is a hallmark of satisfying sexuality (Table 6.3). For playfulness to occur, other aspects of intimacy must be functioning well: trust, mutual acceptance, focus on pleasure, freedom to be you, and valuing your partner and relationship. By its nature, playfulness is idiosyncratic; for example, using teasing nicknames such as "Big Ben" for your penis and "Grand Tetons" for her breasts. Sexual playfulness can enhance and strengthen intimacy, but its absence can also signal individual stress or relationship problems.

In our culture, "romance" and "sexual experimentation" are code words for adult relationship playfulness. When playfulness and romance die, sexual function will also die.

Table 6.3 Examples of Playfulness and Its Role in Intimacy

34-Year-old male lawyer: "We spend time tickling each other, which is sometimes sexual and sometimes not. We will touch each other sexually while doing normal everyday things. We will 'accidentally' touch and chase each other in the house. I will sneak up on her while she is changing. I will expose myself in the house when we are alone. My wife will give me a sneak peek when she teases. We take showers together and will sometimes wash each other with sexual overtones."

36-Year-old father: "Lately we haven't played much because we had two unplanned pregnancies. I worry about the financial burden of this [providing for the family] and feel I have to be real concerned about my job."

32-Year-old female teacher: "I love to dress up for my husband in lacy clothes one time, then my regular underwear another. I also sometimes beg him in a playful way (I get down on my knees and BEG dramatically!) to dress for me in his tuxedo or leopard skin briefs…that I have to have him this way.…It's a spoof and a tease! But it feels like we're really willing to please each other…that's why I think I so love this.…I also prize the way we can giggle and smile sometimes when we're making love. I feel so special then."

31-Year-old male financial analyst: "Play is a ritualistic part of our sexual seduction.… We will utilize humor from movies (seen or made up). It's fun to tease. Foreplay is interspersed with jokes and comments to relieve tension. We both feel that sex is a time of laughter and enjoyment rather than seriousness."

41-Year-old business man: "We don't play in our sexual relationship. I have always taken sex too seriously to be able to think about being sexually playful. Clearly, we need to change this."

57-Year-old male construction worker: "We are both workaholics, so play is important to relieve stress, fatigue. Sexual activities include cuddling, snuggling…much time in touching, lots of time in bed just visiting."

27-Year-old man: "Sexual play for us? It's our human sundae!"

Couples who are satisfied with their relationships have moments, even if infrequent, of sexual playfulness. It is a hallmark of Good-Enough Sex that fits the couple's real life and is characterized by touch and pleasure. Play makes sex fun. Sexual play can be frivolous and silly but also tender and compassionate. Sex is one of the major forms of play for many adults. Couples who succeed at preserving, even enriching, their romance and sexual regularity, are couples who invest, by instinct or by conscious design, playful energy into their sexuality.

Sex and Spirituality

The meaning of spirituality and sexuality is very individualistic. For a number of men, there is a special, spiritual dimension to sex. This can be true for men who practice traditional religious faith or for those who are not religious. Historically, humanity has connected transcendence with sexuality and fertility with power. Most religions bless marriage as a special relationship. For example, in Roman Catholicism, marriage is a sacrament that is explained as a special way to experience God. The requirement for a sacramental marriage is that it be consummated with sex. It is fascinating to consider that sex is essential for marriage, and marriage is a sacrament, so sex as part of marriage is a special way to experience the transcendent. In a different vein, Buechner, writing in *Now and Then* (1991), suggests, "Here and there, now and then; this is where God is to be found."

Whether one is traditionally religious or not, a good number of men (and women) say that, on occasion, they have experienced an intuitive sense of union through sex. For the man who entrusts his deeper self with his partner, this vulnerability, and the vulnerability of sex itself, can facilitate a spiritual feeling of connection, merging, feeling that your partner is your soul mate, a coming together. Sex can transcend everyday life and have a special meaning for the man and for the couple. An example is being sexual after a major life event such as your wedding, the birth of a child, the wedding of a child, or the birth of a grandchild. Sex is a special part of a very special event. Another example is being sexual as a way of gaining comfort and support after hearing of the death of a friend or as a way to affirm life meaning after attending a funeral of an in-law. Spirituality and an experience of transcendence is a common meaning for sex for many men and women.

Adopting Good-Enough Sex Before a Crisis

Primary prevention is almost always the best strategy. Adopting the Good-Enough Sex model in your 20s and 30s is the optimal strategy.

Don't wait until there is a problem, and don't let a sex problem become chronic and severe. However, in your 40s and 50s, when you have your first acute sexual problem, it is not too late to treat this as a wake-up call and transition to the Good-Enough Sex approach. Even if sexual problems are severe and chronic for 20 years, you can adopt the Good-Enough Sex approach, but it's harder to overcome the history of blame, demoralization, frustration, and avoidance. Make it easy on yourself, and switch to the Good-Enough Sex model as soon as possible (Exercise 6.3).

Exercise 6.3: Implementing the Good-Enough Sex Model

Healthy concepts and intentions are important but they are not enough. You need a clear, specific implementation plan.

Do this exercise first on your own and then with your partner. Review the 12 dimensions of the Good-Enough Sex model. Choose two (three at the most) that are personally relevant in changing your sexual attitudes, behaviors, and feelings. Be clear and specific about what you will change to; it is not enough to drop an old, myth-based dimension. You want to adopt new cognitions, behaviors, and emotions.

The second phase of this exercise is to share your insights and plans with your partner and ask her cooperation in implementing these new attitudes, behaviors, and feelings. For example, if you choose to integrate and flexibly use the three arousal styles, you as a team would plan how to do that. You could purposely initiate all three styles, or switch styles, during a sexual encounter, or each of you could play out a role-enactment scenario. You could strive to make all three arousal styles inviting or you may find that one of you has a strong preference for one style but is open to one other.

However you decide to proceed, there needs to be a mutual commitment to implementing the new dimension. Adopting new attitudes and openness to feelings is very important, but unless you actually have new experiences the good intentions and energetic feelings will break down.

In this exercise, focus on identifying a new sexual voice incorporating at least two dimensions of the Good-Enough Sex approach. It is a couple task to integrate the new attitudes, behaviors, and feelings into your couple sexual style.

What If You Don't Have an Intimate Partner Now?

If you are a man without a partner, the Good-Enough Sex model may seem irrelevant. However, not having a partner right now for whatever reason may actually be an advantage, because you do not have the immediate pressure to integrate the model. You can gradually implement this framework and principles with the virtual partner in your mind. That's right: consider the 12 features of this model and focus on the sexual cognitions, feelings, and behaviors in your virtual relationship. At first this may seem peculiar, but remember that sex is always a relationship dynamic, and there may be several virtual partners you can relate to. You may, in your memory, be thinking about a past relationship, perhaps with someone who sexually hurt or rejected you. Or you may consider navigating a sexual relationship with an idealized or romanticized partner in the present. Or you have a hoped-for future relationship. You can develop increased sexual health while you internally implement the Good-Enough Sex model with your virtual partner. You will be better prepared for the real-life relationship that will eventually come your way.

How Is Good-Enough Sex Great Sex?

Because many—when they first hear us propose putting into practice Good-Enough Sex—think we're encouraging acceptance of mediocre or second-rate, bland, take-what-you-can-get, boring sex, here is a brief summary of how our model is radically different, and the blueprint for great sex—without the unrealistic hype (Table 6.4).

What makes Good-Enough Sex great is that it is not great in the perfectionistic performance sense but in the sense of emotional acceptance and relationship playfulness, cooperation, intimacy, pleasure, and eroticism. Yes, it is a case where reality really is better than fantasy.

Table 6.4 Good-Enough Sex Is Great Because...

You feel more self-assured and proud of yourself as a sexual man because the Good-Enough Sex model is based on science and realistic expectations.

You gain a sense of acceptance because you view sex in realistic terms, seeing sex as a part of unfeigned life and an honest intimate relationship.

You accept yourself and your partner as authentic persons, not mythic figures.

You understand and view your honest sex life as a normal part of life, not hype with its pressure to be someone you are not and pressure to sexually perform in ways that don't fit your actual body and your genuine self.

You feel comfortable with your partner because you endeavor to cooperate with her as an intimate team. Together you are open to a variety of "meanings" in your sexual life—fun, pleasure, comfort, tension reduction, playfulness, consolation, spirituality.

You can accept variable sex with its special times and intimacy as well as mediocre times without disappointment and panic because together you find flexible ways of making love that fit your life's situation.

You feel more confidence about your sexual function and flexible because you understand that there are multiple reasons for having sex and multiple ways of becoming aroused. You can be flexible because you are an intimate team and have options and choices for pleasing yourself and each other.

You feel anxiety free because your focus as a couple is mutual pleasure, not the Hollywood movie pressure of perfect performance.

Closing Thoughts

The Good-Enough Sex model is a direct challenge to the traditional male perfect intercourse performance model. The Good-Enough Sex approach will facilitate long-term comfort, intimacy, confidence, and satisfaction. Valuing variable, flexible male and couple sexuality allows you to maintain a vital sexual life in your 40s, 50s, 60s, 70s, and 80s.

CHAPTER 7

Fitness, Physical Well-Being, and Sexual Function

Men's sexual health is anchored in a fit, healthy body. Physical well-being and fitness are essential for your emotional health and illustrate the integration of the mind–body connection for male sexuality. The guideline is simple: anything good for your physical body will be good for your sexuality, and anything that subverts your physical body will subvert your sexuality.

Fitness is an important concept for men of all ages but is particularly crucial for middle years (over age 40) and older men (over age 60). The best way to conceptualize physical well-being and fitness is the concept of primary prevention, with secondary intervention for acute problems. Unfortunately, what often happens is that health problems become chronic and severe and cause sexual dysfunction.

Prevention

Prevention is the optimal strategy. Primary prevention concentrates on behavioral health habits—sleep, exercise, eating, drinking, drug use, and smoking. A paradox of healthy behavioral habits is that when practiced well they contribute a positive, but relatively small amount, to sexual function. However, problematic or dysfunctional health habits can have a major negative impact on sexual function. For example, chronic disturbed sleep patterns—i.e., sleeping less than 5 hours a night—can cause depression, irritability, and inhibited sexual desire. Cocaine abuse can cause desire, arousal, and orgasmic dysfunction. Smoking interferes with vascular function, which can be a major cause of erectile dysfunction. You owe it to your physical well-being to confront and change these destructive patterns. You will have a secondary reward—renewed sexual vitality. Changing health habits requires discipline and a commitment to a gradual change process and maintaining healthy habits.

Healthy Sleep Patterns

Healthy sleep patterns—regular sleep–wake times, deep sleep, and dreaming, which is physically and psychologically reenergizing, sleep patterns that result in feeling psychologically rested—all contribute to a sense of physical and psychological fitness, which in turn promotes sexual desire and function. Healthy sleep patterns are the foundation of physical well-being. It means establishing a rhythm of going to sleep and awakening on a regular schedule (7–9 hours a night), not drinking or using over-the-counter medications to induce sleep, and engaging in relaxing, nonconflictual activity for 30 minutes before going to bed. Practice mental and physical relaxation techniques. If you do not go to sleep within 20 minutes or wake tossing and turning, get out of bed and do something relaxing until you're tired. In the morning, have a positive waking ritual.

Physical Exercise

The second most important physical health factor is exercise. Exercising is an excellent example of the importance of finding a healthy balance. When people think of optimal exercise they think of young, competitive athletes in exceptional physical condition. Such an extreme is not necessary for good sexual function; rather, a balanced level of physical exercise is important.

Unfortunately, the typical pattern for adult men is a sedentary lifestyle, with a lack of any exercise program. This can cause lethargy, poor physical conditioning, inefficient respiration, general fatigue, lack of sexual energy, and poor vascular and cardiac function—all detriments to healthy sexual function. The other extreme is caused by excessive exercise—overconditioning. This can result in a compulsive use of activity to avoid dealing with emotions and people, not enough time or energy for a genuine sexual relationship, fear of aging and diminished physical capacity, and competitiveness with other men, attached to a fear of loss. Still other men are weekend warriors. Sedentary during the week, these men engage in physical activity on the weekend, with an increased risk for overexertion and physical injury.

A Healthy and Balanced Exercise Program

In terms of exercising, the key is regularity and frequency rather than intense, intermittent workouts. Begin slowly and gradually. Find an exercise routine you can maintain such as walking, swimming, working out at a health club, or aerobics or yoga classes. Engage in the exercise at least three times a week, optimally six; work with a group or exercise buddy to stay accountable; acknowledge the multiple benefits of activity and fitness.

The key element in a healthy exercise program is following age-appropriate guidelines and a regular frequency of activity. An exercise fitness program will be different for a 20-year-old man, a 40-year-old, a 60-year-old, and an 80-year-old man. All men need regular exercise and a sense of physical fitness to promote a healthy sexual body. For some men the key is exercising in a gym; for others it is a group sport like basketball or hockey; for others, it is having an exercise buddy, whether a male friend or spouse; for others, an aerobics or yoga class; and for still others, training for a marathon. Men who prefer exercising on their own have to be highly motivated and disciplined to maintain a regular pattern. In healthy, balanced exercise, frequency and regularity are the keys to success. Activities that condition your respiration, cardiac, and vascular systems are good for sexual vitality and function.

Eating Habits and Your Healthy Weight Range

Balance is also a crucial factor in healthy eating habits. Our culture is obsessed with diets. The great majority of diets emphasize one or two aspects of eating, such as low carbohydrate or high carbohydrate intake, minimal calories, no sugar or no meat, or only cooking with olive oil. The theme of many diets is the promise of quick weight loss: "Lose 30 pounds in 30 days!" or "Achieve optimal weight in just two months!" Very few weight-loss diets have relapse prevention or maintenance programs. In truth, you want a balanced, sensible eating plan combined with an exercise routine in which you lose 1–2 pounds a week. The seasoned, balanced approaches recommend smaller portions and regular exercise as the successful weight management approach. Find your healthy weight range, which is the weight you are able to maintain over months and years. This is quite different from ideal weight that you can achieve on a rigorous diet and exercise program but will not be able to maintain.

In terms of having a healthy sexual body, eating habits and weight loss involve two major factors. The first is actual weight and accepting a positive body image. The essence of sexual response is touch rather than visual stimuli. However, when you feel heavy and negative about your own body, this will reduce both your sense of sexual desirability and your sexual desire. Second, high levels of weight can cause medical problems such as adult-onset diabetes, high blood pressure, and heightened levels of cholesterol. Treating these illnesses usually entails the need for medication. Both the illness and the medication side effects can interfere with vascular function, which subverts sexual response.

Alcohol and Drugs

Drinking and drug use are more complex health habits. Many men learn to be sexual while drunk or drinking. For many young men, alcohol provides "liquid courage" to overcome inhibitions and self-consciousness. Drugs are used for the same purpose. However, from a physiological perspective, alcohol is a central nervous system depressant that subverts sexual response. In younger men, the positive psychological effect of alcohol disinhibition ("greasing the sexual wheels") overrides the negative physiological effect. However, with aging, alcohol has a more negative sexual impact. Many middle-aged men find that one drink (or at the most two) can be beneficial in reducing sexual self-consciousness and put them in a sexual mood, but more drinks negatively impact sexual function.

Alcohol is a depressant that can subvert sexual response. In the long run, alcohol abuse and alcoholism causes erectile dysfunction and inhibited sexual desire. So the paradox is that although men have learned to be sexually functional with the help of alcohol to reduce anxiety and self-consciousness, alcohol subverts sexual response physiologically. As a man ages, the negative physiological effects of alcohol will override the positive psychological effects.

Of adults who drink, approximately one in four abuses alcohol or has an alcohol dependence problem. The National Institute on Alcohol Abuse and Alcoholism suggests that a man who has more than 14 drinks a week (for women, 12) or has 5 or more drinks in one sitting has a significant likelihood of an alcohol abuse problem. Except for very young men, this level of drinking poses a risk factor for sexual dysfunction. In men with a history of alcohol abuse or dependence, it is the norm to experience temporary erectile problems, ejaculatory inhibition, or inhibited sexual desire when they stop drinking. In fact, many AA programs encourage sexual abstinence until the man has a year of recovery because of the fear that he'll react to sexual dysfunction by returning to drinking.

A dilemma for men who stop drinking is that they are not able to function sexually in a sober state because they learned sexual response when drinking. The answer is not to go back to abusive drinking. It takes most men (and couples) 3–6 months to develop a comfortable, functional couple sexual style in a sober state. The healthy psychobiosocial strategy is to realize that it will take months to learn to be comfortable and confident with sober sex. If the man does not give in to panic, he learns that a comfortable, aware approach to desire, arousal, and orgasm without alcohol provides a solid foundation for healthy sexual function. Learning self-entrancement arousal is frequently an important part of developing sexual function in sobriety.

For the majority of men, there is nothing wrong with one beer or a glass of wine before being sexual, but there is a major problem with using alcohol as a sexual crutch.

The evidence for effects from drugs on sexual function is less clear, but marijuana appears to inhibit sexual desire with chronic use. Appendix B lists resources to consult if you are using non-prescription drugs (legal or illegal) that could interfere with your sexual function.

Smoking

Smoking has no positive benefits and a range of possible negative effects for both your physical and sexual body. Smoking is particularly harmful for your vascular (especially penile vessels) and respiratory systems, which are core to physical sexual function. Unlike moderate drinking, there are no positive physical, psychological, or sexual benefits of smoking. The more chronic and severe the smoking habit, the more likely there will be negative sexual (and general health) effects. The implications are clear—the primary prevention strategy is to not smoke and the intervention strategy is a stop-smoking program.

Medications

Prescribed and over-the-counter medications add to the complexity of a healthy sexual body. The dilemma is that illness has a negative effect on your physical and sexual body, but the side effects of some medications to treat illness are the major physical factor that subverts sexual function. Examples include blood pressure, antidepressant, and over-the-counter cold medications. High blood pressure, depression, and other illnesses sometimes have a negative impact on your physical and sexual body, but many of the medications to treat these problems have negative sexual side effects, especially impacting desire and erections.

Dealing with Illness and Medication Side Effects

There are three integrative strategies to deal with illness and medication issues: (a) be an active, involved patient in understanding and coping with your illness; (b) consult your medical doctor as a couple with a focus on how to be a better patient in terms of health behaviors and use medication with less sexual side effects or an "antidote" medication to counter the negative sexual side effects; (c) accept the limitations of your illness and change your sexual life with alternative sexual scenarios so your sexuality is not controlled by the illness.

The following are examples of each coping strategy. First, find a trusted book or Web site that provides reliable medical information and coping techniques for your specific illness. Also, consider attending a patient education class or joining a support group with others who are coping with this illness.

Second, invite your partner to come with you to your appointment and make it clear to the physician that you want to focus only on medication and sexual health (not couple counseling). This can bring out the best in the physician in terms of information about the illness, medications, health behaviors, and sexual impacts. You can review the medication's negative side effects and discuss alternative medications and whether there are antidotes you might try.

Third, it is often beneficial to change your sexual pattern to reduce the impact of the illness on your sexual function. For example, if you experience arthritic pain at night and find that your body is most flexible early in the morning or after a nap, that's a better time for you to be sexual. If you take your antidepressant medication in the evening and want to be sexual later that night, you might switch dosing times to the morning. Another alternative is to switch to being sexual in the morning. Talk with your partner and doctor about how best to take your prescribed medications.

In deciding which strategies are personally relevant to you, be an active patient in dealing with your illness and medications. Remember that only rare illnesses can stop you from being sexual or control your physical body. The challenge is to adapt to the illness, medication side effects, and the sexual changes so that touch, pleasure, and sex can continue to be a positive part of your life and relationship.

Exercise 7.1: Maintaining a Physical and Sexual Healthy Body

This exercise asks you to do a careful assessment of your sleep, exercise, eating, and drinking patterns and honestly determine whether each component contributes positively to your physical well-being and fitness. If not, the second phase of this exercise is to establish a realistic change plan.

Part I: Taking Stock

Keep a health behavior log on a daily basis for 2 weeks to observe patterns in your health behaviors. Keep the diary under four headings:

Sleep
Exercise

(Continued)

(*Continued*)

Eating

Drinking (include use of legal and illegal drugs).

It is crucial that you be honest with yourself. Establish a time each day—perhaps bedtime—to record your health behavior for the day. Or, keep this data on your PDA, Blackberry, or laptop computer and make entries in real-time.

Sleep: record what time you went to sleep and what time you woke up, whether you slept soundly or had disturbed sleep, whether you experienced worrisome thoughts or nightmares, and how rested and calm you felt in the morning.

Exercise: record the type of exercise you engaged in, for how long, and how you felt physically and psychologically after exercising.

Eating: record both frequency and quantity of eating patterns, whether planned or impulsive; healthy vs. junk foods; and whether you enjoy the eating experience or feel negative or embarrassed about it. Eating is probably the hardest to record because by its nature eating is a more frequent behavior.

Alcohol and drugs: record your drinking and drug use. Be aware of the context—do you drink alone or socially? What are the internal or external factors that contribute to drinking too much? Is your drinking out of control? How do you feel at the time and after drinking?

Review your data with your partner or a trusted friend. What does this reveal about your physical well-being and sense of fitness? Of the four areas, which is the healthiest for you? Which is the most problematic?

If all four areas enhance your physical body and fitness, congratulations. What do you need to do in the coming years to maintain this level of physical well-being? Remaining physically fit is valuable in itself as well as contributing to a healthy sexual body.

Part II: Improving Your Health

If there are one or more areas that are problematic, how can you institute a change plan? We strongly suggest beginning the change process by scheduling a general physical examination with your medical doctor. A crucial sexual health strategy is to develop a comfortable doctor–patient relationship with a trusted physician. It's easier to talk candidly, especially about sex, if your doctor is not a stranger. Show the physician your sleep, exercise, eating, and

(*Continued*)

(*Continued*)

drinking log. The physician will probably do blood tests and other diagnostic procedures and be able to provide you with an objective evaluation of your physical health along with suggestions about health behaviors.

The next step is to change your problematic health habits. Be realistic. If problems are severe or chronic, a self-help approach will not be enough. You would be wise to seek interventions with a behavioral medicine specialist or a therapist with a mind–body approach (professional resources are listed in Appendix 1). In utilizing cognitive and behavioral change strategies, use all the necessary resources you need to successfully address the problem and attain meaningful change. These can include your partner, friends, clergy, psychologist, books, or trusted Web sites. You need to set realistic goals and have a specific change plan. Here are some change strategies to consider:

Changing sleep patterns:
Prepare yourself for sleeping well. Stop exercising, worrying, or drinking at least an hour before going to sleep.
Have a regular sleep time, a relaxing bedtime pattern (read a novel, take a bath or shower, listen to music, cuddle, or be sexual).
If you awaken during the night, refocus on relaxing thoughts and images—the worst time to deal with problems is the middle of the night. If you can't get back to sleep within 20 minutes, get out of bed and be upright (standing or sitting), because when you are laying down, you are more likely to emotionally ruminate. Do something relaxing or constructive until you feel tired again.
Have a morning routine that allows you to begin the day in a pleasant manner (e.g., shower, make coffee, read the comics or sports).
Limit any naps to 30–45 minutes to rejuvenate yourself but not subvert your nocturnal sleep patterns.

Changing exercise patterns:
Choose an exercise you can do at least three times a week, preferably daily. Consult your physician about your exercise plan if you have any health issues. Start slowly and gradually build up time and activity.

(*Continued*)

(*Continued*)

Remember, regularity and frequency are healthier than an occasional intense workout.

Use all your resources to implement a regular exercise routine—whether classes, a group program, or with friends or your partner.

Walking is a good example of an exercise that many men find easy to implement. Whether walking, biking, swimming, or a work-out routine, make this an integral part of your life.

Changing eating patterns:

Find your healthy weight range; resist the temptation to achieve a perfect weight goal.

If you are overweight, there are two chief guidelines—balanced eating and weight loss of 1–2 pounds per week.

Establish one to three foods to eliminate from your eating repertoire. Realize that for most foods the goal is moderation.

Consult a professional nutritionist or a hospital-based weight-loss program.

Drinking and drug use patterns:

Be aware that it is easier to stop drinking than to moderate drinking; learning to moderate drinking requires greater motivation and rigor.

Never drink alone; moderate drinking is much easier in a social environment.

Be especially aware of how you feel before you drink, the initial motivation to drink, what keeps you drinking, as well as when and with whom you drink. Do not drink and drive, use alcohol to self-medicate, or drink as a way to fall asleep.

Address any "red-flag" drinking incidents. The National Council on Alcohol Abuse defines a red flag as an event where you drink 5 or more drinks. If you are doing this, you need to use outside resources to assess and change your drinking pattern.

Lastly, be aware of the relationship between your level of physical well-being and your sexual desire, arousal, and orgasmic response. It seldom is a one-to-one relationship, but be honest with yourself (and solicit your partner's feedback) about whether problematic health behaviors subvert your sexual body and couple sexual function. Respect the common advice of older men who lament, "I wish I'd

(*Continued*)

(Continued)

taken better care of my body when I was younger." Lifelong healthy behaviors are easier than trying to get into reasonable physical condition at the age of 50. It's never too late to adopt healthy behavioral habits.

Emotional Fitness

Emotional fitness is an important dimension to your overall fitness, which will promote sexual health and satisfaction. Emotional fitness is undermined by the stresses of our daily lives, the fatigue it can generate physically and emotionally, and our often frantic lifestyles. You do not need to be a "Type A" man or a workaholic to suffer from emotional stress. We have 30% less leisure time than 25 years ago, and the demands of our jobs and careers have increased in recent years. The pressure for companies to be productive and efficient often means people are working harder for the same or even less pay than 10 years ago. More and more time is consumed by commuting to work, dealing with the complexities of life, and taking care of the activities of daily living all the while trying to be more efficient and effective. Unfortunately, this involves an emotional toll.

Many men take little vacation, usually less than permitted. The axiom that "All work and no play make Jack a dull boy" is too often applicable—and ignored. It is very difficult for many men to balance work, home, parenting, maintaining friendships, having a social life, and time for one's self. For many men, even their leisure activities have pressures of business relationships and business promotion. Such stresses make physical and emotional fitness all the more essential.

Physical fitness is important for sexual functioning, and emotional fitness is important for sexual desire, function, and satisfaction. When you are chronically stressed-out, anxious, fatigued, or resentful of the burdens and responsibilities you bear, these emotional stresses undermine sexual function and satisfaction. So in addition to having a good and consistent physical fitness program, it is also valuable to maintain an emotional fitness program.

Exercise 7.2: Develop Your Emotional Health Fitness Program

Goal: The goal of this exercise is to identify specific strategies to facilitate mental, emotional, and behavioral well-being. Consider the four areas below and write your strategies in the column to the right. Keep it simple so you will be effective.

(Continued)

(Continued)

	Area of emotional health	Strategies
#1	Annual or semiannual vacation: Don't let yourself believe that you are indispensable at work. Rather, decide when and how you will take an annual vacation. Plan two semiannual vacations if you prefer. But take all of your allotted vacation and personal time. Coordinate with your partner so that it is a relaxing and revitalizing time.	
#2	Microvacations: Take a look at your weekly schedule and determine how and when you can take simple microvacations. These are times you are off duty. Enjoy a movie, pleasant dinner with your partner, or a family trip to a museum, concert, or sporting event. The essential feature is you intentionally engage in this activity as a microvacation from stress.	
#3	Take the time for self-care: Sit and relax for a moment; take time for reflection; journal for 15 minutes; take a long, relaxing shower; take a 30-minute nap; walk the dog; stop for a cup of coffee; take time to read the paper; piddle in the garage; or play a videogame.Coordinate these moments with your partner so she knows about and supports your self-care. Encourage her to do the same for herself.	
#4	Stress level management: Take a moment as you commute home from work to measure how stressed you are feeling. Or you might quietly sit with your spouse and hold hands for 2 minutes and physically sense each others' stress. What techniques are most helpful for you to unwind and relax?	

Physical Fitness, Sexual Function, and a Satisfying Sexual Relationship

Enjoying a healthy physical body, a sense of physical and emotional fitness, pleasure-oriented sexual function, and arousing and orgasmic sex promotes sexual satisfaction. Both subjective arousal and physiological arousal add to couple satisfaction. The paradox is that poor physical conditioning, poor health habits, poor emotional fitness, and poor body image have a more negative impact on sexuality than the positive impact of a healthy sexual body, physical fitness, and good physical and mental conditioning. That truth is just one of life's unfair realities. But you can handle it.

Illustration 7.1: Art

Forty-nine-year-old Art was divorced 2 years ago. This divorce was initiated by his wife of 6 years, a totally unexpected and unwelcome second divorce. Art had said for several years that he was glad to be done with his first wife, and this second marriage was the perfect compensation for the wasted years of his first marriage. He dealt with this divorce by eating too much, drinking too much, and hiding out. Art gained over 20 pounds and was increasingly isolated.

His brother and sister-in-law invited Art to their mountain cabin for a weekend. On a leisurely hike they urged him to take back control of his life and physical well-being. Since it was just the three of them sitting on a rock overlooking the valley, Art couldn't avoid this discussion. His sister-in-law was empathic and gentle but confrontational in saying that they cared about him and worried about his health. She also shared with Art that among his ex-wife's complaints were that Art did not value her as a person but as a symbol and that he had increasingly fallen into poor health behaviors, especially smoking, a sedentary lifestyle, and talking about the "good old days" when they first met rather than being in the present as an involved, active spouse. His brother said that although he was saddened by the divorce, Art could reorganize his life physically and emotionally. They had a number of divorced and widowed women they would like Art to meet.

Art needed to take responsibility for his own physical and psychological well-being rather than find a woman to take care of him. This meant carefully considering his personal, health, and social behaviors. Fortunately, Art had a successful career in which he was well-respected by colleagues and clients and that he found satisfying. He'd always maintained a regular sleep pattern in all but the most

(Continued)

(*Continued*)

stressful times. However, now Art needed to attend to his physical body and health behaviors.

His first attempt to change with the exercise component was badly thought-out. Art joined a 7-days-a-week 6 am "boot camp" program. It started with 10 men and 3 women, and by the time Art dropped out at the end of the second week there were only 3 men and 1 woman left. His second effort made much more sense—a walking group that met daily for 45 minutes beginning at 7:30 am, 6 days a week. The expectation was that Art would show up at least 4 days; 6 was optimal. This group had had people join and leave but had been in existence for over 4 years. Art enjoyed both the camaraderie and listening to fitness stories and ideas.

Over the last 2 years, Art's main eating had been fast food and pizzas. His wisest decision was to consult a nutritionist, who provided information and eating suggestions. Art e-mailed her his eating diary on a weekly basis and they met every month to discuss specific eating changes. His second best move was to join a healthy cooking class at the YMCA. He met some interesting people and was surprised to discover that at 49 he enjoyed learning to cook.

Art was pleasantly surprised to find that if he only drank outside the house in social situations, his drinking was quickly and easily reduced. He also discovered that he could save money by not having alcohol in his home. However, quitting smoking was a much tougher task. Although Art had attended three stop-smoking programs that used a number of medical and over-the-counter resources (e.g., the patch), he had relapsed, although not back to his two packs a day habit. Art tells anyone who will listen that "Smoking is the hardest addiction to break, so don't start."

A powerful side effect of Art's changing health behaviors was new social contacts and a positive focus rather than obsessing about the divorce. People admired Art's determination to regain physical well-being and his dedication to his fitness program. In fact, it was someone from the walking group who introduced Art to his present girlfriend. Their first date involved hiking a popular mountain trail. Art was especially pleased to have a partner who would support and reinforce his efforts to gain and maintain fitness and physical well-being.

Closing Thoughts

Physical and emotional well-being, conditioning, and fitness contribute directly to a healthy physical body and indirectly to a healthy sexual body.

Physical health, like sexual health, is multicausal and multidimensional. The good news is that maintaining fitness and physical well-being will promote sexual function for all men, but particularly for men after 40. The challenge is to not take your physical well-being for granted but to maintain healthy sleep, exercise, and eating and drinking patterns, abstain from smoking, and take time to relax. Your vascular and neurological systems remain functional into your 70s and 80s but are less efficient. So in maintaining sexual desire and function, psychological, relational, and especially psychosexual skill factors play a more important role. Physical, emotional and sexual well-being are integrally connected, so take good care of yourself.

CHAPTER 8

Lifelong Healthy Sexuality—You Are a Sexual Man Until You Die

At each age—childhood, adolescence, early adulthood, middle age, older age—your experiences and learnings provide an ongoing challenge for your sexual health. Whether they are helpful or difficult experiences, learn to value these as contributions to being a sexual man. A good number of 50- and 60-year-old men will say that they feel more confident, proud, and satisfied with their sexuality as they have gotten older. When you maintain reasonably good physical health, sex has its own positive qualities regardless of your age. You gain wisdom, understanding, and acceptance that may not be age appropriate to younger men. Appreciate your maleness and your sexuality at every age of your life.

We give special attention to the challenges to sexual health with older age. Adapting to the various sexual health opportunities and challenges at each age is a part of flexible sexual health. For older men, sex is more genuine, more of an intimate, interactive experience. You need each other more than in your 20s. Sex is less predictable and controllable but also more involving and satisfying. You can learn to piggyback your arousal on hers. Focus on intimacy, pleasure, eroticism, and satisfaction. A crucial concept is viewing the woman as your intimate, erotic friend. Valuing Good-Enough Sex comes to fruition in your 50s, 60s, 70s, and 80s. Men who cling to the rigid, performance-oriented traditional male sex role stop being sexual in their 50s and 60s. Men who adopt the new model of healthy male and couple sexuality continue to enjoy a variable, flexible sexual life into their 80s. You are a sexual man from the day you are born until the day that you die.

The 20s and 30s

Many of the concerns and worries of your teen years probably continued into young adulthood. You may worry about normalcy in a sexual relationship, including the frequency that you're sexual, your lovemaking skills, how to sexually please your partner, the normalcy of your sexual fantasies, and how to handle disappointments with your sexual function (such as premature ejaculation). Many men experience the issue of how to regulate strong and powerful sexual impulses. Questions about sexuality take on a new dimension with fatherhood and parenting. Healthy male sexuality involves acknowledging, at least to yourself, the multiple concerns and worries you may have, consciously resisting the mythic message that men are not supposed to have questions or concerns, and seeking integration of sexuality into your real life.

The 40s and 50s

In your 40s and 50s, worries commonly center on physical changes and what they mean sexually. With the maturity of midlife, questions frequently arise about your career, the meaning of life, and the deeper integration of your sexuality into your intimate relationship. An awareness that your life may be half over and questions of purpose are common. At the same time, your physical body is mellowing and concerns about sexual function may be accentuated by common medical problems that may arise such as high blood pressure, weight gain, or cardiovascular problems. Such concerns can raise self-doubts and worries of declining health and sexuality.

There are small, typical changes in sexual functioning as men grow older. When you remain in good health and ensure age-appropriate physical conditioning, any and all of these changes are subtle and easily adapted to (Table 8.1).

Your spouse may also be experiencing similar concerns, including menopause, changes in body image, and sexual self-doubts. While men worry about midlife and aging, these changes can offer new opportunities for couples to deepen their emotional connection, acceptance, and intimacy. These are the very qualities that enrich sexuality. Midlife and aging are a clear example of how concerns and vulnerabilities may serve as opportunities for growth and satisfaction.

The 60s and Beyond

In the 60s and beyond, medical problems become common, and their effect on sexual functioning can become a major worry. Adapting to illness and

Table 8.1 Normal, Healthy Changes in Sexual Function Among Aging Men

Slightly decreased number and frequency of morning erections.

Mildly decreased sexual desire.

Mental arousal mellows in intensity presumably due to subtle neurological changes.

Mild decrease in penile sensitivity presumably due to changes in neural thresholds.

To obtain an erection, direct penile stimulation is usually required; desire is not sufficient to initiate erections.

Delayed erection is normal (the erection is slower; it may take 2 to 3 times longer than youth, i.e., 5–30 seconds to begin erectile response), presumably due to mild, decreased penile sensitivity. With fatigue, obtaining an erection may take longer.

Erections may be less firm and, for some older men, full rigidity may occur only seconds before ejaculation. Some men are able to maintain an erection for a longer period of time prior to ejaculation.

Ejaculatory urgency ("the need to ejaculate") may be reduced. Some men may not ejaculate each time.

The awareness of impending orgasm may be muted. Ejaculation may be more single-staged as ejaculatory inevitability may be less well defined and briefer, which appears to be related to decreased production of ejaculatory fluids.

Ejaculation duration may last for only 1–2 seconds (instead of 2–4 seconds in younger men), with 1 or 2 ejaculatory expulsive contractions of the urethra (instead of the 3 or 4 major contractions in youth) and orgasm intensity may be reduced. Some older men may have no prostatic contractions with ejaculation (semen may "ooze out"). Some men occasionally have orgasm without ejaculation.

After ejaculation/orgasm, detumescence of your penis and testicular descent are more rapid due to decreased amount of vasocongestion.

The amount and viscosity of ejaculatory fluid (semen) is decreased.

The quantity of viable sperm becomes reduced, which may limit male fertility.

The refractory period increases in length (e.g., in 20s, minutes; over 55, may be 12 to 24 hours or longer).

Rare rash-like "flush" in neck, trunk, shoulders, thighs, and forearms during sexual excitement compared to youth (due to reduced vasocongestion).

their treatments such as medication side effects that alter sexual functioning are common. Worries about the physical and sexual health of your partner are also common. With acceptance and flexibility, the physical limitations with aging are challenges that can facilitate deepening intimacy. Sexual enjoyment and satisfaction can characterize every age and every stage in life.

How to Approach Healthy Sexuality in Later Life

From the perspective of normal development and aging, consider how to integrate this knowledge into your sexual health as an aging man. Not only are children and adolescents sexual, but there is sex after college, and there is sex after 60. You are a sexual man from the day you're born to the day you die. You can enjoy sexuality throughout your life.

Adopt a Flexible Approach

Do not fall into the trap of believing that sex is not possible in your 60s, 70s, and 80s. The key is adopting a broad-based, flexible, variable approach to male and couple sexuality. Our mantra of intimacy, pleasuring, eroticism, and satisfaction comes to fruition with the aging process. Men who cling to the rigid performance-oriented traditional male sex role usually stop being sexual in their 50s or 60s. You want to adopt the Good-Enough Sex model so you continue to enjoy sexuality into your 80s or longer.

Better Quality of Sex with Age

The traditional cultural theme is that a real man is totally sexually confident and performs with the regularity and predictability of his teens and 20s. The erroneous belief is that anything less is a failure. Other, more sophisticated, men realize that sex is different in their 60s and still enjoy sex but are disappointed and believe they have to settle for second-class sexuality. We believe just the opposite. Sex after 60 is more genuine and human, more of an intimate, interactive experience. You need each other in a way that you didn't in your 20s. Although sex is less predictable and controllable, in many ways it is more affirming, involving, and rewarding. For individual and relationship satisfaction, it is very much a first-class experience.

Many women surprise their partners by saying that they enjoy sex now more than they did 30 years ago. A woman likes the fact that you need her stimulation for arousal and orgasm. Give-and-take sex can be a powerful aphrodisiac for you and for her. A wise man learns to piggy-back his arousal on hers. Through most of your sex life, a man's arousal is easier, quicker, and more predictable than a female's. Now you can enjoy and take advantage of this role enhancement. It is the perfect example of being intimate, interactive friends. You need each other and can enjoy each other more as pleasuring and eroticism build more slowly. This process, which involves more genital (especially penile) stimulation, can be particularly enjoyable.

Men under 35 enjoy receiving penile stimulation—whether manual or oral—but only when they are already aroused. Being receptive and responsive to penile touch as a way to develop and reinforce arousal is a new experience for most men. The healthy approach is to accept and enjoy this variable, flexible sexual response. This includes accepting creative and sometimes unpredictable sexual scenarios. A common mistake aging men make is to jump on their developing erection so they can insert before they lose the erection. This is equivalent to the "sexual drag racing" of younger men, who are afraid of premature ejaculation, going to intercourse as soon as possible to be sure they ejaculate inside the woman.

Sexual Wisdom

As men mature and become sexually wiser, they find that sexual response and control are based on relaxation, slowing down expands the pleasuring/eroticism process, and learning to understand your body and sexual response increases psychosexual skills. Men over 60 learn to accept and enhance the body's sexual response. Rather than trying to start intercourse when you can, the sexual technique is to transition to intercourse when you should. Arousal (subjective and objective) is conceptualized on a 10-point scale, where 5 is the beginning level of arousal signaled by start of an erection, 7 is higher arousal with a firm erection, 9 is high levels of erotic flow, and 10 is orgasm. Rather than transition to intercourse at 5, we suggest transitioning at 7 or 8. The strategy many couples use is for the woman to decide when to initiate intercourse and to guide intromission. This stops you from playing the spectator role and allows you to fully engage in the process of giving and receiving pleasurable and erotic touch.

When we present professional workshops about sex after 60, our colleagues are often quite skeptical about these concepts and techniques. Since we are growing older, we can truthfully say that theoretically, clinically, and personally we find the quality of men's sexual life to be special and satisfying. Men can take satisfaction in beating the odds to maintain a vital sexuality in their 60s, 70s, and 80s. Regrettably, by age 65, one third of men have stopped engaging in couple sex; this rises to over 50% by age 70. Men who cling to the traditional perfect intercourse performance model usually stop being sexual in their 50s or 60s. Men who value our Good-Enough Sex model; who see the woman as his intimate, erotic friend; who integrate intimacy, pleasuring, and eroticism; who celebrate variable, flexible male and couple sexuality; and who integrate their sexuality into their real lives are the men who enjoy intimacy and sexuality into their 80s or longer.

Illustration 8.1: George: Healthy Sex in a Second Marriage

Like most men, George did not expect to be a widower. His first wife, Angie, was 3 years younger and health conscious. However, breast cancer is a very unfair disease, particularly so in Angie's case. She waged a courageous 4-year struggle with the cancer, but lost. Three months before her death, George and Angie had a highly emotional but crucially important talk about her impending death and her hopes for him as a widower. She urged him to stay in close contact with their 31-year-old daughter and two grandchildren. Angie reassured George that she would not find his remarrying disloyal. In fact, she urged him to remarry and create a new life, not in comparison with their life but as a new chapter in his life.

(Continued)

(*Continued*)

As a 63-year-old widower, George was surprised at the number of opportunities to meet available women his age, younger, and older. However, George decided to follow the advice given to him by the minister and reinforced by his daughter to go through the grieving process and establish his own life before seeking a new life partner.

Eighteen months after Angie's death, George began to date. Although tempted to play the sexual dating game, George opted for serious (lover) relationships. His guideline was not even to raise the issue of remarriage until he knew the woman for at least 6 months. He dated three women—two in their 50s and one in her 60s. He enjoyed a sexual relationship with each woman, but for a variety of reasons decided that each would not be a good life partnership.

George met Liz, a 61-year-old divorced woman, through a community tutoring program to teach English as a second language. George was impressed by Liz's devotion to helping others. After dating for 6 months, he introduced Liz to his daughter's family and he met her two adult children. One of the things he most liked was that Liz was so different from Angie—there was no reason for comparison. Liz was four inches shorter, had been divorced for 20 years, had her own successful consulting business, and her sexual preference was for partner-interaction arousal as well as role-enactment arousal. Angie had focused on intimacy-based scenarios and self-entrancement arousal.

Their sexual relationship was vital and energizing but was not the major factor in George's desire to marry Liz. George wanted to enjoy the intimacy and security of being married. George was a man who genuinely valued the companionship and commitment of marriage. Liz wanted George to realize that second marriages are more of a challenge, and she wanted to be sure that both of them were willing to put in the psychological time and energy to ensure that they would beat the odds and have a satisfying, stable second marriage. They wanted sexuality to play a 15–20% role in making theirs a satisfying marriage.

George realized that a second marriage after 60 had to stand on its own merits because it was unlikely that adult children would be major supporters. None of their children were in opposition (George and Liz were lucky), but they had their own lives and were not looking for a substitute mother. The grandchildren were much more open to a new grandmother.

In developing their unique sexual style, George and Liz recognized that they did not have to be clones of each other either emotionally

(*Continued*)

(*Continued*)

or sexually. George had been used to a sexual scenario that featured a quick transition from touching the woman and going to intercourse as soon as he felt she was ready. George worried that if he prolonged touching, he could lose his erection—a major fear. Liz had a different preference in terms of pleasuring, orgasm, and intercourse. She enjoyed a slow, mutual buildup of pleasure and eroticism and particularly enjoyed stimulating George manually and orally, which built her arousal. Although Liz could be orgasmic during intercourse (she especially enjoyed simultaneous manual clitoral stimulation with George inside her), Liz found it easier and more erotic to be orgasmic with either rubbing or manual stimulation (although she enjoyed giving oral stimulation, she did not enjoy receiving cunnilingus). George found this new pleasuring/erotic scenario very inviting, and it reduced pressure for intercourse performance. Even more important, George learned to piggyback his arousal on Liz's. Although George strongly preferred to go to intercourse on his first erection, he was open to Liz's stimulation to help him get a second erection if his erection went on break. George no longer panicked about the waxing and waning of erections.

The hardest thing for George to get used to was Liz's playful way of teasing and initiating. He learned to view this as an invitation to play and share pleasure, not a demand for quick sexual intercourse. Liz enjoyed both receiving and giving erotic, non-intercourse sex. George was able to accept the giving scenario but never became comfortable with receiving manual or oral sex to orgasm. It made him feel too self-conscious and sexually selfish. If the scenario did not flow to intercourse, George preferred to have a sensual cuddle and end in that manner.

George was aware not to compare his relationships with Angie and Liz, either emotionally or sexually. He realized that there was no positive benefit and it could be emotionally dangerous. These were two very different chapters of his life, each with its own value.

Health, Illness, and Side Effects of Medication with Aging

Healthy sexuality avoids unreasonable extremes. The most common extreme is the pessimistic view of aging as loss; the other extreme is thinking that you can have perfect health and perfect sex until 100. Strive for realistic acceptance of your aging body and positive, realistic expectations of sex in your 60s, 70s, and 80s.

A crucial component of realistic acceptance is that the majority of men at 60 are taking at least one medication to deal with a chronic illness. By age 70, the great majority are taking medication. Aging itself does not stop sexual functioning. The major factor is illness and the side effects of medications to treat these illnesses. The good news is that illness does not stop sexual response; the bad news is that illness and medication side effects do alter your sexual response.

There are three major strategies in dealing with illness and medications:

- Be an active, knowledgeable patient in dealing with your illness.
- Establish a communicative, consultant relationship with your general physician or specialist in terms of your medication protocol and changes in health behaviors. The optimal way to do this is to consult your physician as a couple.
- Use all of your psychological, relational, and psychosexual skill resources to enhance your sexual response. This can include pro-sexual medications that are integrated into your couple sexual style of intimacy, pleasuring, and eroticism.

To implement these strategies, first, accept that you have an illness. Do not deny it or feel embarrassed. It does you no good to engage in "what if" thinking. Whether or not it could have been prevented is now irrelevant. You have an illness; accept it, accept your distressed feelings, and deal with it.

What does it mean to be an active patient? The typical trap for men is to minimize health issues or avoid them because of anxiety. A good example is the man given a diagnosis of prostate cancer who never makes a follow-up appointment. An active patient would research assessment and treatment options, promptly schedule a follow-up session as well as a second opinion, and carefully evaluate interventions given the type of prostate cancer, his age, and preference for careful monitoring, surgery, radiation, or hormonal treatment. The spouse has an active role in processing information and decision-making, but ultimately it is your body and your decision.

Establish a consultant relationship with your doctor and ask your spouse to attend a joint consultation not only to evaluate medical interventions but also to discuss the sexual implications of the treatment and medications. Physicians usually find sex a difficult topic but are more likely to be helpful if you go together and make it clear that you are not looking for a "magic pill" but wise, sound medical information, focused on treatment options and side effects of medications and health habits. You want to utilize interventions that have the most positive impact on the illness but the least negative impact on sexuality. For example, if you take an antidepressant medication in the evening before going to bed and you prefer to make love at night, you could change your dosing schedule to early in the morning. Another strategy is to enter cognitive–behavioral individual or couple therapy to improve your problem-solving and mood, which may allow a lower medication dose, resulting in lessened sexual side effects.

The third strategy, using all your resources, includes integrating a pro-sex medication (Viagra/sildenafil HCL, Cialis/tadalafil HCL, Levitra/vardenafil HCL, or testosterone) in your couple sexual style of intimacy, pleasuring, and eroticism. Contrary to the marketing ads, the medication will not work as a stand-alone intervention, nor will it return you to the totally predictable, autonomous erections of your teens. In truth, pro-erection medications make your vascular system more efficient so that once subjectively aroused it is easier to obtain and maintain an erection sufficient for intercourse. A man who prefers structure and predictability will find that the 4-hour window of opportunity provided by Viagra facilitates sexual initiation, whereas a man whose partner prefers variability and unpredictability will do better with Cialis, which provides greater freedom and a longer (up to 36 hours) window of opportunity.

The most important concept is to accept the reality of your disease and medication side effects and to integrate it with the Good-Enough Sex approach. Accept both your body and its illness. This serves as a foundation and as a challenge for healthy male and couple sexuality. A good example is diabetes, an illness that Barry has had for over 30 years. His first priority has been to be an active diabetic patient. He abstains from drinking juices, alcohol, and eating sugars; maintains a consistent weight range of 170–175; walks 20–25 miles a week; and rigorously follows his prescribed oral medication protocol. Part of his motivation to be a good diabetic patient is his desire to maintain a vital, satisfying sexual relationship with his wife of 40 years, Emily. Although at present he does not utilize medication for sex, he would not hesitate to do so in the future if needed. Erections and orgasms are no longer the easy, autonomous function he learned in his youth. Both Barry and Emily value their intimate, erotic sexual relationship, finding it more genuine and satisfying then the automatic sex of their early years. We fully expect to enjoy sexuality in our 60s, 70s, and 80s.

The Value of Sexuality in Your Older Age

If you adopt this new model of healthy male sexuality, you can continue to enjoy a variable, flexible sexual life into your 80s. You can take pride in beating the odds and enjoy the pleasures of affectionate, sensual, playful, and erotic touch and intercourse.

What makes sex functional after 70? The mantra is staying physically healthy; accepting your body rather than emphasizing the losses; seeing the woman as your intimate, erotic sexual friend; piggybacking your arousal on hers; realizing that giving pleasure facilitates increased pleasure for you; being open to erotic scenarios and techniques; not transitioning to intercourse until you are highly aroused; enjoying a range of sensual, playful, and erotic non-intercourse scenarios when sex doesn't flow to intercourse; and enjoying afterplay. That's what we mean by a variable, flexible couple sexual relationship.

Exercise 8.1: Enjoying Sex in Your 60s and Beyond

This exercise has two components—a "his" scenario and an "our" scenario. The focus is to play to your strengths as a sexual man in your 60s, 70s, or 80s—no comparisons with youthful sex and no "if only" thinking. You are a sexual man who deserves to anticipate and enjoy sex at this point in your life.

The first scenario is the selfish one. What is your favorite way of initiating a sexual experience, what are your favorite pleasuring and erotic techniques and scenarios, what are your favorite intercourse positions and movements, and what is your favorite way to end a sexual encounter? Don't be shy or self-conscious. Take the personal and sexual risks to make this a really special sexual experience. You can have erotic sex after 60. Women report that a major aphrodisiac is an involved, responsive partner. Rather than being apologetic about slower arousal or needing more direct penile stimulation, you can focus on the new pleasures and flexibility of this sexual scenario. Give yourself permission to be sexually enthusiastic and value sex after 60.

The second phase of this exercise is a special couple sexual scenario. The biggest advantage of couple sex after 60 is that it's more genuine, human, and interactive. The mantra of intimacy, pleasuring, and eroticism reaches fruition after 60 for both the man and the woman. Mutuality and multiple methods of stimulation are the keys to couple sexual satisfaction.

Begin this exercise outside the bedroom—take a walk or sit over a glass of wine and cooperatively construct an inviting way to begin sexually; the type and sequence of pleasurable and erotic stimulation; how to transition to intercourse (who decides and who guides intromission); what positions, types of stroking, and methods of stimulation would make intercourse most exciting; and your favorite way to end a sexual encounter (warm, playful, verbal, go back to stimulation).

The joy of sex after 60 is knowing that you have beaten the odds and embraced a new model of male and couple sexuality that values sharing pleasure and experiencing variable, flexible sex with your intimate, erotic friend.

Closing Thoughts

Valuing intimacy, pleasuring, and eroticism; the focus on desire, pleasure, satisfaction; the woman as your intimate, erotic friend; and valuing Good-Enough Sex comes to fruition in your 60s, 70s, and 80s. If you adopt this new model of male and couple sexuality you can continue to enjoy a variable, flexible, and genuinely human sexuality into your 80s. Truly, you are a sexual man from the moment your life begins, through each stage of your life, and throughout your aging years.

CHAPTER 9

Dealing With Sexual and Health Problems

The fact is that at some point in their lives, over 90% of men report a sexual concern or problem. Obviously, these problems can subvert sexual health. Contrary to the traditional cultural mandate that men are not supposed to have sexual questions, anxieties, or concerns, dealing with sexual problems is almost a universal experience for men. It is crucial to understand and accept this because a sexual problem need not be a shameful secret, create feelings of inadequacy, or seem hopeless.

We will briefly describe common sexual problems and how to address them. Appendixes A and B provide resources to help address and resolve problems (self-help books and Web sites, medical resources, and individual, couple, or sex therapy locators). You are responsible for addressing your sexual problems, and they can be successfully dealt with. Your partner can be a supportive, intimate ally but cannot do it for you. Knowledge is power. Having the understanding, motivation, and resources to deal with and resolve sexual problems will greatly enhance your sexual health and satisfaction.

Common Male Sexual Problems

The most common sexual dysfunctions (SDs) are premature ejaculation, erectile dysfunction, inhibited sexual desire, compulsive masturbation (often to porn Web sites), ejaculatory inhibition, and a sexual secret (variant arousal pattern, preferring masturbation over couple sex, history of sexual trauma, and sexual orientation conflicts). The major sexual health problems are sexually transmitted diseases, poor health habits subverting sexual function, medical illness and side effects of medications, infertility, and fears of aging. The most common relationship problems are dissatisfaction with the partner, affairs, unresolved couple conflicts, as well as not valuing the relationship, or not valuing couple sexuality.

Sexual Problems Are Multidimensional

Professionals debate whether sexual problems should be considered medical problems, psychological problems, or relationship problems. The reality is that sexual problems are multicausal and multidimensional. The biopsychosocial model of understanding, assessing, and treating sexual problems is optimal. In this way, you are cognizant of all the factors influencing male and couple sexuality and using all your resources to successfully address the problem. Unless you comprehensively address problems and devote time and energy to healthy sexuality, you are likely to regress to problematic sexual behavior. You cannot treat sex with benign neglect. A relapse prevention program is crucial; you owe it to yourself and your relationship to maintain sexual health.

Sexual Dysfunction and Dissatisfaction

Traditional myths maintain that women have sexual problems, but men don't. A real man is always ready for sexual performance with no questions, doubts, or concerns. What bravado. A number of studies indicate that sexual dysfunction (SD) is common. Almost every man at some point in his life will experience an SD. At any given point in time, about 35–40% of individuals (31% of men, 43% of women) have an SD (Table 9.1). We live in a culture that idealizes and exaggerates the idea that sex should be spontaneous, perfect, or great every time. Yet it is normal to have sexual difficulties. One study found that 97% of men (95% of women) had an important sexual concern at some point in his life, important enough to want to talk with their doctor. Yet only 23% of the men reported that they did in fact discuss their concerns with a professional clinician.

Men's partners also frequently experience sex dysfunction (Table 9.2). A good number of couples experience multiple, simultaneous sex dysfunctions. For example, she experiences pain with intercourse while he has erectile dysfunction; or he has premature ejaculation and she experiences low sexual desire. It is crucial that you appreciate any sexual difficulty she may experience, because your SD could be a response to her difficulties. Cooperate as a team to work together regardless of the SD. Bring the same acceptance and support to her that you want for yourself.

Table 9.1 Percentage of Men Who Report Chronic Sexual Problems (31%)

	Number	Percentage
Premature ejaculation	1 in 4	29
Performance anxiety	1 in 6	17
Lack of interest	1 in 6	16
Erectile dysfunction	1 in 10	10
Ejaculatory inhibition	1 in 11	8
Sex not pleasurable	1 in 11	8
Pain with coitus	1 in 33	3

Note. N = 1,740, ages 19–59. From *National Health and Social Life Survey*, 1994; Table 10.8A, p. 370.

Table 9.2 Percentage of Women Who Report Chronic Sexual Problems (43%)

	Number	Percentage
Low desire	1 in 3	33
Inhibited orgasm	1 in 4	24
Sex not pleasurable	1 in 5	21
Pain with intercourse	1 in 7	14
Performance anxiety	1 in 10	12
Lubrication trouble	1 in 10	10
Climax too soon	1 in 10	10

Note. N = 1,740, ages 19–59. From *National Health and Social Life Survey*, 1994; Table 10.8B, p. 371

Determining the Causes and Effects of SD

There are a number of possible causes and effects of SD—physical, psychological, and relational. If you have a persistent SD, you and your partner can decide what you want to do to address it and whether you would benefit from professional consultation.

Physical Factors

Table 9.3 helps you consider the possible physical causes of SD.

Medical Illness and Side Effects of Medications. Medical illness does not stop sexual function, but it usually does alter it. Whether diabetes, high blood pressure, heart disease, cancer, hormone imbalance, or multiple sclerosis, the first task is to be an active, knowledgeable patient. Obviously, cure is the ideal outcome, but many diseases are chronic and must be successfully managed. You can live your life with the disease: it need not control your life or your sexual relationship. You need to be a disciplined patient—follow the medical protocol, take prescribed medication (Segraves & Balon, 2003), and follow healthy behavioral habits.

Table 9.3 The Physical Types of SD

Consider possible medical and physical causes for your difficulty. Talk to your physician if you have concerns or want to rule out a medical factor.

1. Bio-neuro-hormonal system: Do you have congenital problems in your genetic, circulatory, neurologic, hormonal, or urologic system? These sources are very rare.

   Yes _____ No _____
   What illness: _____

2. Physical illness → A number of illnesses can cause SD. If you have, or suspect you have, one of the illnesses below, it is important to talk with your doctor. Illnesses that can cause sexual dysfunctions:
   Cancer/chemotherapy
   Cardiac disease
   Chronic pain
   Chronic renal failure
   Diabetes mellitus
   Epilepsy
   Hormonal problems
   Hypertension
   Hypogonadism
   Hypopituitarism
   Hypothyroidism
   Lipid abnormalities
   Multiple sclerosis
   Peyronies disease
   Polyneuropathy
   Prostatitis
   Respiratory illness
   Sexually transmitted disease
   Sleep apnea
   Systemic lupus
   Vascular disease

   Yes _____ No _____
   What illness: _____

3. Physical injury: Pelvic surgery, prostate surgery, injuries, or neurologic trauma can cause SD.

   Yes _____ No _____
   What injury: _____

4. Pharmacological side effects: A number of medications, over-the-counter drugs, and illegal drugs can cause SD. Have you begun taking (or withdrawn from) an agent such as an antihypertensive medication, mental health medication, or chemotherapy? Some agents include:
   a. Cardiovascular drugs: antihypertensives, diuretics, antiarrhythmics.
   b. Antidepressant medications (e.g., SSRI: fluoxetine/Prozac; MAOIs: phenelzine; heterocyclics: amitriptyline/Elavil; clomipramine/Anafranil).

(Continued)

Table 9.3 (*Continued*)

    c. Antipsychotics (e.g., thioridazine/Mellaril; trifluoperazine/Stelazine).

    d. Antianxiety (e.g., alprazolam/Xanax; clonazepam/Klonopin)

    e. Illicit drugs: marijuana (decreased desire); MDNA (ED, orgasmic delay)

        Yes _____   No _____

        What agent: _____

5. Health habits: Do you have problematic health patterns such as smoking, poor cardiovascular conditioning, overtraining (e.g., marathon), sleep deprivation, drinking, weight problems, or drug abuse?

        Yes _____   No _____

        What issue: _____

The most common medical cause of SD is side effects of medications. This is especially true of antidepressant and hypertensive medications, but a large number of prescription and over-the-counter medications can have negative sexual side effects. We have two suggestions for how to address this problem. First is to consult with your physician (or pharmacologist or trusted medical Web site) about all the medications you take and their possible sexual side effects. Side effects are quite variable for the individual so you need to be a personal scientist regarding your illness, medications, and medication side effects.

Second, is to consider a number of possible coping strategies. These include switching medications or taking the medication at a lower dose if medically possible; dosing at times where sexual side effects are minimized; using a pro-sex medication to compensate for the side effect; spending more time on pleasuring and asking your partner for more erotic stimulation; adding a second medication (an antidote); and on weekends when you are most likely to be sexual, taking a "drug holiday" from the problem medication. In consulting your internist or specialist about illness or medication issues, we suggest going to the consultation with your partner and emphasizing that you want to be a good patient as well as maintain a healthy sexual life.

Physical/Medical Problems.   Maintaining a healthy sexual body is crucial. Anything that interferes with your physical well-being will interfere with your sexual well-being. One issue for men is not seeing their doctor regularly, out of anxiety or machismo ("It's only a sprain"). Women see the doctor four times more often than men. If you think there is a possible physical cause of SD, it is important that you discuss the concern with your physician. Let's begin by looking at your relationship with your physician and your attitudes and beliefs about physical and sexual health.

Speaking with Your Physician. Talking about sexual problems and concerns is an uncomfortable topic in most settings, including speaking with your physician. Although almost all individuals and couples have sexual problems and concerns at some point, physicians and other health care professionals rarely recognize sexual problems or dysfunctions in their patients.

Rather than faulting your doctor, recognize that he or she lives in the same society with the same sexual discomfort. Most physicians assume that if sexual concerns are important to the patient, you will initiate the discussion, whereas you may assume that since the doctor has the ability to treat sexual problems, it is up to him or her to ask the questions. Unfortunately, these attitudes serve to continue the silent avoidance of sexual problems.

Take the Lead. We suggest that you take the lead because your doctor probably will not (Table 9.4). Don't be distressed if at first he or she seems uncomfortable—few physicians have received training in sexual medicine. Most doctors want to be helpful and are willing to sort out medical aspects with you, especially about an acute illness, medications, and sexual side effects. What they don't want to do is assume the role of sex counselor.

Your doctor does not have to be comfortable talking about sexual concerns to be a really good doctor, but it helps. By the way, most physicians are uncomfortable talking with couples; the medical model focuses on individual appointments, but your leadership will serve you well. Give your doctor the chance to help.

The guideline is "fix and foster." The physician can treat (fix) a medical illness, increase or decrease medication, help you manage your illness, and suggest changes in health behaviors. However, it is up to you and your partner to change psychological, relational, and psychosexual skill components to "foster" sexual function and satisfaction.

Table 9.4 Suggestions for Starting the Discussion with Your Physician

"I want to talk to you about a sexual concern, but I am uncomfortable."

"I would like to ask you about a sexual problem that worries me. Do you think you can help?"

"Can you refer me to a sexual medicine specialist or to a sex therapist?"

"As I've come to learn more about my illness, I realize that there are a number of potential sexual problems. Can you refer me to a sexual specialist?"

"I'm afraid I have a sexually transmitted disease [or a prostate infection or a lowered sexual desire because of the medication I'm taking]. Should I be tested, have a physical exam, or can you just treat it?"

Table 9.5 Guidelines for Seeking a Medical Evaluation for SD

It is good health practice to have a regular physician (family practice, internist) with whom you are comfortable, and to have a general physical examination regularly. How regularly?

If you are in good health and

1. you are younger than 30 years old, have an exam at least every 5 years.
2. 30–45 years old, have an exam at least every 4 years.
3. 45–60 years old, have an exam every 2 years.
4. 60 or older, have an exam every year.

Consult your MD if

1. you are taking medication on a regular basis.
2. you have a family history of:
    a. significant medical illness (such as diabetes, cancer).
    b. severe developmental illness (such as cystic fibrosis, multiple sclerosis, thyroid, or other endocrine problems).
    c. genetic problems (heart disease, obesity, neurological).

Thank your doctor for being willing to talk with you about sexual concerns or for giving you a referral to a specialist. Then, as you leave the office, congratulate yourself for taking the lead and being your own sexual health advocate.

When to Seek a Medical Evaluation. Table 9.5 presents guidelines for wisely seeking a medical evaluation for a sexual concern. Your doctor can not only determine whether there is a physical cause (Table 9.5) but also offer a medical or pharmacological treatment. For example, to treat a prostate infection, your doctor can prescribe medication. Your physician could also be your professional case manager, referring you to other trustworthy physicians who specialize in sexual medicine, as well as psychologists, marital therapists, or sex therapists.

A physical examination is very important for your physical and sexual health because your doctor can monitor you for common illnesses that run in families such as high blood pressure, diabetes, heart disease, and cancer. The number one type of men's cancer is prostate cancer (41% of all cancers among men); lung cancer is number 2 (13%) and colon cancer is number 3 (9%; Jemal et al., 2006). Early detection is the most important factor in cancer treatment.

What's Involved in a Medical Evaluation. Your general physician, who knows you and your medical history best, is the first choice to discuss your sexual concerns. You may be referred to a urologist, endocrinologist, or sexual medicine specialist for further evaluation. Medical evaluation for SD typically consists of three steps.

History. Your doctor will discuss your personal medical history, a brief sexual history, basic information about your sexual function, other symptoms or aspects of your medical situation, your thoughts regarding the cause of the SD, and how distressed you are. Your doctor is trying to gain a comprehensive understanding of your situation as well as rule out medical possibilities that could cause your SD.

Physical Examination. Your doctor will examine you, focusing on your genital area, and will check your prostate gland for signs of infection. You should be doing regular testicular self-exams.

Testing. Simple blood and urine tests may be done to make sure that there is no systemic problem (such as thyroid or testosterone deficits). These diagnostic tests vary according to your age and family history.

Psychological Causes and Effects

Table 9.6 considers psychological and relationship causes and effects of SD.

If you suspect psychological or relationship features may either cause or result from an SD, talk with your partner. If you cannot work together to ameliorate the SD, be wise and consult with a psychologist, marital therapist, or sex therapist (see Appendix A).

Table 9.6 The Psychological-Relationship Types of SD

1. Psychological system: Do you have a chronic, psychological character pattern or significant mental health problem such as bipolar, obsessive/compulsive, dysthymia, or generalized anxiety disorder?

    Yes _____ No _____

    What problem: _____

2. Individual psychological issues: Do you have current psychological stresses such as depression, anxiety due to work stresses, parenting, losses?

    Yes _____ No _____

    What issues: _____

3. Relationship issues: Are you and your partner experiencing relationship distresses such as unresolved emotional conflicts, alienation, loneliness?

    Yes _____ No _____

    What issues: _____

4. Psychosexual skills deficit: Do you doubt your lovemaking skills? Do you lack knowledge about your body, your partner's body, or hold unreasonable expectations about sexual performance? Do you lack essential sensual skills for arousal or interpersonal skills such as warmly talking of sex and cooperating to make sex comfortable?

    Yes _____ No _____

    What issues: _____

Effective Treatments for Male SD

Premature (Rapid) Ejaculation

The most common male sexual problem—premature (rapid) ejaculation (PE)—affects approximately 3 out of 10 adult men. Metz and McCarthy (2003) outline the possible causes and effects for PE and a range of medical, psychological, psychosexual skill, and relational approaches to resolving PE.

PE Treatment. For most men, PE management involves becoming skilled at key concepts including learning ejaculatory control as an intimate team, particularly identifying the point of ejaculatory inevitability; learning to relax your body, especially your pelvic muscles; learning self-entrance-ment arousal rather than being totally dependent on partner-interaction arousal; expanding your arousal continuum; reintroducing intercourse in the woman-on-top position using minimal intercourse movement at first so that your penis acclimates to being inside her vagina; and slowing down the pleasuring and intercourse process and savoring pleasurable sensations. If desired, use a low dose of an antidepressant medication with your doctor's direction to slow down your ejaculatory response, but be cautious. There is no magic pill and remember the axiom "If you only take a pill, you gain no skill." As you gain comfort and confidence with the psycho-sexual skills involved in ejaculatory control, you can gradually fade out the medication. Maintain positive, realistic expectations—the lovemak-ing experience typically lasts 15–45 minutes, with 2–12 minutes involving intercourse itself.

When PE is caused by a medical problem, your physician will work with you to treat the physical cause. For example, acquired PE caused by a pros-tate infection can be treated with antibiotics, and normal ejaculatory control can return. And when PE is lifelong and severe, some medications (e.g., off-label SSRI) can slow down arousal for many men. For most men, how-ever, the issue is learning the psychosexual skills for arousal regulation.

Other treatments for PE: Some men try a penile desensitizing cream or spray, a penile rubber ring device, Velcro testicular band, or a condom containing an analgesic (e.g., lidocane) to prevent rapid ejaculation (by diminishing the pleasurable sensations in the penis), although this approach usually does not work. Besides, it is not good strategy to undermine your pleasure and arousal to gain control. Strategies such as detailed psycho-sexual skills, oral medications, and couple cooperation are very helpful.

Erectile Dysfunction

Since the introduction of Viagra in 1998, public and professional dis-course about erectile dysfunction (ED) has totally changed. People used to believe that 90% of ED was psychological. The new belief (myth) is that 95% is physical and that Viagra, Levitra, or Cialis is the answer. Our culture swings from one simplistic extreme to the other. In fact, ED is the prime example of the need for and validity of a biopsychosocial approach to assessing and treating sexual dysfunction (Metz & McCarthy, 2004).

ED Treatment. The key to understanding ED is in male sexual socialization—young men learn sexual response as very easy, totally predictable, and the most important factor is that it is autonomous—he can experience desire, arousal, and orgasm and need nothing from his partner. In part, this is due to vascular and neurological systems functioning most efficiently in his teens and 20s, and partly because masculinity and sexual performance are so highly valued. However, the totally predictable, autonomous sexual performance model is not the right model for middle-aged men and those in serious relationships.

The healthiest approach is the Good-Enough Sex model of male and couple sexuality (Metz & McCarthy, 2007). It is crucial to evaluate general medical conditions, especially vascular, neurological, and hormonal function. It is just as crucial to evaluate psychological and relationship factors that subvert sexual function as well as those that promote healthy sexuality—especially valuing sex as an intimate, interactive process and seeing the woman as your erotic friend, not someone to perform for or be afraid of. Pro-erection medication can be a valuable treatment resource, but not a stand–alone intervention. The medication has to be integrated into your couple style of intimacy, pleasuring, and eroticism.

Psychosexual skills and couple interventions (e.g., Metz & McCarthy, 2004) include understanding that relaxation and sensuality are the foundation for sexual response and easy erections; practicing the wax and wane of erection exercise so you don't panic if your erection goes on break; verbally and nonverbally making requests of your partner for erotic stimulation; learning to piggyback your arousal on hers; not transitioning to intercourse until arousal is high and letting her guide intromission; engaging in multiple stimulation during intercourse; if eroticism doesn't flow to intercourse comfortably, transitioning to either an erotic, non-intercourse scenario or a warm, sensual scenario. The most important concept is to accept the 85% Good-Enough Sex approach rather than the demand for 100% perfect intercourse performance. Your penis and couple sex are variable, flexible, and human—you are not a performance machine.

When ED is caused by a medical problem, it is crucial that you and your physician work together to determine the specific cause. Medical treatment will vary depending on this determination. For example, ED caused by neurologic impairment from prostate surgery will be treated differently from than

ED caused by a loss of interest in sex resulting from an abnormal level of the hormone testosterone. Medications like Viagra may be effective treatments for neurologic impairment, whereas abnormally low testosterone is treated with testosterone injections or gel or transdermal patches applied at the skin.

Determining the source of testosterone deficiency is essential, because abnormally low testosterone may result from different sources, ranging from physical or emotional exhaustion, side effects of medication, chemical abuse, testicular cancer, a pituitary tumor, or even misuse of hair lotions for baldness. To treat low testosterone without abnormal lab findings and without identifying the source to guide therapy may be short-sighted. In the medical literature, the incidence of ED caused by endocrine disorders varies between 1 and 35%. Testosterone replacement therapy does not benefit men with normal serum levels. In fact, in men with ED with normal serum levels, testosterone can compound the problem by increasing sexual desire without increasing performance. Testosterone therapy is indicated in men whose testosterone values are below normal levels. This treatment is focused on increasing desire and, indirectly, increasing erectile capacity.

Pro-Erection Oral Medications

Medications such as Viagra, Levitra, and Cialis help initiate and maintain erection by relaxing the corpus cavernosum smooth muscle in your penis. Viagra (sildenafil) is the oldest of these drugs. Levitra (vardenafil) similarly enhances penile blood flow and, more recently, Cialis (tadalifil) has been marketed as the "weekender" for its long-lasting results. All three medications enhance blood flow to the penis by blocking the PDE-5 enzyme. These medications can be used for ED whether its cause is physical, psychological, or medication related. Other medications are apomorphine (a dopaminergic agonist), yohimbine (an alpha-2 receptor blocker), and phentolamine mesylate (an adrenergic blocker). Their effectiveness is usually less than the PDE-5 enzyme inhibitors like Viagra.

Strengths and Weaknesses of Viagra, Levitra, and Cialis. It appears that these medications are approximately equal in efficacy. About 60–85% of the time, when you take the drug and there is adequate penile stimulation, you will have an erection sufficient for intercourse.

There are some differences in the medications. For example, Viagra and Levitra work in about 30 to 60 minutes, whereas Cialis works in as little as 15 to 30 minutes. Cialis and Levitra can be taken with food, but Viagra's effect is slowed by a high-fat meal. The erection-enhancing effect may last for approximately 4 hours with Viagra and Levitra and 24 to 36 hours with Cialis. The blue vision or light sensitivity some men experience with Viagra and Levitra does not occur with Cialis. Each medication sometimes (5–15% of men) has side effects such as headache, facial red-ness, upset stomach, and sinus congestion. Cialis also blocks an enzyme that is found in smooth muscles of internal organs, which may explain why Cialis's most troublesome side effect is back pain in 5–6% of men. None of the three medications can be taken safely with nitrates (e.g., Imdur or nitroglycerine).

The choice of medication will depend upon your and your doctor's pref-erences as well as your partner's input—her feelings and preferences are vital. Remember that a medication's effect can vary person to person. With your doctor's supervision, try the one of your choice and adjust the dose or try another to seek the effect you want. Remember, it is crucial to integrate the medication into your couple sexual relationship.

Intracavernous Drugs

There are several intracavernous drug therapies for erectile dysfunction (e.g., Caverjet). By means of an injection in the base of the penis, these vasoactive drugs act on the penis to produce an erection. Among these agents are E1-prostaglandin (PGE1, alprostadil), papaverine, and phentolamine.

These agents are also combined. Most used is Trimix (papaverine + phentolamine mesylate + PGE1). The different drugs are injected alone or in combination in the penile corpus cavernosum. According to dif-ferent authors and to the diverse drugs used, the incidence of complica-tion varies between 1 and 10%. There is a high dropout rate from these treatments presumably because of their inconvenient injection delivery system.

A medical alternative to needle injection is the Medicated Urethral System for Erection (MUSE), which inserts a small alprostadil supposi-tory into the penile urethra. Reports of efficacy vary between 7 and 65%. The most common adverse effects are penile pain (36%), urethral burning (13%), dizziness (4%), orthostatic hypotension (3%), and syncope (0.4%). Priapism is very rare.

Combination ED Medical Treatments

Some physicians experiment with combination treatments. In a severe and complicated case, injection medications (e.g., alprostadil) are com-bined with a number of oral agents (e.g., Viagra) and devices (e.g., vacuum device) to overcome physical (e.g., vascular, neurologic) or psychologi-cal (performance anxiety, depression) limitations. Couple sex therapy is invaluable to integrate these and other medical treatments into your relationship.

Devices for ED.   In addition to pharmacologic treatments, devices are sometimes used, although scientific validation of effectiveness is limited.

- Penile brace: Nonsurgical prostheses include splints such as Rejoyn, a soft rubber brace that holds the flaccid penis rigid and is available in drugstores. The brace exposes the tip of the penis to allow for pleasure. Some women find the device uncomfortable during intercourse. These are available without prescription.
- Vacuum constriction devices: Vacuum constriction devices draw blood into the penis, causing an erection, and trap the blood there in order to maintain the erection. These devices include a plastic tube that fits over the penis in order to create an airtight cover. A vacuum is created around the penis by motor or manual pumping. When erection occurs, the tube is removed and a fitted rubber band is placed on the penis at the base to retain the erection for approximately 30 minutes. These devices require a prescription. Many men stop using these devices due to lack of comfort on the part of either the man or the woman.
- Surgical penile prostheses: Rigid or flexible rods may be surgically implanted into the penis to make it mechanically erect. There are inflatable models that allow for artificial engorging and deflating of the penis by means of a hydraulic system composed of tubes implanted in the penis and a fluid reservoir (bulb) implanted in one of the testicular sacs (the testis is removed). The tubes are then inflated by squeezing the bulb and deflated by a valve in the bulb. These surgeries permit the penis to be reliably inserted into the vagina. Because implants are irreversible, an implant is the last option for treating ED.
- Penile vascular surgery: When there is irreversible damage to the penile arteries and veins, penile vascular reconstruction surgery may be attempted. The results of such surgery are usually poor, but its effectiveness may improve with increased medical knowledge and surgical experience.

Inhibited Sexual Desire

Inhibited sexual desire (ISD) is much more common for men than commonly believed. The most striking fact is that when couple sex stops, in over 90% of the cases it's the man's decision—made nonverbally and unilaterally. Not only does intercourse stop, but so does sensual, playful, and erotic touch. If sex doesn't involve intercourse, many men want to avoid all intimacy. When it's intercourse or nothing, nothing ultimately wins.

The major cause of male ISD is loss of comfort and confidence with erections. Sex has become a source of frustration and embarrassment, not pleasure. The essence of sexual desire is positive anticipation and the sense that you deserve to enjoy sex at this point in your life and in this relationship. This is replaced by the cycle of anticipatory anxiety, tense and performance-oriented intercourse, and increasing frequency of failures and eventually avoidance. The pass–fail perfect intercourse model subverts male sexual desire. You are only one failure from feeling like a sexual loser.

ISD Treatment. So how can the man (and the couple) revitalize sexual desire? The keys are to rebuild positive anticipation of sharing pleasure and eroticism; to value your partner as your intimate, erotic friend; to adopt the Good-Enough Sex model of pleasure-oriented couple sex; to experiment with blending self-entrancement arousal, partner-interaction arousal, and role-enactment arousal; to change health behaviors so you have more sexual energy; to view intercourse as a natural continuation of erotic flow and a special erotic technique, not a pass–fail test; to emphasize a variable, flexible approach to couple sexuality; to utilize testosterone to enhance sexual desire; and to maintain a regular rhythm of sensual, playful, and erotic connection and intercourse.

Ejaculatory Inhibition (EI)

Ejaculatory inhibition (EI) is the unspoken male sexual dysfunction, often misunderstood as ED. Among men over age 50, EI affects as many as 1 in 8 men. Again, the best assessment/treatment model is a couple psychobiosocial approach. There are many possible causes and dimensions of EI from depression, to excessive masturbation, to side effects of medications to fatigue. The most common cause is not valuing couple sex, instead falling into a mechanical intercourse routine that is no longer exciting and arousing. Men typically transition to intercourse at the start of an erection, with a subjective arousal of 4 or 5, and approach intercourse as simply a matter of thrusting. When orgasm isn't attained, the result is frustration and loss of erection.

EI Treatment. Key treatment strategies include using multiple methods of stimulation during both pleasuring and intercourse; piggybacking your arousal on your partner's; transitioning to intercourse when you have higher subjective arousal (7 or 8); using erotic fantasies to heighten subjective arousal; being aware of and using orgasm triggers (i.e., the cues/resources you use during masturbation to allow you to let go and "come"); making requests of your partner for erotic stimulation as well as taking personal and sexual risks (including self-stimulation mixed with partner stimulation to enhance arousal); and allowing yourself to go with the erotic flow rather than try to force orgasm.

Men's Sexual Difficulties

Sexual Secrets

There is a saying from 12-step programs, "You're only as sick as your secrets." Men guard their sexual secrets from everyone—their partners, physicians, and best friends. Yet, these secrets control their sexuality (Table 9.7). The combination of eroticism, secrecy, and shame powerfully reinforces the secret sexuality.

Addressing male sexual secrets usually requires more than a self-help approach; it requires individual or couple therapy.

Variant Arousal. It is estimated that as many as 4% of men have a variant arousal pattern, called a *paraphilia*. Paraphilia or variant arousal involves a restricted sex arousal pattern, distinguished by the focus that triggers arousal. Examples include fetishism (e.g., foot, shoe, cross-dressing), sado-masochism (pain), and urophilia (urination or "golden shower").

A paraphilia is a recurring arousal dependency (not simply a prefer-ence) on an impersonal or anti-intimate object to facilitate sexual arousal. In mild cases, fantasy alone may be sufficient to become aroused and ejac-ulate; in severe cases, the paraphilic behavior is required to ensure sexual arousal.

Sexual Arousal Problems Vary in Severity. Sexual arousal disorders are not dichotomous (either–or). Paraphilias vary in severity according to (a) the level of dependency for sexual arousal; that is, whether it is "almost never" needed for arousal versus "always" needed; and (b) the range of enactment of the paraphilic content as fantasy versus behavior (see Figure 9.1).

A variant arousal pattern that is not necessary for arousal/orgasm and never enacted is harmless unless it is upsetting (e.g., distraction from intimacy). As the level of severity increases, or if the arousal pattern is

Table 9.7 The Most Common Secrets

Variant or deviant arousal pattern

Sexual compulsivity: preference for masturbatory sex rather than couple sex, especially involving excessive use of the Internet and pornography

Sexual and emotional affairs

A history of sexual trauma that has not been well processed or accepted

Conflicts regarding sexual orientation

anti-intimate or illegal, it is important for a man to seek professional help to prevent harm to others as well as improve his sexual quality of life.

Sexual Variant Problems Are Intimacy Challenges. A paraphilia that is severe (that is, requires behavior) is inevitably an intimacy disorder—it causes the man to devalue interactive couple sex and usually interferes with sexual intimacy (e.g., distresses his partner). Examples include foot fetishes, cross-dressing, and serious (non-playful) bondage. The best way to approach these issues is for the man to take responsibility for his sexuality and set realistic change goals. The second step is to involve his partner as an intimate ally. A couple sex therapist can be an excellent resource (Appendix A).

Illegal Sexual Behavior. Thoughts and fantasies are not illegal even if the content is about a harmful or illegal behavior. However, for some men, unregulated thought or fantasy of illegal sex behavior can lead to harmful or illegal behavior. If you are concerned about your thoughts or feelings, there is help available (Appendix A). As many as 1% of men have a deviant arousal pattern—a pattern that is acted out and illegal, a sex offense. The most frequent illegal sexual behaviors—sex offending—which harms

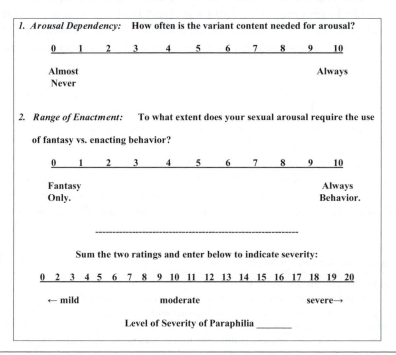

Figure 9.1 Severity of Variant Arousal Patterns (Paraphilia).

others are exhibitionism, voyeurism (spying or "peeping"), frotteurism (rubbing against an unsuspecting other), and the most harmful, pedophilia (sex abuse of children) (Finkelhor, 1993). Such illegal sexual behaviors must be confronted and require professional intervention. Sadly, most men do not heed this advice, deny the deviant behavior, and only address it after someone threatens to report him to the police or he is arrested.

Perhaps three fourths of men with a paraphilic arousal pattern are not sex offenders. In many cases, the paraphilic content is not illegal (e.g., a foot fetish, cross-dressing) or is limited to fantasy (cognition) only. Other men with a deviant arousal pattern do not act on it (for example, a man may fantasize about exhibiting himself but does not). On the other hand, not all sex offenders have a paraphilia (e.g., antisocial [sociopathic] behavior or the sexual impulsivity of men suffering bipolar disorder). However, the majority of men who sexually offend are enacting a harmful paraphilia.

What to Do If You Have Sexually Harmed Someone or Have Thoughts About Doing So. If you have had thoughts or sexual fantasies about abusing children or another criminal sexual behavior, or have been tempted to act on those feelings, you can prevent abuse by seeking professional help. If you have enacted a paraphilia that is illegal (e.g., pedophilia, voyeurism, frotteurism, exhibitionism), you must seek professional help. Realize that you may, or have, seriously hurt others by the abuse and fear you create. Do not let shame about your behavior or denial of its seriousness prevent you from seeking therapy. Confronting the problem is motivated by respect for yourself and others. You can prevent or stop offending, and therapy and/or medication is better treatment than legal trouble. There is help. Appendix A can guide you to find expert professional help.

Realize that to seek help may not be a simple thing for you to do because of your fears, shame, or denial of its seriousness. When you seek help there may be consequences. If you are offending or have offended against children or vulnerable adults, realize that under some situations helping professionals in every U.S. state are required to report abuse of children to legal authorities. We recommend that you talk with the helping professional about their abuse reporting obligations before providing details about your history. If you are offending against adults, the helping professional with whom you will work is not usually required to report you to authorities. You can greatly benefit from specialized professional help. Take responsibility for your problem and seek help. The well-being of others and your sexual health depend on it.

Sexual Compulsivity

Sexual compulsivity ("addiction") often involves a secretive variant arousal pattern while devaluing couple sex and presents a major dilemma.

Sex drive, when not integrated well, leads to various forms of compulsive sexual behavior. Perhaps the most common manifestation is pornography misuse, or what is popularly called *porn addiction*. Other behaviors include excessive use of strip bars, lap dances, prostitution, swinging, massage parlors, and pick-up clubs. There is both an individual and a relationship dimension to compulsive sexual behavior. Usually the man denies that a problem exists and wants to keep his partner in the dark. This short-term strategy, taking the easy way out, usually backfires and the woman feels lied to and betrayed in addition to dealing with the hard issue of the secret arousal pattern.

Sexual Compulsivity as an Individual Problem. Sexually healthy men learn the three emotional and sexual regulatory skills—(a) respecting and regulating lust, the biological imperative; (b) balancing sexual objectification and personalization; and (c) differentiating and integrating emotions and sexual feelings; that is, managing emotional sexualization. When these skills are not integrated, you can easily develop sexually obsessive fantasies or compulsivity, involving high frequency of masturbation. How can you recognize whether you have a sexually compulsive behavior problem (Table 9.8)?

Men who turn to sex as a panacea for their emotions, stress, or pain are trapped in a self-defeating sexually compulsive pattern (Leedes, 2001). The behavior expresses unspoken, usually unrealized, and unacknowledged feelings. These men feel lonely, living in a world that feels unyielding; seek to find acceptance in the world they experience as harsh; or seek to find control and freedom in a world that can be overpowering (Cooper & Marcus, 2003). Invariably, there is pain and suffering beneath the sexual acting out. Compulsive sex behavior is extreme emotional sexualization. A superficial macho rationale is used to justify compulsive sex (for example, "This is part of being a real man"; or, "I'm expected to go to strip bars to entertain clients").

Sexually compulsive men have significant difficulty forming close attachments and valuing relationship intimacy. As many as 95% of sexually compulsive men fear genuine intimacy, fear being "seen" or known; do not trust that genuine love can exist; and fear losing emotional control. The sexual compulsivity hides sadness, anger, and fear of being alone and crushes loving feelings.

Sexual Compulsivity Is a Relationship Problem. Compulsive sexual behavior is detrimental for men, but it also subverts intimate relationships by creating a relationship conflict. Pornography misuse and other sexually compulsive behaviors depersonalize women's bodies and treat women as

Table 9.8 Recognizing Compulsive Sexual Behavior

Compulsive sexual behavior involves detrimental and excessive preoccupation with sexual content such as:

- excessive sexual fantasies (e.g., visual docking on a woman's breasts, butt, or other physical characteristics [other than during lovemaking] for more that 5 seconds or replaying a sexual fantasy to the point of distraction from work tasks or alienation from your sexual partner;
- extreme frequency of masturbation (e.g., 3 times per day) without the demonstrated ability (e.g., no masturbation for 1 month) to cease;
- inability to limit Internet pornography (e.g., to less than 1 hour per week);
- seeking the services of a prostitute;
- frequenting strip bars more than 3 times a year, especially going alone;
- significant financial expenditures beyond your financial means;
- excessive or rigid sexual demands (rather than requests) with your partner;
- extra-relationship affairs;
- having more sexual interest in, and/or emotional vulnerability to, women other than your partner.

sex objects. Women's eroticism can objectify men's bodies but is secondary to romanticizing a man as handsome and attractive, successful, sensitive, and emotionally strong. Without healthy understanding of men's sexual nature, and without a man regulating his sex drive and integrating it with his relationship, intense conflicts over meaning can develop between a man and a woman. It is easy for women to interpret (misinterpret) a man's interest in pornography as infidelity, a betrayal of the relationship.

We believe that the ultimate issue in a relationship is for a couple to integrate eroticism into their relationship in a pro-intimate way, in whatever mutually satisfying form that may take. Otherwise, erotica can serve an anti-intimate role and subvert their emotional relationship. When emotional and sexual intimacy develops, we weave the other person into our life.

The Facts About Compulsive Sexual Behavior. Compulsive sexual behavior is almost exclusively a male problem; the ratio of male to female occurrence is more than 4 to 1. It is estimated that 6–8% of men are addicted to sex (Cooper & Marcus, 2003). More than two thirds of people with sexual acting-out problems use the Internet as a venue. Twenty percent of "netizens" engage in some sort of online sexual activity. Over 15% of Internet pornography viewers have compulsive problems. The Internet has exceptional power to elicit sexual compulsivity because of its easy accessibility, unlimited variety of content, anonymity, privacy, and its invitational nature, with the false promise of no real-life consequences (Cooper, 2002).

What to Do If You Think You Have a Sexual Compulsivity Problem   Because of the potential for sexual compulsivity to (a) become more expansive, (b) prevent you from developing an authentic relationship, and (c) cause serious harm to your relationship, it is important to find a competent professional to help you assess whether you would benefit from treatment for sexual compulsivity. It is important that you find a psychologist or marital therapist who has training in sexual issues and uses a sex-positive and pro-intimacy approach (consult Appendix A).

Sexual and Emotional Affairs

The issue of extra-relationship affairs is one of the most complex and value-laden in the sexual field. An affair can be anything from paid sex to a one-night stand, an ongoing sexual affair, or a deeply emotional, long-standing relationship (Table 9.9). Typically, a man has an affair for sexual release, because of opportunity, or to create a crisis to address individual, relational, or sexual problems. A woman may become involved in an affair to mollify sexual self-doubts (feeling sexually unattractive or inadequate), because of a relationship crisis, or as a catalyst for divorce. Subsequent marriage with the person with whom you had an affair (a common male pattern) has a significantly greater likelihood (over 80%) of ending in divorce.

A high-opportunity/low-involvement encounter (this is the most common type of male affair) is the one-night stand, prostitute, or other sexual experience that requires low emotional investment. Sex is the straightforward goal. The second type of affair is an ongoing, compartmentalized affair; examples include meeting once a month at a motel for sex, spending time with your sexual friend when traveling for business, meeting at a conference twice a year to have sex, going to Las Vegas each quarter and meeting for dinner and sex. The third type of affair poses the greatest threat to your relationship: a comparison affair. Whether for 2 weeks or 2 years, this relationship meets more of the person's emotional and sexual needs than his primary relationship. The comparison affair is the most common type of female affair. Men have a harder time dealing with a partner's affair because it is a reversal of the traditional double standard and involves both emotional and sexual betrayal. Men often say their affairs are just about sex or don't mean anything—they just couldn't say no to the opportunity.

Table 9.9 The Three Kinds of Extra-Relationship Affairs

High-opportunity/low-involvement affair: Sexually driven encounter.
Compartmentalized affair: What happens there stays there.
Comparison affair: Is there a better partner out there for me?

Approximately 20–25% of men engage in some type of affair and approximately 10–15% of women do (Allen et al., 2005). Contrary to popular mythology, the most common time for an affair is early in the relationship, not after many years. Rather than there being one cause and one outcome, the truth is that affairs are multicausal, multidimensional, play out in many different ways, and have very different outcomes.

The Affair. A discovered affair throws both people and the relationship into a crisis. As usual, we suggest primary prevention. Very few couples talk about vulnerabilities to affairs—there is a vague assumption that since they love each other, an affair won't happen. Many people think that if you have a good relationship, this would protect you from an affair or if you have good sex, you won't have a reason for an affair. Hopes and intentions are not enough—there is a poignant saying "The road to Hell is paved with good intentions."

Affairs are usually quite disruptive for the primary relationship. It needs to be dealt with rather than denied or handled in an overly dramatic manner. The first issue is to understand the role of the affair from the perspective of both the involved partner and the injured partner and how the affair affects the relationship, especially in the long term.

Although some affairs function as a catalyst for divorce, an affair is not an automatic ticket to divorce. Many affairs serve as a crisis to facilitate a couple in addressing major marital problems. An affair can also be a flag for psychological problems such as alcohol or drug abuse, obsessive–compulsive disorder, or the displacing of other emotions (e.g., anxiety) to sexual acting-out.

The most common outcome for a male high-opportunity/low-involvement affair is that the partner eventually accepts it (in truth, you cannot change the past); the man says it didn't mean anything and commits to not repeating it. For female affairs, especially comparison affairs, the outcome is more variable.

How Healthy Couples Prevent or Handle an Affair. We suggest that you and your partner adopt a clear understanding and agreement about affairs involving three steps:

1. Clarify your awareness of what type of mood, person, and situation would cause you to be vulnerable to an affair and then share this information with your partner.
2. Have an agreement that if you (or she) are in a high-risk situation, you will talk to your partner about the implications for you, her, and your relationship of acting on this opportunity. Most men say

they just fell into an affair. This technique requires you to process what is happening rather than act secretly and impulsively.

3. Follow the 24-hour rule if an affair occurs. Discuss the sexual incident with your partner within 24 hours. Affairs grow in secrecy. The cover-up is often more damaging than the affair (recall the Clinton–Lewinsky affair).

If an affair has occurred, it needs to be dealt with, not denied or avoided. Rather than obsessing about details, the injured partner "beating up" on the involved partner, or engaging in an emotional out-of-control attack and counterattack cycle (similar to the format of many talk shows), we suggest a step-by-step approach to understanding the meaning of the affair, appreciating and accepting each others' feelings, and learning from it. Appendices A and B suggest resources for the couple to recover and grow from an affair.

The Man's Affair.   Men want their wives or partners to accept that an affair (the most common male affair is the high-opportunity/low-involvement followed by a sexually focused, ongoing, compartmentalized affair) was a mistake, that it was just about sex, not emotion, and not really a threat to his primary relationship. In fact, a significant majority of marriages and relationships do survive a male affair, although the woman feels hurt, angry, and betrayed.

The most damage is caused by the cover-up (e.g., denying it when confronted), which increases feelings of emotional betrayal, mistrust, and justifies an affair by placing blame on your partner. Many men do not even consider what they did as an affair—especially if it involved paid sex or the Internet (cybersex) rather than an in-person affair. Yet, the partner does. In truth, the sexual incident is a major distraction from the couple intimate bond as well as a threat to the trust bond.

The Woman's Affair.   Recovery and forgiveness from a man's affair, especially a non-emotional affair, is the usual outcome. It is more difficult to recover from a woman's affair. There are two major reasons for this:

1. A female affair is a reversal of the traditional double standard.
2. The most common type of female affair is the comparison affair, where more of the emotional and sexual needs are met in the affair than the marriage.

In other words, this was a "lover affair" and the man feels put down, compared, and betrayed. It does not help that the advice from male friends and relatives is the supermacho approach—beat her up and go after him.

Often, men focus on false pride rather than understanding the causes and dimensions of the affair and processing them so that he can make a wise decision regarding how to address the reality of the affair both personally and as a couple.

Couples can and do recover from a female affair, but it requires psychological time and energy. Often, the man stays stuck in the sense of betrayal and his anger subverts the understanding and healing process. Usually, couple therapy is the wisest resource. The therapy structure of processing emotions, understanding the meaning of the affair, rebuilding trust and intimacy, revitalizing marital sex, and having a clear agreement to not have future affairs is the wisest approach. Of course, for some situations the affair is a way to leave the marriage or the affair destroys the marital bond. We encourage men not to give into their angry impulses but to make wise decisions regarding how to deal with a partner's affair.

Sexual Trauma

Approximately 1 in 7 men report a history of sexual abuse either in childhood or adolescence (Finkelhor, 1993). There is a stigma attached to this abuse because this is not supposed to happen to males, and the child may worry about what it means because the vast majority of sex perpetrators are male (adult or older adolescent). In general, males are more secretive about and ashamed of sexual abuse. The public generally thinks that abuse happens to girls, not boys. Yet, the reality is that boys are sexually abused, usually by men or older adolescent males they know, such as camp counselors, teachers, youth ministers, relatives, or friends of the family. The great majority of abuse involves hands-on incidents (manual, oral, or rubbing stimulation or anal intercourse). This can involve the boy in either the active or passive role. Men often deny or minimize the experiences, feeling stigmatized because it was a same-sex experience or because they were aroused and orgasmic (so how could that be abuse?). The essence of abuse is that the adult male's or female's sexual needs are met at the expense of the boy's or adolescent's emotional needs.

While the focus of sex abuse is the sexual behavior, the potential lasting effect is a psychological one: the betrayal of trust. Boys (and girls) expect that significant adults—father, mother, older relative, teacher, clergyman—will protect them, not violate them. The confusion and conflict between what might be experienced as physical pleasure with bewilderment, profound anxiety, and shame is traumatic and can have profound and persistent detrimental effects.

Men deal with abuse/trauma less well than women. Men treat it as a shameful secret that is an attack on their masculinity or somehow their fault (blaming the victim) or use it as a macho badge of distinction: "My teacher wants me sexually." In order to regain psychological and sexual health, you need to be able to process the abuse. Talk with a psychologist for perspective. Be aware that "living well is the best revenge." You deserve to view yourself as a strong, resilient man and to have a sexually healthy life as an adult.

Sexual Orientation Conflict

Conflicts and secrets regarding sexual orientation are difficult issues, filled with misunderstandings and stigma. Orientation is not an either–or reality, with labels like heterosexual, homosexual, bisexual, transsexual, asexual. Orientation is not a noun but an adjective, a human quality. A number of studies (Kinsey, Pomeroy, & Martin, 1948 Laumann et al., 1994) suggest that only a small number of men and women have no thoughts, feelings, fantasies, or experiences with people of their same sex. Most individuals are complex in their sexual experiences, feelings, and fantasies, and there is a great deal of variation. Sexual orientation is to a large extent biologically grounded and not subject to change. Lifestyle preferences may change, but basic orientation does not. Consider, for example, if you are predominately heterosexual, what would it take to change you into a comfortable homosexual?

Society tends to label orientation according to either sexual behavior or lifestyle. Notice, however, that sexual orientation is not simply behavior (e.g., an adolescent masturbating with another) or a simple feature of your personality. Rather, sexual orientation involves the composite of your level of attraction to women or men, your self-identity, who you have sex with, the primary focus of your sexual fantasies, the gender of your emotional friends, as well as your social comfort preferences (Exercise 9.1). You can see, then, why only a few men (and women) are exclusively gay or straight and why most of us are complex in our sexual cognitions, feelings, and actions.

One in 3 men have had some type of same-sex experience (usually in childhood); often they are fearful that a sexual dysfunction or concern means they are really gay. The best data (Laumann et al., 1994) available show that over half of men have had thoughts, feelings, or fantasies about being sexual with another man, between 25 and 30% of men have had a same-sex experience to orgasm (most often in childhood, adolescence, or young adulthood), perhaps 10% of men in one year have had more sexual experiences with men than women, and 3–6% of men have a core homosexual (gay) orientation. Rather than being a mental illness or a failed masculinity, scientific findings confirm that men with exclusive homosexual orientation are biologically hard-wired, as are those men with exclusive heterosexual orientation.

The guilt and anxiety about these normal same-sex thoughts, feelings, fantasies, and experiences cause more distress than the experiences themselves. These are normal and experimental experiences. Homosexual orientation is a strong physical attraction and emotional and erotic commitment to sex with men. The key to sexual acceptance is to process your experiences and learnings with a sense of acceptance.

Exercise 9.1: Identifying Dimensions of Your Sexual Orientation

Directions: For the dimensions below, describe yourself in terms of your past, the present, and your desired feelings in the future.

Orientation dimension	Past	Present	Future
Sexual attraction or desire for another (man, woman)			
Your sexual identity or self-identification of who you are: gay, bisexual, heterosexual			
Your sexual behavior with women, men, or both			
Your sexual fantasies of women, men, or both			
Your emotional preferences and comfort with women, men, or both			
Your social preferences for friends and social acquaintances			

Other Concerns of Men

Sexually Transmitted Diseases

The reality of the twenty-first century is that 40–50% of men will contract an STD in their lives. The most common STDs are chlamydia, herpes, and HPV (genital warts); the latter two cannot be cured but can be medically managed. Syphilis and gonorrhea can be medically treated when diagnosed early. The most highly feared STD is HIV/AIDS, which is life threatening. The good news is that STDs are now viewed as a medical problem, not a moral problem or a disease that only attacks bad people.

You need to take care of your physical and sexual body, which involves being tested and treated for STDs and preventing future STDs by practicing safer sex. Obviously, the best prevention is for both you and your partner to undergo an STD screen and HIV test and to value your monogamous relationship. However, life often gets in the way of these rational sexual guidelines. We suggest that couples speak to a doctor together and establish clear guidelines on how to deal with herpes or HPV on an ongoing basis, whether that means that the man has to use a condom, avoid infected areas, or avoid sexual contact when an outbreak is beginning. STDs are a reality of sex in the twenty-first century. You want to deal with this as a health issue and not let it control your self-esteem or sex life.

Dealing With Infertility

Infertility is extremely stressful for couples and their sexual relationships. Traditionally, infertility has been seen as a woman's problem and concern. However, at present the estimate is that about one third of infertility factors involve a male cause, one third a female cause, and one third a combination of factors. Male sexual self-esteem is particularly vulnerable when there is a male infertility factor.

The crucial concept is to approach infertility as a health issue and as an intimate team. Blame or guilt will not help you individually or as a couple to deal with the infertility process. Approximately 4 out of 5 couples pursuing infertility treatment develop a sexual dysfunction if treatment extends more than 2 years. Having intercourse on a rigid timetable reduces both desire and erection. Sex is no longer fun, it is a task, and often disheartening when two weeks later you discover that once again your efforts to get pregnant have failed.

Consulting a couple counselor with a subspecialty in dealing with infertility issues can help you work as an intimate team. Infertility causes stress to the man, woman, and couple and is best addressed as a couple issue. Don't fall into the traditional gender trap where the man minimizes individual and couple concerns and views his partner as overly emotional, even hysterical. If your relationship is to survive the stress of dealing with infertility, you need to do this as an intimate team.

Male Menopause?

Physiologically, there is no male menopause. Andropause (male menopause) would involve significant change in endocrine (hormone) levels. Proclaiming that there is a male menopause may sell magazines, but it is not a fact. The fact is that for a physically healthy man, testosterone declines approximately 0.8% per year for men between the ages of 40 and 80. What physicians address with testosterone replacement is a significant decline induced by illness or medication side effects.

Think of your physical changes with aging as a mellowing. Physiologically, your vascular and neurological systems remain functional but are less robust and efficient. Actually, your hormonal system changes the least. If you do experience very low testosterone levels, we suggest consulting an endocrinologist with a subspecialty in male sexual health to discuss testosterone replacement therapy (typically via gel or injection).

Men commonly do experience a mid-life adjustment that is primarily psychological. Rather than being the crisis portrayed in the media, this is a mid-life reflection on your life's meaning and purpose, including relationship and sexual issues. For some, this may set off a crisis, but for the vast majority of men, it is a time of healthy reevaluation. "What is really important?" "Is this all there is?" "What do I want to do with the rest of my life?" "What do I value about intimacy and sexuality?" This is a healthy search for meaning, often facilitated by life events such as job stagnation or successes, children leaving home, or a death in the family.

For most men, mid-life is a major opportunity in your search for meaning. Your life and relationship often benefit. This process can result in growing wisdom, including sexual acceptance and satisfaction.

Fears of Aging

A common myth is that men reach the height of their sexual function at 18 and it's all downhill after that. Another myth is that men lose their sexual appeal and confidence at 50. What nonsense. The reality is that if you adopt the Good-Enough Sex model, you can enjoy sex in your 60s, 70s, and 80s. You are a sexual man until the day you die.

Fears of aging are more accurately fears of illness. As we age, illness becomes more common, and as illness increases, sexual dysfunction may as well. Men who report "fair" or "poor" health are four to five times more likely to experience sexual dysfunction (low desire, erectile dysfunction, ejaculatory inhibition) as men in excellent health (Laumann et al., 1994).

Maintaining a healthy body whether at 55, 65, 75, or 85 is extremely important. Just as important is to focus on what you can change—psychologically and relationally—in particular, psychosexual skill factors. Fears of aging are irrational. Unrealistic fears of sexual decline can set up a self-fulfilling prophecy. If you expect that you'll lose it, you probably will. Accept your aging body and accept a more human, variable, and flexible male and couple sexuality with aging. Remember, physiologically and sexually, the guideline is "Use it or lose it."

Relationship Concerns

Partner Problems That Subvert Sex. Be aware that your sexual health is essentially influenced by your partner's sexual health—physically, emotionally, and interpersonally. When your partner has a health problem that subverts her sexual health, it is essential that you become her support person so you can adapt together. Be an intimate team and utilize flexible sexual scenarios in dealing with depression, anxiety, menopause, cancer treatment, or arthritis. Her problems are yours, and yours are hers—you are an intimate team.

Relational Problems That Can Subvert Sexuality. When a marriage works well, it meets the man's needs for intimacy and security better than any other relationship. Healthy sexuality plays a 15–20% role in couple satisfaction. However, couple problems can subvert sex, and sexual problems can subvert couple satisfaction. Relationship problems can play an inordinately powerful role in sexual dissatisfaction and dysfunction, and sexual dynamics play an inordinately powerful role in relationship dissatisfaction and alienation.

The major problems are dissatisfaction with your partner, not valuing the relationship, or not valuing couple sex. Our recommendation in all these areas is to see this as a couple issue and to seek couple therapy when the problem is still acute rather than waiting until the problem is chronic and severe.

Healthy relationships involve a strong identity as a couple, the ability to recognize and address differences and conflicts, and the ability to communicate with and influence your mate. This includes acknowledging your partner's strengths as well as vulnerabilities and feeling respectful and loving in spite of the problems. Also important is maintaining a commitment to the vitality and security of the relationship. The couple bond involves respect, trust, and intimacy. Communication often breaks down to good–bad power struggles: "I'm right, you're wrong." You view your partner as your worst critic.

We propose a very different communication/problem-solving model, a four-phase process. The first phase is listening to each other's feelings and perceptions in a respectful, caring manner. The second phase is generating practical and emotional alternatives to resolve the problem. The third phase is reaching an understanding/agreement that ideally resolves the problem in a manner that meets both your needs but at a minimum that each of you can live with. The fourth phase is to implement the agreement and if necessary make changes so that it really is helpful. A crucial concept in dealing with personal and relational problems is that about 30% of problems are resolvable, 50–60% are modifiable, and 10–20% need to be accepted and lived with. Contrary to pop psychology, few problems have a perfect resolution. With genuine intimacy and communication, these realities are acceptable.

Valuing Your Relationship and Partner Sex

In movies and traditional male culture, the sexual charge comes from a premarital relationship or an extramarital affair. You almost never see marital sex in a movie. Newness, illicitness, and adventure are highly valued sexually. A marital or serious relationship is often taken for granted, and the sex settles into a functional routine rather than an involving, erotic experience. Men cheat themselves by settling for a marginal relationship and a mediocre sex life. Typically, it is the woman who complains about a stable but unsatisfying relationship. When she threatens to leave or actually leaves, it is a wake-up call for the man, but often too late. Sex is not the only ingredient in a healthy relationship, but sexual avoidance is a major relationship drain.

Future Relationship Vitality

If men approached their careers like they approach their intimate relationships, there would be a dramatic rise in bankruptcies in our culture. You can learn to value your intimate, erotic relationship rather than treat it with benign neglect. Like every other component in life, you have to put time and energy into your relationship to keep it vital, satisfying, and secure (Exercise 9.2).

Exercise 9.2: Identifying Sexual Problems and Creating a Change Plan

To make these concepts personal and concrete, identify sexual problems in your life. We encourage you to use the biopsychosocial approach to assessment. Are there psychological concerns/problems—attitudes, behaviors, or emotions—that interfere with relationship and sexual satisfaction? What about illness, side effects of medication, or health habits that subvert sexual function? Are there relationship factors that subvert sexual function and satisfaction? Don't deny; be honest with yourself and ask for feedback from your partner. Write out in a clear, specific manner what factors—psychological, physiological, and relational—interfere with sexual function and satisfaction.

The second phase of this exercise is even more important. What do you need to do individually and as a couple to address these problems? Can you do it on your own, or would a wiser course be to consult a therapist or physician? Most men prefer to solve problems on their own, but often the wisest choice is to use all your resources—your partner, physician, information from books or trusted Web sites, and/or an individual, couple, or sex therapist (resources are listed in Appendices A and B). You deserve to have a healthy, satisfying life and sexuality. You can confront problems and make positive changes.

Illustration 9.1: Drew

Fifty-eight-year-old Drew was terribly disappointed in himself and his life. At 21, Drew was sure that everything would work out for him. He'd just graduated college, left a dysfunctional family situation behind, was planning to take a professional job in a new city, and expected to have a great time sexually as a single man, with the intention of marrying and having a family in his late 30s.

Now Drew was a twice-divorced man who was alienated from his 26-year-old daughter from his first marriage, was coparenting his 13-year-old son from his second marriage, and who needed to disclose to a new partner that he had the herpes virus, although it had been 10 years since the last outbreak. In addition, Drew was anxious about erectile dysfunction and took Viagra (without telling his partner) to insure that he would not lose his erection. For Drew, sex was more about performance for the woman and avoiding embarrassment than pleasure.

Drew's younger brother, pleased both emotionally and sexually with his second marriage, asked to talk to Drew. Drew really liked his brother's second wife and suggested that she join the conversation. Drew didn't want anyone to feel sorry for him but he did want relational advice and support. The most helpful thing his brother said was that he too had herpes (approximately 1 in 5 adult men do) and that it wasn't a source of shame or embarrassment for him in his marriage. The most helpful thing his sister-in-law said was that she saw him as a smart, attractive person who she would be glad to introduce to single and divorced friends, but that Drew needed to stop apologizing for himself and his situation. With a great deal of embarrassment, Drew told them about his anticipatory anxiety and Viagra use. His sister-in-law was a nurse and she reassured Drew that at least 50% of divorced men his age had mild erectile anxiety and that women were more aware and sophisticated about erectile function and dysfunction than he realized. It need not be a shameful secret.

Drew was committed to stop apologizing for himself. He wanted to only date women he was attracted to both physically and emotionally, who he was comfortable with and trusted to be his intimate, erotic friend. Drew was amazed to discover that this more honest, positive approach increased his attractiveness to women. At a minimum, Drew wanted a sexual friendship; ideally, he wanted an intimate, serious relationship where sexuality would play a positive role rather than be a pass–fail performance test.

Valuing sexual health requires you to take steps to continue your growth and not relapse (Exercise 9.3). You—with your partner's support—can create an individualized plan to maintain gains, generalize them, and develop specific strategies to prevent relapse.

Exercise 9.3: Your Relapse Prevention and Sexual Growth Plan

Continue to use the concepts, guidelines, and techniques that you are learning from this book and to engage in assessment and change exercises. Maintaining healthy sexual attitudes, behaviors, and feelings is crucial. If you simply consider this book a good read and put it on the shelf, you'll relapse back to poor sex habits, which will cause frustration for you and even more frustration for your partner.

You owe it to yourself and your relationship to continue to value healthy male sexuality, especially maintaining positive, realistic sexual expectations.

Following are 10 relapse prevention guidelines. Our suggestion is to choose two to four strategies that are personally relevant to you that will facilitate maintaining healthy male sexuality.

1. Set aside quality couple time and discuss what you need to do individually and as a couple to maintain a satisfying intimate relationship.
2. Plan a sensual pleasuring date or a playful, erotic date every 4 to 8 weeks where you have a prohibition on intercourse. This allows you to experiment with new sensual stimuli (alternative pleasuring position, body lotion, or new setting) or a playful, erotic scenario (being sexual in the shower, a different oral sex position or sequence, one-way rather than mutual sex). This reminds you to value sharing pleasure in addition to intercourse and develop a broad-based, flexible sexual repertoire.
3. Have a formal follow-up meeting every 6 months, either by yourselves or with a therapist to ensure that you remain aware and do not slip back to unhealthy sexual attitudes, behaviors, or feelings. Set realistic individual and couple goals for the next 6 months.
4. Good-Enough Sex has a range from great to disappointing. Five to 15% of sexual experiences are dissatisfying or dysfunctional. That is normal, not a reason to panic or feel like a failure. The single most important technique in relapse prevention is to accept and not overreact to experiences that are unsatisfying or dysfunctional. Maintaining positive, realistic expectations

(Continued)

(*Continued*)

about couple sexuality is a major resource. Take pride in having an accepting and resilient couple sexual style.

5. Accept occasional lapses, but do not allow a lapse to become a relapse. Treat a dysfunctional sexual experience as a normal variation, a mistake to learn from. You are a sexual couple, not a perfectly functioning sexual machine. Whether it is once every 10 times, once a month, or once a year, you will have a lapse (dysfunctional or dissatisfying sex). You can laugh or shrug off the experience and make a date in the next one to three days when you have the time and energy for an intimate, pleasurable, erotic experience.

6. Skim through the book and make a summary list of the items that are helpful for you, that you can refer to and review periodically. For example, it was good to learn that Americans don't have this wild sex life; there is a clear need for sexual self-discipline; you want to remember to value pleasure as much as function. Your partner can make a list as well and then share and discuss why these points are important for you to remain aware of and implement.

7. The importance of setting aside quality time, especially intimacy dates and a weekend away without the children, cannot be emphasized enough. Couples report better sex on vacations, validating the importance of getting away, even if only for a weekend.

8. There is not one right way to be sexual. Each couple develops their own unique style of initiation, pleasuring, erotic scenarios and techniques, intercourse, and afterplay. Rather than treating your couple sexual style with benign neglect, be open to modifying or adding something new or special each year.

9. Develop a range of intimate, pleasurable, and erotic ways to connect, reconnect, and maintain connection. These include five dimensions of touch: affectionate, sensual, playful, erotic, and intercourse. The more ways there are to maintain sexual connection, the easier it is to avoid relapse.

10. Keep your sexual relationship vital. Continue to make sexual requests and be open to exploring erotic scenarios. The importance of maintaining a sexual relationship that serves a 15–20% role of energizing your couple bond and facilitating special feelings of desirability and satisfaction cannot be overemphasized. Couples who share intimacy, nondemand pleasuring, erotic

(*Continued*)

(Continued)

> scenarios and techniques, and planned as well as spontaneous sexual encounters have a variable, flexible sexual relationship. This is a major antidote to relapse.

Closing Thoughts

The majority of men—whether single, married, divorced, or widowed—will experience psychological, physical, or relational concerns and problems in their life, including sexual difficulties. A key factor is to address these problems rather than deny or feel controlled by them. Change is a one-two combination of taking personal responsibility for your behavior and approaching the woman as your intimate ally in addressing and changing problem areas. The goal is not to be the perfect man or the perfect sexual performer but to integrate sexuality into your life and relationship so that it plays a 15–20% role in your well-being and life satisfaction.

CHAPTER 10

Valuing an Intimate, Erotic Sexual Life

This book has been a pleasure to write and fulfilling for many reasons. Foremost among these is to present for you a new model of healthy male and couple sexuality that incorporates important professional and personal learnings from our more than 60 years of experience.

When we were growing up, what we learned about male sexuality was thoroughly different from what we have written in this book. For Barry there was no formal sex education from school, family, or religion. For Mike, there was family silence and good anatomical sex education flavored with wariness and teacher embarrassment in a church-sponsored grade school. The informal sources—jokes and bragging from older boys—emphasized proving yourself sexually with a strict prohibition on asking any questions or voicing any doubts.

Although many, including us, object to the confusing, contradictory sex messages that now flood our culture, we cannot afford to regress to the old days of ignorance and silence. Younger people have to adapt to the pervasiveness of sexual themes in music, movies, TV, and advertising that was less pervasive in years past, but there are also healthier resources—if young people can find them.

Most of the sex resources, especially media and self-help books, focus on female sexuality issues. The male issues that receive the most attention are erectile dysfunction and premature ejaculation. The emphasis is on a medical approach, directed solely to the man, with a promise of a return to perfect sexual performance. In our view, this sets up the perfect storm, which intimidates rather than empowers the man, resulting in embarrassment, inhibited desire, emotional and sexual avoidance of partner sex, and feelings of inadequacy.

We are strong advocates for addressing sexual dysfunction and concerns as an intimate team rather than autonomously. We advocate a psychobiosocial approach to sexual dysfunction—using all your resources to gain and maintain sexual comfort and confidence. The crucial concept is the Good-Enough Sex model, which accepts the inherent variability and flexibility of the couple sexual experience in contrast to the traditional male perfect intercourse performance model. The essence of sexuality is giving and receiving pleasure-oriented touching. You are not a sex performance machine. Good-Enough Sex is first-class sex for men, not settling for less, feminine, or mediocre. Men who adopt this approach in their 30s will inoculate themselves against sexual problems with aging.

Primary prevention is the best strategy. However, we are realistic in accepting that most men will not be open to this approach until their 40s or 50s. The mantra of intimacy, pleasure, eroticism, and positive, realistic expectations comes to fruition in your 60s. As relationships become serious and the man ages, there is greater acceptance of sex as an interpersonal process rather than an autonomous process. This naturally transitions into accepting sexuality as inherently variable and flexible and enjoying this rather than clinging to the traditional double standard/perfect intercourse criterion that subverts male sexuality with aging.

We want to strongly reinforce two themes:

1. Valuing the Good-Enough Sex model of male and couple sexuality, and
2. The crucial importance of building a resilient sexuality.

Building Good-Enough Sex

Sex is a positive, lifelong developmental process that brings challenges that are different for a 30-year-old man, a 50-year-old man, and a 70-year-old man. These challenges are met in the context of Good-Enough Sex so that sexuality is a positive part of you as a man and plays a 15–20% role in enhancing your life and relationship. Your real life changes, as does real-life sexuality. Sex can and will fit into your real life rather than be a separate, compartmentalized part.

Resilience and Sexual Satisfaction

If you want sex to remain vital and satisfying, you cannot rest on your laurels or take sex for granted. Each of us is in a long-term marriage— Barry for over 40 years and Mike for over 20 years. Neither of us takes our marriage or marital sex for granted. Treating relationship sex with benign neglect is a self-defeating strategy. The advantage of a new relationship is that by its nature you put time and energy into it. Romance and passionate sex are major drivers for a new relationship. You owe it to yourself, your partner, and your relationship to maintain energy and vitality so that sex continues to enhance your couple bond.

Illustration 10.1: Donovan

Thirty-eight-year-old Donovan, a married African-American small business owner, felt extremely lucky and blessed in his life and sexuality. Donovan had grown up on the mean streets of Detroit in a working-class, single-mother household. He remembers hearing as an 11-year-old that "marriage was for White folks, sex was for Black folks." Donovan had very limited contact with his biological father but had an excellent role model (his mother's father). The grandfather was a retired auto worker in a long-term marriage. His grandfather urged Donovan to take pride in himself and his life, which included getting a good education, staying away from drugs and crime, and not having children until he was married and had a career. He was Donovan's major sex educator, reinforcing the school's teaching about safer sex and condoms, and adding important values and realistic expectations. Donovan learned that masturbation was normal and healthy; to use contraception and condoms to prevent STDs and pregnancy; to treat a woman as a sexual friend; to not be manipulative or abusive; to understand the differences between sex and a loving, committed relationship; and to value marriage, marital sex, and children. This was a very different message than Donovan received from peers and the media but one that was congruent with his life plan of being an educated, middle-class adult. He wanted a satisfying, stable marriage and family; a vital, satisfying sex life; and a non-violent middle-class life. Donovan loved his mother very much but did not want to repeat her life pattern.

At 38, Donovan took great pride in his life, marriage, and marital sex. He owned a small business in Chicago, was active in the community and with his two children, and was proud of his wife, their marriage, and the healthy role of sex in their life. Donovan felt that they were a good marital and sexual model for their children and was pleased his grandfather lived to see his established adult life. Donovan still tears up when he recalls the grandfather's words two weeks before he died, "I'm proud of you and the life and family you've created."

In terms of sex, Donovan valued both intimacy and eroticism and viewed his wife, Leticia, as his intimate and erotic friend. Her

(*Continued*)

(Continued)

parents were very concerned—she had divorced after 14 months of a very tumultuous marriage to her college boyfriend. They worried that Leticia was marrying down with Donovan and that this was a rebound marriage. In fact, Donovan and Leticia had talked about these and other difficult life and relationship issues and felt ready to make a marital commitment. Sex was certainly a driver in their dating relationship. They felt desired and desirable and very much enjoyed the romantic love, passionate sex, and idealization in this phase of their relationship. However, they were aware that this special, fun time would evolve (as it does in all relationships). Both Donovan and Leticia were committed to developing a deeper, intimate, interactive couple sexual style that would be vital and satisfying.

The hardest issue for Donovan and Leticia to deal with was finding the degree of intimacy that allowed them to feel connected and be able to communicate (verbally and nonverbally) about erotic scenarios and techniques. They wanted to maintain sexual attraction and value each other as intimate, erotic friends. The danger of too little intimacy is lack of empathy and safety, and too much intimacy can cause you to de-eroticize your partner. Donovan and Leticia chose a complementary couple sexual style where each had a bridge to sexual desire and a sexual voice and preferences while also maintaining a genuine couple bond that integrated intimacy and eroticism.

Nondemand pleasuring, touching both inside and outside the bedroom, with awareness that not all touching would lead to intercourse, worked very well for them. Leticia put greater value on sensual touch and Donovan particularly enjoyed receiving manual stimulation to orgasm when Leticia was not into a mutual sexual experience.

Donovan liked the idea that there were their own as well as shared bridges to desire. Even more, he valued that sex was a way of sharing pleasure and reinforcing intimacy. He really enjoyed parenting but was very pleased that he'd had a vasectomy after the birth of his last child, so they didn't have to worry about an unplanned pregnancy. Donovan realized that he valued sex as a tension reducer more than Leticia, but she accepted this as a legitimate, healthy function of sex. Donovan liked "quickies" and this was part of their varied sexual repertoire.

Both of them looked forward to sharing intimacy and sexuality into their 60s, 70s, and 80s. Donovan realized that it would be a different mix of intimacy and eroticism, but wanted sex to remain vital and satisfying.

Barriers to Being a Healthy Sexual Man

When the media discuss elements that undermine healthy male sexuality, the emphasis is on medical factors and aging. That simplistic approach is misleading. The best way to understand male sexual health is the developmental, biopsychosocial model of Good-Enough Sex. This is also the best model for understanding barriers to healthy sexuality and how to overcome them.

Attitude

Let's examine psychological barriers first. The prime negative psychological factor is attitude. Desire is the core component in healthy sexuality. The core of desire is positive anticipation and feeling that you deserve for sex to be a positive in your life and relationship. This attitude is more important than your testosterone level or the state of your erection. Another key psychological factor is your openness to variable, flexible sexual response rather than panicking if the encounter does not easily flow to erection, intercourse, and orgasm. Performance anxiety and trying to force an erection interferes with the comfort, pleasure, arousal, and erotic flow of variable, flexible sexual response. You need to stay psychologically focused on the pleasure process rather than distracted by the performance focus.

Physical Barriers

Body Acceptance. The crucial biological factor is to realistically accept your sexual body at each stage of your life. As you age, do not emphasize the loss of autonomous response. Your body mellows and is a less efficient performance machine, but as long as you maintain good health and healthy habits your body will continue to be capable of pleasurable, functional sexual response. The psychological challenge is to enjoy each chapter of your physiological body response. Our favorite analogy for life-long sexual gratification is that in youth you are a competitive sprinter, but with aging you can enjoy the pleasure of a well-paced jog. Prevention is the best strategy, and the best way to reduce physical barriers is to emphasize maintaining physical wellness.

Dealing with Illness. The second most common physical barrier is illness and side effects of medication. The challenge is to be an active patient, consult your physician as a couple to explore changing medication and health behaviors, and positively adapt to an illness rather than be controlled by it. Illness and side effects of medication do not stop sex, but your sexual body needs to accept the illness and adapt to it. The challenge is to focus on psychological, relational, and, especially, psychosexual skill factors to compensate for less robust physical sexual response.

Positive Aging. The third physiological barrier is that your body becomes less forgiving as you age. The best example is drinking. As a young adult, you could engage in heavy drinking without negative sexual effects. By your 30s or 40s, your physical body rebels, and so does your sexual body. One glass of wine can be relaxing and reduce self-consciousness; a bottle of wine will make you sleepy and impair your arousal and erection function even if you feel sexy. Good health habits become increasingly important to your sexual health with aging.

Cooperation with Your Partner as an Intimate Team

You need your partner to be your intimate and erotic friend. The cooperative, intimate, interactive approach to sexuality becomes dominant with a serious relationship and with aging. The wise man learns that an involved, aroused partner is the main aphrodisiac and learns to piggyback his arousal on hers.

Couple identity, cooperation, and intimate communication are core in implementing a psychosexual skills approach to maintaining sexual vitality and satisfaction. This means accepting that variable, flexible couple sexuality is more satisfying than male autonomous sexual performance.

The core change is sharing with the woman rather than performing for her. Men learn sex as their domain and their responsibility. The challenge is to expand your experience of sex as an equitable, mutual, pleasure-oriented, shared domain. It is a much easier adaptation for women than men. The male culture belittles this as feminizing male sexuality. This is foolishness. The equity approach to sexuality facilitates a genuine human expression of both male and female sexuality. In terms of both quality and satisfaction, intimate, interactive sex is more satisfying. Relational sex beats autonomous sex.

Equitable Partners

A key relational sex challenge is to feel open and vulnerable with your partner. As a teenager and young adult, you urged the woman to be sexually open and to let go sexually. As adults, the best sex is when both of you are open to giving and receiving pleasurable and erotic touch. Usually, the problem is not with the woman but with social pressure on the man to cling to the traditional male role. The challenge for you is to be the equitable partner, not the dominant partner.

Your partner is receptive to the Good-Enough Sex experience partly because it removes her performance pressures to do the "right things" to please you and to be a sexy model you can't resist (like in the women's magazines). Even more important, healthy women value intimate, interactive sexuality. The challenge is to accept her influence and implement this new approach of male and couple sexuality. Ideally, a man would share this new understanding with male friends and enjoy their support for this new sexual approach. Unfortunately, even among well-educated, psychologically minded men there remains a vast gulf between ideal and real. You are a very lucky man if you have supportive friends. For the great majority of men, they need to turn to their partner as the prime support in adopting this new equitable approach to male and couple sexuality.

You want to make Good-Enough Sex a positive, integral part of your life with the hope that sexual comfort, function, and satisfaction will continue to grow. Sexuality is an ongoing, dynamic process. You cannot afford to treat sex with benign neglect or to rest on your laurels. You need to continue to put psychological energy into your sexuality if it is to remain vital and satisfying. Awareness and good intentions are very helpful but they are not enough. Use the following exercise to design a specific relapse prevention plan that you are committed to implementing. Talk to your partner about how she can be supportive as well as keep each of you accountable to maintain and cultivate healthy male and couple sexuality.

Exercise 10.1: Your Healthy Sex Date

Our favorite technique is a 6-month "healthy sex" date. This could involve setting aside 30–60 minutes with your partner to reaffirm what is going well in your sex life and to raise any concerns or problems. The bottom line question: Is sex playing a positive 15–20% role in your life and relationship? If not, or if there are problems, what can you and your partner do to enhance sexual satisfaction? Be clear and specific, making sure you have a system to promote successful implementation of a change and maintenance plan.

The second phase is to set a new positive, reasonable sexual goal for the next 6 months. This makes real and concrete the concept of sexual growth. Keep it simple; don't make it a big job. The goal could be nitty-gritty, such as buying a new pleasuring lotion or trying the sitting–kneeling intercourse position, or it could be to introduce a major change such as enrolling in a "passionate couple" enhancement weekend program, taking a 4-day trip without the children for

(Continued)

(*Continued*)

the first time in 5 years, or going as a couple to your wife's internist to discuss how to cooperatively manage her arthritis so intimacy and sexuality can play a positive role in her life and your relationship. Remember the guideline—integrate sex into your real life and real-life into your sexuality in each phase of your life.

Valuing Sex

People say the problem with men is that they are too sexually focused. In the integrated Good-Enough Sex model, we have proposed a different approach to valuing healthy male and couple sexuality. We urge you to value all three aspects—intimacy, pleasuring, and eroticism. We urge you to value a pleasure-oriented, variable, flexible sexuality and to engage your partner as your intimate, erotic friend. Most of all we urge you to value the Good-Enough Sex model—this is the key to lifelong, satisfying male and couple sexuality. Good-Enough Sex is the greatest sex. See for yourself.

Closing Thoughts

We hope this book has been worthwhile for you in terms of valuable information, healthy principles, concepts, guidelines, exercises, and case studies. Just as important, we urge you to continue utilizing strategies and techniques you find relevant to your situation so you continue to grow, prevent relapse, and strengthen your male and couple sexuality. You want sexuality to play a positive 15–20% role in your life and relationship now and in the future. You want to feel proud of yourself as a sexual man.

Epilogue
The Nuts and Bolts for Your Sexual Health

Let's recap the major points for integration in promoting your sexual health. Hopefully you have already adopted many of these concepts; others may still require attention and improvement. Periodically you can review these summary points to both appreciate your level of sexual health and to keep a focus on maintaining and generalizing your gains.

1. Be proud of yourself as a man. This involves valuing your masculinity and living your life as a model of a healthy man. Be self-accepting and take pride in your sexuality. Value your masculinity and sexuality—even when others are negative.
2. Be honest with yourself. Start with accepting that your sexual thoughts and feelings are normal. Then evaluate your thoughts and feelings by these healthy criteria: (a) Do your thoughts, feelings, and behaviors help you to feel proud of yourself as a sexual man? (b) Are your thoughts, feelings, and behaviors respectful of others? (c) To what extent do your thoughts, feelings, and behaviors build mature intimacy with your partner?
3. Accept childhood and adolescent sexual experiences without shame. Otherwise, anxiety or shame about these experiences can inhibit affirmation of your adult sexuality.
4. Remember that sexuality is a lifelong developmental process, with changing and growing sexual satisfaction throughout your life.
5. Keep your head "screwed on straight." Be conscious about filtering the negative sexual messages in our commercial society that are aimed at getting your attention rather than promoting sexually healthy attitudes and values. Be aware of your sexual cognitions,

how they influence your feelings, and their role in your behaviors. This awareness facilitates making sophisticated choices for sexually healthy thoughts, feelings, and actions.

6. Respect your biological imperative and regulate your sexual emotions and behaviors. If you minimize this biological force and do not accept the need to regulate your sex impulses, your sex drive will betray you and at some point will get you into trouble. Respect the power of sex: (a) respect your body's drive for sex; (b) be aware of your automatic predisposition to objectify sex; and (c) monitor the tendency to emotionally sexualize other emotions. Remember that healthy male sexuality is self-regulated to promote your individual and relationship health.

   Self-awareness is a powerful tool for your sexual health. Self-regulation requires you to be aware and engage in healthy self-talk: "What's happening is sexually intriguing—I like looking and it titillates me." This awareness empowers you to take control: "I'll refocus so I do not bait myself with sexual lust." Appreciate the calming (not eradication) of your sex impulses. Remember, the role of healthy sex is to promote individual and relationship well-being.

7. Take good care of your body as the solid foundation for your sexual health. Remember that what is good for your body is good for your sexual health, and what is harmful to your body is harmful to your sexuality. Adapt to the physical challenges in your life, especially with illness and aging.

8. Let your sexual mantra be to pursue sexual pleasure and eroticism as an intimate team. Therein lies genuine sexual and relationship satisfaction.

9. Adopt the Good-Enough Sex model. Review and refresh your understanding of the features of this model (as your life, body, and relationship change).

10. Value intimate, erotic partner sex. Be realistic, fitting sex into your honest lives. Remember that it is normal for sexual quality to vary. Flexibility and variability are characteristics of couples who are sexually satisfied. Sex is about cooperation and sharing sexual pleasure, not in chasing perfect sexual performance.

11. Be aware that there are multiple negative messages about sex in our culture. You need to affirm that your sexuality and sexual relationship is good, healthy, and important to your relationship. God created sex. Don't let anyone denigrate your healthy

sexuality. You will benefit from giving yourself a pep talk every now and then. Remind yourself:

- Feel proud that you are a sexual man.
- Your body is good.
- Your sex drive is good.
- Your desire for intimacy and eroticism is good.
- Your partner is your intimate friend; be an intimate team with her.
- Sex is of lifelong importance.

12. Live your life as a leader—personally as well as sexually. Be a role model of healthy sexual attitudes and behaviors. Because we men are seldom honest with each other, it is powerful to be able to set a positive example for other men, for your spouse, and for your children. This can be as simple as talking honestly with other men, respectfully asking a buddy to stop hitting on a woman who is obviously uncomfortable, saying that you respect and value your sex life with your wife. Don't act like a prude; rather, look for opportunities to be positive, to model your strong value of sex and the importance of sexual satisfaction as an intimate team, and to show respect for the complexity of sex and your sexual relationship.

13. Remember key concepts:

- Sex is good.
- Integrate your sexual thoughts, feelings, and behaviors.
- Regulate, don't castigate.
- Fit your sex life into your daily life; bring your daily life to your sex life.
- Positive, realistic expectations enhance your sexuality.
- Sexual problems are normal during your life. Address them— resolve, modify, or adapt to them.
- Ultimately, sex is about your relationship: be an intimate team.
- Good-Enough Sex is great sex because it is honest and genuine.
- You are a sexual man from the day you are born to the day you die.

Take a moment to focus on one or two goals for your sexual growth. Write these down. Examples include:

- Talk with your partner about your satisfaction with her. Reinforce being an intimate team.
- Pay more attention to your sexual attitudes and focus of attention and consider how they affect you.

- Set up an appointment as a couple with a sex therapist to discuss a sexual concern or dysfunction.
- Write down your sexual expectations of your body and partner sex and evaluate whether they are reasonable.
- Repeat one of the exercises in this book.
- Consider how you might become more of a sex-positive leader with your buddies or children.
- Accept your sexual past for what it was, appreciate where you are now, and commit to your growing sexual health in the future.
- You want sexual health and satisfaction to play a positive 15–20% role in your life and relationship.

You are a sexual man. Be healthy. Feel proud.

Choosing an Individual, Couple, or Sex Therapist

This is a self-help book, but it is not a do-it-yourself therapy book. Men and couples are often reluctant to consult a therapist, feeling that to do so is a sign of craziness, a confession of inadequacy, or an admission that your life and relationship are in dire straits. In reality, seeking professional help is a sign of psychological wisdom and strength. Entering individual, couple, or sex therapy means that you realize there is a problem and you have made a commitment to resolve the issues and promote individual and couple growth.

The mental health field can be confusing. Couples therapy and sex therapy are clinical subspecialties. They are offered by several groups of professionals including psychologists, marital therapists, psychiatrists, social workers, and pastoral counselors. The professional background of the practitioner is less important than his or her competence in dealing with your sexual health and any specific problems.

Many people have health insurance that provides coverage for mental health and thus can afford the services of a private practitioner. Those who do not have either the financial resources or insurance could consider a city or county mental health clinic, a university or medical school outpatient mental health clinic, or a family services center. Some clinics have a sliding fee scale (the fee is based on your ability to pay).

When choosing a therapist, be assertive in asking about credentials and areas of expertise. Ask the clinician what the focus of the therapy will be, how long therapy can be expected to last, and whether the emphasis is specifically on sexual problems or more generally on individual, communication, or relationship issues. Be especially diligent in asking about credentials such as university degrees and licensing. Be wary of people who call themselves personal counselors, sex counselors, or personal coaches. There are poorly qualified persons—and some outright quacks—in any field.

One of the best ways to obtain a referral is to call a local professional organization such as a state psychological association, marriage and family therapy association, or mental health association. You can ask for a referral from a family physician, clergyman or rabbi, or trusted friend. If you live near a university or medical school, call to find out what mental and sexual health services may be available.

For a sex therapy referral, contact the American Association of Sex Educators, Counselors, and Therapists (AASECT) through the Internet at www.aasect.org or write or call for a list of certified sex therapists in your area: P.O. Box 5488, Richmond, VA 23220; phone: (804) 644-3288. Another resource is the Society for Sex Therapy and Research (SSTAR) at www.sstarnet.org.

For a marital therapist, check the Internet site for the American Association for Marriage and Family Therapy (AAMFT) at www.therapistlocator.net or the Association for Behavioral and Cognitive Therapies (ABCT) at www.abct.org. Another good resource is the national Registry of Marriage Friendly Therapists, who are dedicated to helping marriages succeed if possible: www.marriagefriendlytherapists.com. If you are looking for a psychologist who can provide individual therapy for anxiety, depression, behavioral health, or other psychological issues we suggest the National Registry of Health Service Providers in Psychology: www.findapsychologist.org.

Feel free to talk with two or three therapists before deciding with whom to work. Be aware of your level of comfort with the therapist, degree of rapport, whether the therapist has special skill working with couples, and whether the therapist's assessment of the problem and approach to treatment makes sense to you. Once you begin, give therapy a chance to be helpful. There are few miracle cures. Change requires commitment and is a gradual and often difficult process. Although some people benefit from short-term therapy (fewer than 10 sessions), most find the therapeutic process will require 4 months or longer. The role of the therapist is that of a consultant rather than a decision-maker. Therapy requires effort, both during the session and at home. Therapy helps to change attitudes, feelings, and behavior. Although it takes courage to seek professional help, therapy can be a tremendous help in evaluating and changing individual, relational, and sexual problems.

Finding a physician who is male friendly and interested in male sexual health is a challenge but is worthwhile for you and your physical and sexual health. Choose an internist or family physician who is board certified and is interested in treating you as a whole person, not just a series of symptoms. In choosing a specialist—urologist, endocrinologist, neurologist, addiction medicine, or sexual medicine—you can consult your general physician or obtain a referral through your local medical society, hospital, nearby medical school, or through trusted friends.

Resources

Suggested Reading on Male Sexuality

Joannides, P. (2006). *The guide to getting it on*. West Hollywood, CA: Goofy Foot Press.

McCarthy, B. W., & McCarthy, E. (1998). *Male sexual awareness*. New York: Carroll & Graf.

Metz, M. E., & McCarthy, B. W. (2003). *Coping with premature ejaculation: Overcome PE, please your partner, and have great sex*. Oakland, CA: New Harbinger.

Metz, M. E., & McCarthy, B. W. (2004). *Coping with erectile dysfunction: How to regain confidence and enjoy great sex*. Oakland, CA: New Harbinger Publications.

Milsten, R., & Slowinski, J. (1999). *The sexual male: Problems and solutions*. New York: W.W. Norton.

Zilbergeld, B. (1999). *The new male sexuality*. New York: Bantam Books.

Suggested Reading on Female Sexuality

Foley, S., Kope, S., & Sugrue, D. (2002). *Sex matters for women: A complete guide to taking care of your sexual self*. New York: Guilford.

Heiman, J., & LoPiccolo, J. (1988). *Becoming orgasmic: Women's guide to sexual fulfillment*. New York: Prentice-Hall.

Suggested Reading on Couple Sexuality

Holstein, L. (2002). *How to have magnificent sex: The seven dimensions of a vital sexual connection*. New York: Harmony Books.

McCarthy, B., & McCarthy, E. (1998). *Couple sexual awareness*. New York: Carroll & Graf.

McCarthy, B., & McCarthy, E. (2002). *Sexual awareness.* New York: Carroll & Graf.

Schnarch, D. (1997). *Passionate marriage: Sex, love and intimacy in emotionally committed relationships.* New York: Norton.

Other Notable Sexuality Readings

Fisher, H. (2005). *Why we love: The nature and chemistry of romantic love.* New York: Henry Holt.

Glass, S. (2003). *Not "just friends."* New York: Free Press.

Maltz, W. (2001). *The sexual healing journey.* New York: HarperCollins.

McCarthy, B., & McCarthy, E. (2003). *Rekindling desire.* New York: Brunner/ Routledge.

Michael, R., Gagnon, J., Laumann, E., & Kolata, G. (1994). *Sex in America: A definitive survey.* New York: Little, Brown.

Perel, E. (2006). *Mating in captivity: Reconciling the erotic and the domestic.* New York: HarperCollins.

Suggested Reading on Relationship Satisfaction

Chapman, G. (1995). *The five love languages: How to express heartfelt commitment to your mate.* Chicago: Northfield Publishing.

Doherty, W. (2001). *Take back your marriage.* New York: Guilford.

Gottman, J., & Silver, N. (1999). *The seven principles for making marriage work.* New York: Crown Publishing.

Love, P. (2002). *The truth about love.* New York: Simon & Schuster.

Markman, H., Stanley, S., & Blumberg, S. L. (2001). *Fighting for your marriage: Positive steps for preventing divorce and preserving a lasting love.* San Francisco: Jossey-Bass.

McCarthy, B., & McCarthy, E. (2004). *Getting it right the first time: Creating a healthy marriage.* New York: Brunner/Routledge.

McCarthy, B. W., & McCarthy, E. (2006). *Getting it right this time.* New York: Routledge.

Suggested Reading and Resources for Mental Health

Bourne, E. (2001). *The anxiety and phobia workbook* (3rd ed.). Oakland, CA: New Harbinger Publications.

Burns, D. (1989). *The feeling good handbook.* New York: Penguin.

Staff of Parragon Publishing. (2002). *New guide to relaxation.* Bath, UK: Paragon Publishing.

Internet Sites: Mental Health

Obsessive Compulsive Foundation: http://www.ocfoundation.org/

National Institutes of Mental Health (NIMH) home page: http://www.nimh. nih.gov/

NIMH, Anxiety: http://www.nimh.nih.gov/anxiety/anxietymenu.cfm
NIMH, Depression: http://www.nimh.nih.gov/publicat/depressionmenu.cfm

Internet Sites: Health

National Institutes of Health (NIH): http://www.nih.gov
National Institute on Alcohol Abuse and Alcoholism: http://www.niaaa.nih.gov
WebMD—for many illnesses, including diabetes, cancer, heart disease: http://www.webmd.com
Sex Addicts Anonymous: http://www.sexaa.org

Videotapes: Sexual Enrichment

Holstein, L. (2001). *Magnificent lovemaking.*
Sinclair Institute (Director). (1991). *Sex: A lifelong pleasure series.* (Available from the Sinclair Institute, P.O. Box 8865, Chapel Hill, NC 27515)
Sommers, F. *The great sex video series.* (Available from Pathway Productions, Inc., 360 Bloor Street West, Suite 407A, Toronto, Canada M5S 1X1)
Stubbs, K. R. (1994). *Erotic massage.* (Available from the Secret Garden, P.O. Box 67, Larkspur, CA 94977)
The couples guide to great sex over 40, vols. 1 and 2 (1995). (Available from the Sinclair Institute, P.O. Box 8865, Chapel Hill, NC 27515)

Professional Associations

American Association for Marriage and Family Therapy (AAMFT): www.therapistlocator.net
American Association of Sex Educators, Counselors, and Therapists (AASECT): P.O. Box 54388, Richmond, VA 23220-0488, www.aasect.org
Association for Behavioral & Cognitive Therapies (ABCT): 305 Seventh Avenue, New York, NY 10001-6008. Phone (212) 647-1890, www.abct.org
Sex Information and Education Council of the United States (SIECUS): 130 West 42nd Street, Suite 350, New York, NY 10036. Phone (212) 819-7990, fax (212) 819-9776, www.seicus.org
Society for Scientific Study of Sexuality (SSSS): P.O. Box 416, Allentown, PA 18105-0416. Phone (610) 530-2483. www.sexscience.org
Society for Sex Therapy and Research (SSTAR): www.sstarnet.org

Sex "Toys," Books, and Videos

Good Vibrations Mail Order: 938 Howard Street, Suite 101, San Francisco, CA 94110. Phone (800) 289-8423, fax (415) 974-8990, www.goodvibes.com

References

Allen, E., Atkins, D., Baucom, D., Snyder, D., Gordon, K. & Glass, S. (2005). Interpersonal, intrapersonal, and contextual factors in engaging in and responding to extramarital involvement. *Clinical Psychology: Science and Practice, 12*(2), 101–130.

Bancroft, J. (Ed.). (2003). *Sexual development in childhood*. Bloomington, IN: Indiana University Press.

Bancroft, J., Herbenick, D. L., & Reynolds, M. A. (2003). Masturbation as a marker of sexual development: Two studies 50 years apart. In J. Bancroft (Ed.), *Sexual development in childhood* (pp. 134–155). Bloomington, IN: Indiana University Press.

Basson, R. (2002). A model of women's sexual desire. *Journal of Sex & Marital Therapy, 28*(1), 1–10.

Brady, J. P., & Levitt, E. (1965). Scalability of sexual experiences. *Psychological Record, 15*(2), 275–279.

Buechner, F. 1991. *Now and then: A memoir of vocation*. New York: HarperCollins Publishers, p. 89.

Buss, D. (1995). Psychological sex differences: Origins through sexual selection. *American Psychologist, 50*(3), 164–168.

Cooper, A. (Ed.). (2002). *Sex and the Internet: A guidebook for clinicians*. New York: Brunner-Routledge.

Cooper, A., & Marcus, I. D. (2003). Men who are not in control of their sexual behavior. In S. B. Levine, C. B. Risen, & S. E. Althof (Eds.), *Handbook of clinical sexuality for mental health professionals* (pp. 311–332). New York: Brunner-Routledge.

Ellis, B.J., & Symons, D. (1990). Sex differences in sexual fantasy : An evolutionary psychological approach. *Journal of Sex Research, 27*(4), November, 527–555.

Epstein, N. B., & Baucom, D. H. (2002). *Enhanced cognitive–behavioral therapy for couples: A contextual approach*. Washington, DC: American Psychological Association.

Finkelhor, D. (1993). Epidemiological factors in the clinical identification of child sexual abuse. *Child Abuse and Neglect, 17,* 67–70.

Fisher, H. E. (2005). *Why we love: The nature and chemistry of romantic love.* New York: Henry Holt.

Fisher, H. E., Aron, A., Mashek, D., Li, H., & Brown, L. (2002). Defining the brain systems of lust, romantic attraction, and attachment. *Archives of Sexual Behavior, 31*(5), 413–419.

Frank, E., Anderson, C., & Rubinstein, D. N. (1978). Frequency of sexual dysfunction in normal couples. *New England Journal of Medicine, 299*(3), 111–115.

Friedrich, W. (2003). Studies of sexuality of nonabused children. In J. Bancroft (Ed.), *Sexual development in childhood* (pp. 107–120). Bloomington, IN: Indiana University Press.

Friedrich W. (1997). *Child sexual behavior inventory: Professional manual.* Odessa, FL: Psychological Assessment Resources.

Goldman, R., & Goldman, J. (1988). *Show me yours: What children think about sex.* Victoria, Australia: Penguin.

Greenwald, E., & Leitenberg, H. (1988). Long-term effects of sexual experiences with siblings and nonsiblings during childhood. *Archives of Sexual Behavior, 18,* 389–399.

Guttenmacher Institute. (1998). *Facts in brief: Teen sex and pregnancy.* Retrieved , 12/7/2006 from http://www.agi-usa.org/pubs/fb_teen_sex.html

Hamann, S., Herman, R.A., Nolan, C. L., & Wallen, K. (2004). Men and women differ in amygdala response to visual sexual stimuli. *Nature Neuroscience, 7*(4), 411–416.

Haugaard, J. J. (1996). Sexual behaviors between children: Professionals' opinions and undergraduates' recollections. *Families in Society: The Journal of Contemporary Human Sciences, 77,* 81–89.

Jemal, A., Siegel, R., Ward, E., Murray, T., Xu, J., Smigal, C., et al. (2006). Cancer statistics. *A Cancer Journal for Clinicians, 56,* 106–130.

Kinsey, A. C., Pomeroy, C., & Martin, C. E. (1948). *Sexual behavior in the human male.* New York: W. B. Saunders.

Larsson, I., & Svedin, C. G. (2002). Teachers' and parents' reports on 3- to 6-year-old children's sexual behavior: A comparison. *Child Abuse & Neglect, 26,* 247–266.

Laumann, E. O., Gagnon, J. H., Michael, R. T., & Michaels, S. (1994). *The social organization of sexuality: Sexual practices in the United States.* Chicago: University of Chicago Press.

Leedes, R. (2001). The three most important criteria in diagnosing sexual addictions: Obsession, obsession, and obsession. *Sexual Addiction & Compulsivity, 8*(3–4), 215–226.

Lopez Sanchez, F., Del Campo, A., & Guijo, V. (2002). Prepubertal sexuality. *Sexologies, 11,* 42, 49–58.

Masters, W. H., & Johnson, V. E. (1966). *Human sexual response.* Boston: Little, Brown.

Metz, M. E., & McCarthy, B. W. (2003). *Coping with premature ejaculation: Overcome PE, Please your partner, and have great sex.* Oakland, CA: New Harbinger.

Metz, M. E., & McCarthy, B. W. (2004). *Coping with erectile dysfunction: How to regain confidence and enjoy great sex.* Oakland, CA: New Harbinger.

Metz, M. E., & McCarthy, B. W. (2007). The "Good-Enough Sex" model for men's and couple satisfaction. *Sexual and Relationship Therapy, 22,* 351–362.

Michael, R. T., Gagnon, J. H., Laumann, E. O., & Kolata, G. (1994). *Sex in America: A definitive survey.* New York: Warner Books.

Reynolds, M. A., Herbenick, D. L., & Bancroft, J. (2003). The nature of childhood sexual experiences: Two studies 50 years apart. In J. Bancroft (Ed.), *Sexual development in childhood* (pp. 134–155). Bloomington, IN: Indiana University Press.

Rutter, M. (1982). Developmental neuropsychiatry: Concepts, issues, and prospects. *Journal of Clinical Neuropsychology, 4*(2), 91–115.

Sandfort, Th. G. M., & Cohen-Kettenis, P. T. (2000). Sexual behavior in Dutch and Belgian children as observed by their mothers. *Journal of Psychology and Human Sexuality, 12*, 105–115.

Segraves, R. T., & Balon, R. (2003). *Sexual pharmacology: Fast facts.* New York: W. W. Norton.

World Health Organization (WHO), United Nations (1975). Education and training in human sexuality: The training of health professionals. WHO technical brochure # 572. Geneva: WHO, p. 14.

Index

A

AAMFT. *see* American Association
for Marriage and Family Therapy
(AAMFT)
AASECT. *see* American Association
of Sex Educators, Counselors, and
Therapists (AASECT)
ABCT. *see* Association for Behavioral
and Cognitive Therapy (ABCT)
Acquired Immunodeficiency Syndrome
(AIDS), 171
Actions, 23–24
Adolescent sexual behavior, 52
Affairs, 167
  comparison, 166
  extra-relationship, 166
  man's, 168
  prevent or handle, 167–168
  woman's, 168–169
Afterplay phase, 66
Age
  appropriate sexual
    expectations, 106
  fears, 173
  Good-Enough Sex model, 173
  health, 141–143
  illness, 141–143
  medications, 141–143
  normal changes, 137

positive, 186
quality of sex, 138
sexuality value, 143–144
sexual man, 135–145
sexual satisfaction, 106
AIDS. *see* Acquired Immunodeficiency
Syndrome (AIDS)
Alcohol, 106, 124–125
  abuse, 106
Alprostadil, 158
Ambivalence, 41–42
American Association for
Marriage and Family Therapy
(AAMFT), 194, 199
American Association of
Sex Educators, Counselors,
and Therapists
(AASECT), 194, 199
Anatomy and physiology, 63–66
Andropause, 172–173
Antidepressant medications, 142
Apomorphine, 157
Appropriate sexual feelings, 5
Arousal, 72
Association for Behavioral and
Cognitive Therapy (ABCT), 194
Attachment, 78–79
Attitude, 185
Autonomous, 31
  function, 102

B

Balance, 32
Barriers, 7–8, 40–42, 185–186
Basson, model of female arousal, 71–72
Behavioral health habits, 121–122
Behavioral skill, 28–29
Behaviors, 23–24. see also specific type
Biopsychosocial model, 11–12
Body acceptance, 185
Boys
    childhood sexual experiences, 38
    learn about sex, 38
    to men, 37–58
    sexual behaviors
        aged 2–5, 46
        aged 6–12 years, 46–47
Bragging, 8–9
Bravado, 8–9

C

Caverjet, 158
CBE. see Cognitive-behavioral-
    emotional (CBE) model
Child abuse, 163
Children
    confusion and uncertainty, 57
    learn about sexuality, 44
    sexual behaviors
        adult reactions, 46
        evaluate, 47–48
        health continuum, 48
        natural and healthy, 47
        observed, 45
        with peers, 50–51
        scientific learnings, 45–46
Chlamydia, 171
Cialis/tadalafil HCL, 143,
    156, 157
Clitoris, 71
Coached, 3
Cognitions, 23
Cognitive-behavioral-emotional (CBE)
    model, 22–24
    couple, 103
    men's sexual health, 11
    skills, 24, 102–104

Cognitive-behavioral individual or
    couple therapy, 142
Cognitive skills, 24
Communicating emotions, 27
Communication, 186
Communication/problem-solving
    model, 174
Comparison affair, 166
Compulsive sexual behavior
    factors, 165–166
    recognizing, 165
Confidence, 1, 3, 4
Confusion, 41–42
    childhood, 57
Cooperation, 103–104, 186
Coping strategy, 126
    SD, 151
Copulation, 78
Counseling and sexual health, 3
Couple CBE, 103
Couple identity, 186
Couple relationship, 112–113
    sex integration exercise, 114–115
Couples sexuality
    core, 93
    flexible, 110–111
    suggested readings, 197–198
Couples therapy, 142, 193
Criminal sexual behavior, 163
Cultures
    matriarchal, 62
    patriarchal, 62

D

Desire, 65
    female, 7, 71–72
Developmental readiness, 50
Deviant sexual pattern, 162–163
Dissatisfaction, 148
Do-it-yourself vs. self-help, 193
Drinking, 106, 124–125
    changing, 129
Drive, 79–80
Drug use, 124–125
    changing, 129
Duplicity, 41–42
Duration of sex, 74

E

Eating habits
changing, 129
healthy weight range, 123–124
ED. *see* Erectile dysfunction (ED)
EI. *see* Ejaculatory inhibition (EI)
85% approach, 108
Ejaculation, premature (rapid), 155
Ejaculatory inhibition
(EI), 160–161
Emotional distress, 104–105
Emotional fitness, 130
Emotional health fitness program
development exercise, 130–131
Emotional intimacy
pathways, 84
vulnerability, 28
Emotional satisfaction, 84–85
Emotional sexualization, 79–81
Emotional skill, 24, 28
Emotional skills, 164
Emotions, 24
communicating, 27
Empathy, 28, 104–105
Empty nest couple, 115
E1-prostaglandin (PGE1,
alprostadil), 158
Equitable partners, 186–187
Erectile dysfunction (ED), 67, 155–157
combination medical
treatments, 158
devices, 159
Good-Enough Sex model, 156
intracavernous drug therapies, 158
treatment, 156–157
Erection, 64
chemistry, 68
physiology, 67
Eroticism, 90, 92, 93
evaluating, 83
materials, 73, 74
use and misuse, 82
valuing, 181–188
Excitement, 65
Exercise program (physical)
changing, 128–129
healthy and balanced, 123

maintaining sexual healthy
body, 126–127
physical body, 122
Exercises (mental)
exploring sexual body, 68–71
Good-Enough Sex model
implementation, 118
healthy sex date, 187–188
listening and feelings, 26
maintaining sexual healthy
body, 126–127
peer sexual experiences, 51–52
relapse prevention, 177–179
sexual growth plan, 177–179
sexual history, 54
sexual knowledge
questionnaire, 1–2
Exhibitionism, 163
Expectations, 9, 30–31
Extra-relationship affairs, 166

F

Fantasy, 9, 12–13, 73
Fears
aging, 173
of failure, 108
Feelings, 24, 25
expressing, 27–28
guiding principle, 27
illustration, 25
listening exercise, 26
Female
affair, 168–169
anatomy, 63–66, 70–71
desire and sexual response, 7
frequency of masturbation, 75
vs. male sexuality, 59–86
physiology, 63–66
sexuality, 71–72
suggested readings, 197
Fetishism, 161
First intercourse, 52–53
Fisher, Helen, 77
Fitness, 121. *see also* Exercise
program (physical)
sexual function, 121–134
Five purposes for sex, 29–30

Fix and foster, 152
Flexible approach, 138
Flexible couple sexuality, 110–111
Flexible sexual experiences, 108
Frequency, 74
Frotteursim, 163
Function
   vs. performance, 31, 107–108
   vs. pleasure, 107–108
Future relationship vitality, 175

G

Gender
   arousal differences, 71–72
   difference, 59–60, 62, 114
     emotional and sexual
      satisfaction, 83–84
     fantasy, 73
     physiological differentiation, 63–64
Generous sexual
   cooperation, 109–110
Genital warts, 171
Genuine satisfaction, 89
Give-and-take sex, 138
Glans, 70
Golden shower, 161
Gonorrhea, 171
Good-Enough Sex model, 14, 35, 94,
   107, 182
aging, 173
aspects, 188
building, 182
before crisis, 117–118
ED, 156
fruition, 135
great, 119
illustration, 94–96
implementation exercise, 118
male and couple satisfaction, 101
male and couple sexuality, 99–120
man without partner, 118–119
medication side effects, 143
partner receptivity, 187
purpose, 99
quality, 108
80s, 138

50s or 60s, 139
Good physical health
   sexual health, 106
Great sex, 13

H

Health
   aging, 141–143
   behaviors
     changing, 132–134
     habits, 106
     log, 126–127
   couple sexuality
     aspects, 188
   female sexual response, 72
   habits, 106
     problematic, 128
   improving, 127–128
   insurance, 193
   Internet sites, 199
   male sexuality
     aspects, 188
     core concepts, 17
     mantra, 88
     pride, 3
   satisfying sex, 6
   sleep patterns, 122
Healthy sex
   after 60, 137
   barriers, 7–8, 185–186
   date exercise, 187–188
   experiences, 51
   illustration, 18–20
   mantra, 87–97
   second marriage, 139–141
Herpes, 171
Her *vs.* his sexuality, 59–86
High-opportunity/low-involvement
   encounter, 166
History of sex
   learning, 60, 62
His *vs.* her sexuality, 59–86
HIV. *see* Human immunodeficiency
   virus (HIV)
Homosexuality, 55–56
Hormonal system, 68

HPV (genital warts), 171
Human immunodeficiency virus
     (HIV), 171
Human sexual response
     cycle, 65

I

Illegal sexual behavior, 162–163
Illness
     aging, 141–143
     dealing with, 185–186
     managing, 142
     medications, 125–126
Individual sexual health, 29–30
     concept, 18
Infertility, 172
Infidelity. *see* Affair
Inhibited sexual desire (ISD), 159–160
Integrated eroticism, 88–89
Integration, 93
     components of sexual health, 12
     sexual personality, 30
Intercourse, 52–53
     first time, 53
Internet sites
     health, 199
     mental health, 198–199
     pornography, 165
Intimacy, 87–88, 91
     playfulness, 116
     team, 13, 102–110, 186
     valuing, 181–188
Intracavernous drug therapies
     for ED, 158
ISD. *see* Inhibited sexual desire (ISD)

L

Labia, 71
Laumann, Edward, 73
Learned behavior, 49–50
Learning about sex, 37–44
Levitra/vardenafil HCL, 143, 156, 157
     strengths and weaknesses, 157–158
Libido self-regulation, 79–80
Lifelong healthy sexuality, 7, 94, 135–145

Listening exercise, 26
Love, three forms, 77–79
Lovemaking skills, 74
     forms, 77
     learning, 72–73
     satisfying sex, 6
Lust
     regulating, 79–81
     self-regulation, 79–80

M

Male
     affair, 168
     bravado, 41
     vs. female
          relationships, 62
          sexuality, 59–86
     menopause, 172–173
     pride, 1
     and sex media, 8
     sexual confidence, 100
     sexual dysfunction, 155–161
     sexual health
          CBE, 11
          creating model exercise, 10–11
          essence, 93
          factors, 11
          hallmark, 56–58
          healthy thinking, 17–35
          media presentations, 53
          model, 9–10, 11
          psychological dimensions, 11
          suggested readings, 197
     sexuality, 99–119
          satisfaction, 101
     sexual problems, 147–148, 155–161
     socialization, 88
Mantra healthy sexuality, 87–97
Masculinity pride, 1. *see also* Male
Masturbation, 7, 52, 74–75
     men and women's frequency, 75
     reasons, 76
Matriarchal cultures, 62
McCarthy, Barry, 14
Media
     men and sex, 8

presentation of male
sexuality, 53
as sex educators, 39–40
Medical problems
SD, 149, 151–152
Medicated Urethral System for Erection
(MUSE), 158
Medications, 125
aging, 141–143
illness, 125–126
managing, 142
over-the-counter, 125
side effects
Good-Enough Sex
model, 143
SD, 149
Men. *see* Male
Mental health
Internet sites, 198–199
suggested readings, 198
Metz, Michael, 14
Mixed feelings, 25–26
MUSE. *see* Medicated Urethral System
for Erection (MUSE)
Mutual intimacy, 89

N

National Health and Social Life
(NHSL), 73
National Registry of Healthy Service
Providers in Psychology, 194
Natural sexual behavior, 47
Netizens, 165
Neurologic system, 68
NHSL. *see* National Health and Social
Life (NHSL)
Nondemand pleasuring, 88, 91–92
Normal and healthy, 37–58

O

Objectification, 79–80
Older age, 143–144. *see also* Age
Orgasm, 31, 66, 76, 90
Orientation identity features, 55–56
Over-the-counter medications, 125

P

Papaverine, 158
Paraphilia, 161, 162
severity, 162
Parents as sex educators, 38
Partner
interaction arousal, 33, 113
problems, 173–174
receptivity to Good-Enough Sex
model, 187
value, 34, 174–175
Passionate couple, 187–188
Patriarchal cultures, 62
PDE-5 enzyme inhibitors, 157
PE. *see* Premature (rapid)
ejaculation (PE)
Pedophilia, 163
Peeping, 163
Peer sexual experience exercise, 51–52
Penis, 64
brace, 159
myth, 70–71
physiology, 66–67
size, 70–71
stimulation, 138
vascular surgery, 159
vascular system, 67
Performance, 89
vs. function, 107–108
pressure, 108
PGE1, 158
Phentolamine mesylate, 157, 158
Physical body
exercise, 122
interrelationship with sexual
function, 6
Physical fitness, 121
emotional fitness, 130
SD, 149
sexual function, 121–134
sexual health, 106
Physical problems, 185
SD, 151–152
Physician
discussion, 152
finding male friendly, 195
speaking with, 152

Plateau, 66
Pleasure, 31, 88
   vs. function, 107–108
Poisonous thinking, 20–22
Pornography, 12–13
   addiction, 164
   continuum, 83
   misuse, 164–165
   sex, 30
   use and misuse, 82
Positive aging, 186
Premature (rapid) ejaculation (PE), 155
Prescribed medications, 125
Prevention, 121
Pride
   healthy men, 3
   masculinity, 1
   sexuality, 1, 3
Primary prevention, 182
Problematic health habits, 128
Problem-solving, 142–143
Pro-erection oral medications, 157
Professional associations, 199
Pro-sex medication, 143
Psychobiosocial model, 11–12
Psychosexual skills, 12

Q

Quality with age, 138

R

Rapid ejaculation, 155
Real life *vs.* sex life, 34–35
Referral, 194
Regulating sexual objectification, 80
Rejection, 108
Relapse prevention exercise, 177–179
Relational dimensions, 104–105
Relational problems, 174
Relationship
   concerns, 173–174
   couple, 112–113
   dimension, 12, 104
   intimacy, 104
   men *vs.* women in history, 62

   problems that subvert sex, 174
   satisfaction, 13
   and sexual satisfaction, 102–110
   suggested readings, 198
   understanding core
      dimensions, 102–104
   valuing, 174–175
Relaxation, 107
Religious groups as sex educators, 39
Resilience and sexual satisfaction,
   182–184
Resources, 197–199
Respect, 63
Response cycle, 65
Responsive sexual desire, 71–72
Role enactment arousal, 33, 113
Romantic love, 78

S

Sadomasochism, 161
Same-sex experience, 170–171
Satisfaction, 66, 89, 90, 92
   health, 6
   lovemaking skills, 6
   sex life, 1, 6
   sexuality, 13
   sexual relationship, 132
Schools as sex educators, 38–39
Scrotum, 69
SD. *see* Sexual dysfunction (SD)
Self-awareness, 190
Self-discipline, 28–29
Self-entrancement arousal, 33, 113
Self-help *vs.* do-it-yourself, 193
Self-regulation, 190
   drive, 79–80
   libido, 79–80
   lust, 79–80
Self-talk, 190
Sex, 1–16
   addiction, 163–164
   couple relationship, 112–113
   on demand, 107
   drive, 77–78
   education, 42–44
   and emotional affairs, 166

expectations, 9
40s and 50s, 136
frequency and duration, 74
functional after 70, 143–144
good element, 101–102
and health problems, 147–179
how we learn, 37–41
integration exercise, 114–115
learned behavior, 49–50
and love, 76–77
messages to regulate, 40–41
mixed messages, 40–41
negative messages, 41
normal, 4
over 60, 139, 143
partners, 75
purpose, 29–30
  couple relationship, 112–113
quality with age, 138
reasons, 30
research, 73
resources, 181
60s and beyond, 136–137
  exercise, 144–145
  workshops, 139
society's understanding, 61–62
and spirituality, 117
therapist, 193–195
therapy, 193
  referral, 194
20s and 30s, 136
Sex Information and Education Council
  of the United States (SIECUS), 199
Sexology, 62
Sex "Toys," 199
Sexual arousal, 33
  problems, 161
  styles, 113–114
Sexual awareness, 68–71
Sexual behavior, 41, 73–76
  boys
    aged 2–5 years, 46
    aged 6–12 years, 46–47
  childhood health continuum, 48
  illegal, 162–163
  science, 73
  variations, 60–61

Sexual body
  exploring exercise, 68–71
  understanding, 64–66
Sexual boredom, 34
Sexual compulsivity, 163–164
  individual problem, 164
  relationship problem, 164–165
Sexual concerns, 4–6
Sexual development, 44–55
Sexual dysfunction (SD), 147–148, 161
  addressing, 182
  cause and effect, 149–159
  coping strategies, 151
  history, 154
  medical cause, 151
  medical evaluation, 153
    contents, 153
    when, 153
  medical illness, 149
  medication side effects, 149
  overcoming, 108
  personal medical history, 154
  physical and medical problems,
    151–152
  physical examination, 154
  physical factors, 149
  physical types, 150–151
  psychological causes and effects, 154
  prevalence (frequency), 148–149
  treatment, 155–161
Sexual emotions
  distinguishing, 81–82
  managing, 80–81
Sexual enrichment videotapes, 199
Sexual experiences
  child abuse, 163
  childhood with peers, 50–51
  expressing, 8
  flexible, 108
Sexual fidelity, 76
Sexual function
  changes among men, 137
  fitness, physical well-being, 121–134
  and pleasure, 107–108
Sexual growth plan exercise, 177–179
Sexual health
  components, 7, 11–12

counseled and coached, 3
defined, 4
dimensions, 11–12
good physical health, 106
healthy behavioral habits, 106
learnings, 22, 79–80
lifelong process, 7
maintaining exercise, 126–127
Sexual history exercise, 54
Sexual identity and orientation, 55–56
Sexual integration, 189
Sexual interest, 5
Sexual intimacy
pathways, 84
Sexuality
confidence, 1
his *vs.* her, 59–86
model of, 9–11
personalized, 116
playful, 116
pride, 1
vs. real life, 34–35
satisfying, 1, 13
special, 116
spiritual, 116
value in older age, 143–144
Sexual knowledge
healthy step-by-step progressive, 50
questionnaire exercise, 1–2
Sexually transmitted disease (STD),
171–172
Sexual man, 135–145
Sexual objectification regulation, 80
Sexual orientation
conflict, 170–171
identifying dimensions, 171
identity, 55–56
Sexual pleasure, 31
Sexual practices appeal, 75
Sexual problems
chronic, 149
creating change plan illustration,
175–176
identification exercise, 175
multidimensional, 148
Sexual realism, 65
Sexual regulatory skills, 164

Sexual response
assessing and changing
exercise, 90–92
cycle, 65
female, 7
foundation, 107
Sexual road map, 57–58
Sexual satisfaction, 84–85
age-appropriate sexual
expectations, 106
lifelong, 94
and relationships, 102–110
and resilience, 182–184
understanding, 102
Sexual scenarios creation
exercise, 112
Sexual secrets, 161
Sexual stereotypes, 59
Sexual thoughts, 73
Sexual trauma, 169–170
Sexual variant problems, 162
Sexual wisdom, 139
Sexual worries, 4–6, 56–57
penis size, 70–71
SIECUS. *see* Sex Information and
Education Council of the United
States (SIECUS)
Sildenafil HCL, 143, 155–156, 157, 158
strengths and weaknesses, 157–158
Skin hunger, 108
Sleep patterns
changing, 128
health, 122
Smoking, 106, 125
Societal norms, 12
Society for Sex Therapy and Research
(SSTAR), 194, 199
Society's understanding of sex, 61–62
Sperm, 69
Spying, 163
SSTAR. *see* Society for Sex Therapy and
Research (SSTAR)
STD. *see* Sexually transmitted disease
(STD)
Stevenson, Robert Louis, 7
Surgical penile prostheses, 159
Syphilis, 171

T

Tadalafil HCL, 143, 156, 157
Teenage years, 57
Testicles, 69
Testosterone, 143
    deficiency, 157
Thinking
    enhancing exercise, 20–22
    independently, 20
    male sexuality, 17–35
Thoughts, 23
Touch, 31
    kinds, 32
    role, 107
Traditional sex therapy, 89
Trimix, 158
Trivializing, 8–9

U

Urophilia, 161

V

Vacuum constriction devices, 159
Vagina, 71
Value
    erotic sexual life, 181–188
    intimacy, 181–188
    partner, 34, 174–175
        relationship, 174–175
    sex, 188
    sexuality in older age, 143–144
Vardenafil HCL, 143, 156, 157
    strengths and weaknesses, 157–158
Variable couple sexuality, 110–111
Variant arousal, 161
Variant arousal patterns, 162
Vascular system, 67
    penis, 67
Viagra/sildenafil HCL, 143, 155–156,
    157, 158
    strengths and weaknesses, 157–158
Videotapes for sexual enrichment, 199
Visual pornography continuum, 83
Voyeurism, 163
Vulnerability, 28

W

Websites. *see* Internet sites
Women. *see also* Female
    affair, 168–169
    frequency of masturbation, 75
    sex preferences, 73–76
    sexual anatomy and physiology,
        63–66

Y

Yohimbine, 157